THE SMALL BUSINESS CASEBOOK

THE SMALL BUSINESS CASEBOOK

Sue Birley

MACMILLAN

First edition 1979
Reprinted 1982, 1986

Published by
THE MACMILLAN PRESS LTD
Houndmills, Basingstoke, Hampshire RG21 2XS
and London
Companies and representatives
throughout the world

Printed in Great Britain by
Antony Rowe Ltd
Chippenham

British Library Cataloguing in Publication Data
Birley, Susan J
The small business casebook
1. Small business – Great Britain – Case studies
I. Title
338.6′42′0722   HD2346.G7
ISBN 0–333–26099–6
ISBN 0–333–26100–3 Pbk

To
PROFESSOR BRUCE SCOTT
for starting the ball rolling

Contents

Those cases not written by Sue Birley were prepared under her direction by former
M.Sc. students at the London Business School.

Acknowledgements

My grateful thanks go to Professor Michael Beesley for initiating the project; to David Norburn, Philip Green, David Turpin and Arthur Moore for providing four of the cases; and to Michael Beesley, Peter Gorb, Bill Porter, David Norburn and Bob Hamilton for reading and commenting on the drafts. I am grateful to M. Sc. and Sloan students at the London Business School for being willing guinea-pigs, and to Linda Harris, Sue Coan and Ann Clapp for patiently typing the many drafts. I should also like to thank the owners and managers of all the companies for being so helpful in providing material to allow others to learn from their experiences.

Finally, I wish to thank the *Financial Times Ltd* for permission to quote an extract from an article by Margaret Reid published on 7 September 1977.

S.B.

Introduction

The small business is a vital part of the economic and social life of the community, and yet it is only recently that academics, businessmen and others have begun to recognise that small business is rarely large business in microcosm. The motivations of the owner–manager, the skills and resources available to him, and the pressures exerted on him by the environment are often quite different from those of the functional manager in the larger firm. The cases in this book examine these differences while at the same time giving the student an opportunity to study the critical factors in the development of the small firm.

There are, of course, factors that the small business and the large business have in common. Business policy is the study of the total business, and the techniques of analysis which are used do not vary with the size of business. Thus, this book also affords an opportunity to practise these skills.

The cases are intended for students – any student who will eventually find himself working in a managerial capacity. Very few students will become small businessmen, but almost all will come into contact with them frequently during their working life, whether as customers, suppliers, advisers, investors or even competitors. Despite this, most students have no idea of what such a business is really like. Management teaching encourages the view that profit, systems and structure are the measures of an efficient and healthy business and yet these can be anathema to the small-firm owner. He may be happier in apparent chaos but in complete control, and so, faced with companies such as Eaves and Washbourne or with entrepreneurs such as Ali Cameron, the student's initial reaction is one of disbelief. The aim of this casebook is to turn such disbelief into understanding so that the student will eventually be able to interact with the small-business community in a constructive way.

Each case is intended to be taken at three levels. First, the student should be able to identify the general issues that the case is highlighting. For example, Chapter 6 (Regent Printers) looks at the issues of delegation and corporate structure in a rapidly growing firm. Secondly, the student should be able to suggest solutions for the particular problem posed: for example, (again in Chapter 6), what to do with Elroy, who has been promoted beyond the level of his capability but who is viewed by the owners of the firm as part of their extended family. Thirdly, and as a result of his analysis, the student should come to realise that many of the solutions which he suggests come from an external view of the firm, and, if they are to be implemented, may require the introduction of a third party. The question of who this person is and how he should help and persuade the owner is one which not only is important in the particular situation but also is currently being studied by both government and commercial organisations.

Although the book is written as a self-contained course and is used as such at the London Business School, each case can be taken and taught in isolation as part of any general management course. A selection of cases is already being used in a wide range of institutions, from colleges of further education to business schools and for students from Higher National Diploma to post-graduate level.

1

The purpose in writing the book was to provide material to promote the teaching of small business to students. This does not, however, exclude its use in teaching the small businessman himself. A number of such businessmen, including the people who have contributed case material, have found it helpful to use the cases as a basis for discussing the strategic issues which they face within their own companies.

All the cases are intended as a basis for class discussion, and not as illustrations of good or bad management.

The Cases

The main theme running through this book is the relationship between ownership and management, since it is these two factors which are the key to many of the issues facing the small firm, such as the source of future funds, succession or the acquisition of new skills and products. The ways in which this relationship can change are highlighted in Chapter 1 (Eaves and Washbourne), which looks at the critical choices to be made as the firm grows from the entrepreneurial stage, through a second generation, to the beginnings of professional management. This case series is useful either as a start to a small-business course or as an overview of the area.

The limited amount of data in Chapter 1 can be contrasted with the amount in Chapter 2 (Seed Oysters). Here the student will initially feel more comfortable but soon begin to realise that in a start-up proposal, particularly for a new technology, he is ill equipped to evaluate the venture. What criteria should he use and how should he weight them? How can he separate a good idea from a bad proposal? How does he decide how much money is really needed? And what should be the relationship between shareholding and the inputs of money, products and skills?

Chapter 3 (M. D. Benedict) takes the student through the first two years of the firm as it struggles to survive. It looks at the characteristics of the partners and poses the question of how much luck and how much skill is needed in the early years of a firm.

Chapter 4 (Cohen and Fowler) is an important one for students – particularly as many of them find it easier to identify with professionals such as Sid or Debbie than with entrepreneurs such as Chris Cameron of M. D. Benedict or Stan Eaves of Eaves and Washbourne, but also because it is the only example of a company with a partnership rather than limited liability. The case series raises two issues which distinguish service firms from the more familiar manufacturing firms. First, there is the question of how to grow when the product is based upon the professional skills of the individual; and, secondly, there is the problem of what management and control systems are appropriate in such situations. It is useful to tie this case series in with the case of Stephenson, Turbridge and Bassett (Chapter 5) to review the question of how to motivate and manage highly qualified and effective professionals.

Motivation is the key to Regent Printers (Chapter 6), a rapidly growing and successful firm. An opportunistic approach to growth is taken here, and successful salesmen are given minority shareholdings and promoted to managing director as new companies are created. Is this the way to promote growth, and should the salesmen's motivation change when a holding-company structure is created?

In the discussion of all the cases so far, the student will be interested because growth is assumed and so change is likely to happen. The case of R. J. Nevill (Chapter 7) will, therefore, seem dull by comparison, since the firm has never really been more than a 'corner shop'. Nevertheless, it is important to recognise that Nevill represents a very

2

large proportion of the small-business population, particularly in the retail trade. Students will feel sympathy with Philip, both because they too would not wish to devote their life to what they consider to be an uninteresting business and because they understand the emotional pressures to which he is being subjected. In a discussion of the problems facing the potential second-generation manager, his choices can be compared with those of Paul Washbourne.

Chapters 8 (Gilbern Cars) and 9 (Morgan Cars) should be taken together, in an attempt to look at the possible reasons for survival of the small firm in a high-technology, capital-intensive industry which is dominated by a few giants.

Up to this point the question of the definition of 'small' has deliberately been avoided. There is no finite point at which small firms suddenly become medium-sized, size, in this instance, being a function of complexity of management systems and structure, of product line or of shareholding. The teacher may choose either of the last two cases to illustrate firms trying to make the transition from small to medium-sized. In the first instance, Barnes and Ward (Chapter 10), an old-established company with, in effect, one product, is jerked out of its slumber by a rapidly changing environment and is forced to become market-oriented. Here the student is left with the haunting question: has the firm slept too long?

By the end of Case C in Chapter 11, Henry Sykes has gone far beyond anything which most people would describe as small. Nevertheless, in the financial world obtaining a public quotation means that a small company has achieved the respectability of medium size. This company is particularly interesting because it was the first to trade shares 'over the counter' through M. J. H. Nightingale and Co. and then to take advantage of Stock Exchange Rule 135(2) to obtain permission to trade shares. But perhaps more important for the student of the small business are two issues which run through the three cases in this series. The first concerns the relationship between the investor and the operator, a relationship which becomes particularly complex when the investor is responsible for both equity and debt capital. The second issue concerns the time it takes to create, and the difficulty which growing and successful firms appear to experience in creating, systems and structures which are acceptable to both the bank and the Stock Exchange.

1 Eaves and Washbourne Ltd

SUE BIRLEY

CASE A

This is the first in a series of cases which deals with the development of Eaves and Washbourne Ltd from 1965, when it began to negotiate the acquisition of an American licence, to 1974, when the chief executive was faced with the need to decide both his own future and that of the company.

The company was formed in 1951 by Stan Eaves (32) and his uncle Ron Washbourne (42) – both of whom had previously worked for a local engineering firm, Coventry Gauge and Tools Ltd – to act as sub-contractors for larger firms in the tooling of jigs and fixtures. Starting from an old stable, the business grew until in 1964 they had sales in excess of £100,000 a year and had moved to a small engineering shop in Deedmore Road, Coventry. Stan recalls the formation of the company: 'I had been thinking of setting up on my own for a long time and the more I looked around for a partner, the more I was convinced that Ron was ideal. Whilst I enjoy working with the machines, Ron is very good at costing and planning engineering jobs. He wasn't too keen at first and so I left my job and set it up, and he joined me when the work had built up a bit.'

Throughout their first thirteen years of trading, Ron, in particular, felt that they should try to move away from their total reliance upon sub-contract work by developing a product of their own. There had never been sufficient capital available to pursue this objective, but late in 1965 they were approached by a former customer, Dr Blythe, with a proposition for a licensing venture. Dr Blythe had a great deal of experience in managing large engineering companies in the area, latterly as managing director of Precision Gears, which had been set up as an American subsidiary of Joseph Lamb to manufacture gear-cutting machines and small transfer machines under licence. As a result of the particular knowledge gained, Dr Bythe, who was in his early sixties, had left Precision Gears in order to set up on his own as a licensed manufacturer of engineering products. A trip to America had resulted in his negotiating the licence to manufacture and sell precision surface-grind machines for Parker Majestic Inc., a small but well-known established family business, which had confined its activities to the domestic American market. On his return Dr Blythe formed Associated Machines and Tools and approached the Department of Trade and Industry (DTI) for financial aid. The DTI proposed to invest £300,000 in a factory in the north-east of England, provided that he found £100,000 from his own resources. With insufficient capital of his own, Dr Blythe broached the possibility of some form of joint venture with Eaves and Washbourne. Whilst the proposal to set up a new factory was too expensive and ambitious at that stage of the company's development, particularly while the range of products was unknown in the UK, the joint venture did seem very attractive.

On 31 December 1965, an agreement was drawn up by Dr Blythe (see Exhibit 1A.1) with the understanding that Associated Machines and Tools would be responsible for generating sales and Eaves and Washbourne for manufacturing, when firm orders were received. At this stage the assets of Associated Machines and Tools comprised a £600 scraping master from Parker Majestic, the licence and a quantity of company letterheads. It was estimated that manufacturing set-up costs would be £20,000, that the first batch would take six months to produce, and at a provisional selling price of £1250, it was agreed that no investment should take place until twelve firm orders had been received.

Paul Washbourne, Ron's son, describes subsequent events:

I had just left Oxford at the time, where I had read French and German. I had joined Adcock and Shipley Ltd, milling-machine manufacturers, and was training to be their European sales representative, which would have involved travelling around the Continent chasing their various agents. As soon as Dr Blythe heard about me he said, 'We've got to have him and make him a director, because, as soon as we get this thing off the ground, we are going to market our surface-grinders all over the world. It will be just the job for him.' Of course, I fell for it and went in on Monday morning to give my notice to Adcock and Shipley, who said, 'You might as well go now, as it is costing us to train you.' Well, it took us two days to find out he was going to break us. He had fantastic ideas and was a real big spender. He had never driven a car, always had a chauffeur, and we used to have to send our Austin Seven van to Rugby (twenty miles away) to collect him each morning – he used to come to work in a morning suit! There was a bit of a slump in the industry at that time, we were short of cash, struggling along, and so a month after I joined we went along to his house to suggest that we forget the whole thing. There was a very nasty scene and he refused to entertain the idea.

Part of the original understanding had been that Eaves and Washbourne would find the initial working capital, including Dr Blythe's salary, and Dr Blythe would concentrate upon prospective customers. To this end he flew to America towards the end of the first week, to see the president of Parker Majestic, to try to get some help with initial orders. He took with a him a 'mayoral chain' on which hung a gold replica of the company's emblem – as a present. Two days later a telegram arrived at Deedmore Road: 'MISSION ACCOMPLISHED.' However, by April no orders had been received and relations between the two parties became very strained, as Ron and Stan, encouraged by Paul, began to consider limiting further cash payments until the situation improved. On 28 April they received a second handwritten agreement from Dr Blythe (Exhibit 1A.2), which, after discussion, they refused to sign, Ron explained,

By June it was obvious that either he had to go or we had. The strain was beginning to affect my health. We thought that it was possible that he was short of money so one Friday afternoon we met and offered to purchase the other third of Associated Machines and Tools for £13,000, the cost as stated on the original agreement. To our immense relief, he agreed. I was afraid that he would change his mind if we waited until Monday to consult our solicitors, and so I drew up an agreement myself [Exhibit 1A.3] at the meeting, which we all signed.

Unfortunately, the agreement failed to specify when the licence and other documents

5

(such as drawings and specifications) should change hands; it soon became apparent that Dr Blythe intended this to happen when the payments were finished – three years later. With the second instalment due in summer 1967, cash had become so short that expansion in the rest of the business was suffering. Accordingly, Stan, Ron and Paul decided to cut their losses once again and stop any further payment to Dr Blythe: suddenly the licence became available! But yet another shock was in store: the termination date had been renegotiated the previous November and brought forward to July 1970 – one year after the final payment to Dr Blythe.

In a last-ditch effort to save something out of the mess, Ron Washbourne went to America to see Norman Parker, the chief executive of Parker Majestic:

It was clear when I got there that they were very confused about the situation, but I was able to reassure them and we renegotiated a twenty-year licence in the name of Eaves and Washbourne.

In the autumn of 1967, Associated Machines and Tools began to manufacture.

Reflecting on the experience, Stan takes a philosophical view:

It was a bit strange that he [Dr Blythe] wanted to join us, but he was getting on a bit and he obviously wasn't going to get anywhere in a big company. I thought it was a good opportunity for us. I had always found him all right as a customer: he was straightforward and hard on the point, and I prefer that way of working. Mind you, I didn't know him on a personal level and I had doubts very quickly when I realised that, although he was a brilliant man and had lots of ideas and experience, he lacked everything at a lower level. He couldn't win with us because he didn't know how to deal with us.

So much time had been spent in worrying about the licence that the rest of the business had been neglected. With the beginnings of an engineering slump, not only was the order level extremely low, but in addition the company was facing severe liquidity problems.

Paul Washbourne explains,

We were bankrupt. The only thing that saved us was that the bank manager had a nervous breakdown and went into hospital – they brought in a new manager who did not really know what was going on and we ran up a huge overdraft. Our accountant left and I got a friend of mine from school to come and take over. He wrote letters to everyone to say, 'I have just taken over, the accounts are in a bit of a mess, but the firm is quite sound; give us a couple of months and we will pay you'.

Desperate for cash, Stan, Ron and Paul went to the Industrial and Commercial Finance Corporation (ICFC), a bank specialising in loans to smaller firms, and were offered £10,000 for half the business, provided that their private houses were placed as collateral. Paul recounts,

We came out of that office having been told that we ought to be ashamed of ourselves: we were not capable of running a company. It was a hell of a shock; we had a meeting in Dad's office and decided that we would have a go. We weren't going to throw half the business away for £10,000. Up until then we had had a very dilettante approach to work. For example, my father would work in the mornings and do charity work in the afternoons. Next morning we were all in at 8.00 a.m. Dad borrowed £5000 from a friend to pay the wages and from then on the turnover and profits gradually improved.

6

EAVES AND WASHBOURNE (TOOLS) LTD
DEEDMORE RD, BELL GREEN, COVENTRY

31st December 1965

1. The writer agrees to purchase for £13,000 (monies proved to have been expended on acquisition of Parker–Wilson Rights etc) 2,600 £1 shares in Eaves and Washbourne Ltd at £5 each.

   In the event of Eaves and Washbourne shares being valued by accountants at a figure in excess (or lower than) £5 each, the number of shares purchased will be adjusted accordingly.
2. Associated Machines and Tools Ltd agrees to issue 90,000 fully paid £1 shares – divided as to 30,000 to Mr R. Washbourne and 30,000 to Mr S. Eaves, 30,000 to G. E. K. Blythe leaving 10,000 £1 shares for issue at a later date in equal amounts of $\frac{1}{3}$ to each of the aforementioned shareholders.

G. E. K. Blythe

R. Washbourne

S. Eaves

Note. This agreement was signed by Dr Blythe, Ron Washbourne and Stan Eaves, but other events overtook the legal process and the shares never actually exchanged hands.

ASSOCIATED MACHINES AND TOOLS LTD
ALPHA WORKS. DEEDMORE RD, BELL GREEN, COVENTRY

28th April 1966

Messrs. Eaves and Washbourne (Tools) Ltd,
Deedmore Road,
Bell Green,
Coventry.

Dear Sirs,

Re: Parker-Majestic Licence

As you are fully aware we are Exclusive Licensees of Parker-Majestic Incorporated of Detroit, Michigan, USA.

From time to time over the past five months we have supplied you with technical data, drawings, machine and material specifications, material and labour cost figures, brochures, material and component samples, operating instructions and a service manual. It is recognised and agreed that the aforesaid information and technical data contain valuable trade secrets of our Licensor company, Parker-Majestic Incorporated. Accordingly it is therefore agreed:—

a) to hold the aforesaid information and technical data in strict confidence.

b) not to disclose the same to anyone outside your organisation.

c) not to use, or permit others to use, the aforesaid information and technical data in the manufacture use or sale of machines similar to the licensed machines and spindles, except as expressly permitted under the terms of Agreement currently under negotiation by our respective companies.

d) in the event of failure to agree upon the terms presently under discussion between our respective companies your Company hereby agrees to return forthwith to Our Company, and this without charge or hindrance all the aforesaid information and technical data the acknowledged property of this company by virtue of its Exclusive licence from Parker-Majestic Incorporated, Detroit, USA. Your company recognises that money damages could not fully compensate Parker-Majestic in the event of failure by your company to comply with its obligation under this Agreement for the all important reason that Parker-Majestic have embodied in the aforesaid information and technical data invaluable 'know how' and 'tricks of the trade' acquired and developed by them over the past fifty-one years of business.

In the event of your company failing to comply with the terms of this Preliminary Letter Agreement or for a period of five years following the operative date of failure envisaged and provided for in (c) and (d) above, you hereby agree not to utilise any of the aforesaid information and/or technical data for a period of five years from the operative date above referred to for the purpose of manufacture. Further, you will not cause or permit any such technical data to be used directly or indirectly in the manufacture of machines, spindles and components thereof similar in design to the Parker-Majestic Licensed Machines and Spindles and component parts thereof (whether or not such machines, spindles and component parts thereof are identical to the Licensed Machines Spindles and Component parts thereof).

Yours faithfully,

Associated Machines and Tools Ltd

We agree to the above conditions and terms:
For Eaves and Washbourne (Tools) Ltd

Director	Witness
Director	Witness

EXHIBIT 1A.3

EAVES AND WASHBOURNE (TOOLS) LTD
DEEDMORE RD, BELL GREEN, COVENTRY

17.6.66.

To: Dr G. K. Blythe.

We hereby agree to purchase from Dr G. K. Blythe the whole of the nominal capital of 100,000 £1 shares in Associated Machines and Tools Ltd including all the Parker-Majestic and other licences acquired by the aforesaid company together with all drawings, catalogues, correspondence and technical data received from Parker-Majestic Incorporated, Detroit, USA.

The consideration payable for the aforesaid acquisition shall be £13,000 (Thirteen thousand pounds).

£3,000 initial payment made today hereby acknowledged.

Six six-monthly payments of £1,666. 13. 4d., the first of such payments to be made on 1st January 1967.

It is understood and agreed that necessary safeguards will be afforded Dr Blythe to ensure the above six bi-annual payments are made on the due dates namely 1st January and 1st July in each of the three years 1967, 1968 and 1969.

R. Washbourne

S. Eaves

G. E. K. Blythe

EXHIBIT 1A.4   Consolidated profit and loss account (£), 1965−7

	1965	1966	1967
Turnover	151,387	171, 271	n.a.
Trading profit for the year	15,161	17,413	(4,152)
after charging			
directors' remuneration	2,880	3,600	3,600
auditors' remuneration	347	280	315
depreciation	5,288	6,584	6,484
amortisation of leasehold premises	550	887	−
bank interest	1,793	1,839	2,100
Profit before taxation	15,161	17,413	(4,152)
Taxation	−	4,600	−
Profit after taxation	15,161	12,813	(4,152)

EXHIBIT 1A.5   Consolidate balance sheet (£), 1965–7

	1965	1966	1967
Fixed assets			
Property	3,000	4,500	3,600
Plant, fixtures and motor vehicles	34,549	38,595	45,301
	37,549	43,095	48,901
Goodwill arising on consolidation	–	–	14,315
Current assets			
Stock and work in progress	15,723	16,499	16,122
Debtors	37,769	40,027	44,952
Cash – building society	106	1,909	2,708
– bank	24	50	401
Total assets	91,171	101,580	127,399
Less current liabilities			
Creditors	20,513	21,242	27,989
Bank overdraft	27,050	25,669	45,773
Taxation	(1,817)	2,783	6,185
Directors' current account	12,112	9,160	1,786
	67,858	68,854	81,733
Net assets	33,313	42,726	45,666
Financed by			
Share capital	10,000	10,000	10,000
Reserves	23,313	32,726	28,575
Directors' loan	–	–	7,091
	33,313	42,726	45,666

10

CASE B

This case continues the development of the company until the end of 1973, focusing upon the establishment of two major subsidiaries. During this period Ron Washbourne suffered a number of severe illnesses and Paul became managing director in all but name, having been given 10 per cent of his father's shares in the business.

The formation of Albion Heat Ltd

Many of the parts which Eaves and Washbourne manufactured required a specialist process of heat treatment provided by Alvis Ltd, a large local firm. For some time Eaves and Washbourne had been considering whether to enter this market, since the apparent lack of price sensitivity made potential profitability extremely attractive (customer price insensitivity was thought to be owing to lack of knowledge of the process itself, coupled with the small price of the treatment relative to the overall cost of the job): this was brought to a head during 1970, when Alvis, which had two heat-treatment plants, decided to close down one plant and cut out all sub-contract work. Albion Heat Ltd was formed jointly by Eaves and Washbourne and Brian Shreeve, the ex-Alvis heat-treatment manager. The investment totalled £1000 for all the furnaces which Alvis no longer required, and £5000 for premises and set-up costs. Paul reflects,

> Whilst we are still good friends, Brian will not have me at any meetings. The original idea was that we should put up £6000 and Brian should take 60 per cent of the shares, as he had the expertise. I persuaded my Dad and Stan that shareholding should equal capital investment and so we ended up with a 50/50 partnership, each investing £3000. I think he still feels a bit sore about it. Nevertheless, it was a very good decision. Things didn't turn out as Alvis hoped; within a month we were doing sub-contract work for them, and within three months we were making a profit on their business alone.

The acquisition of Cross Road

During summer 1972, the lease for the factory site at Deedmore Road ran out, and, as it seemed unlikely that it would be renewed, the company looked around for alternative accommodation. A site was purchased at Cross Road, near the city centre, for £80,000, comprising $1\frac{1}{2}$ acres (30,000 square feet) and divided into five small industrial units. In the event, the lease at Deedmore Road was renewed, but by subletting four of the five units the company was able to cover the mortgage costs and make a profit.

At the same time the original partnership, which had never been totally stable, became very shaky. Paul Washbourne describes the situation:

> It only kept going because Stan Eaves, while he doesn't have a weak character, will always give in. My father was the strength of the company. He did all the organisational work, planning and the quotations, and Stan just used to tear around the factory wrapping up parcels, loading lorries and worrying. If they both hadn't been so easy-going, the partnership would have broken up years ago. Anyway, I'm not so easy-going and I used to have terrible rows with Stan. He's got no education, no organisational ability whatsoever and he admits it. He was happy when they had

ten people and he was doing a bit himself. He hates making a profit, because he doesn't like paying tax. It got to such a pitch that he was trying to buy us out and we were trying to buy him out: we were thinking of splitting the firm down the middle. The only trouble with that was that we would have had to liquidate the firm to create two new ones and the capital gains tax on the growth since 1951 would have been enormous – Stan didn't like that.

Stan comments,

I prefer to be entirely on my own. I don't really like having to ask anyone anything – not that I mind seeking advice, but I don't like being in a position where I can't do what I want when I have made up my mind.

Paul and I can't work together. he jumps in where even angels fear to tread and if things come off, that is fine – but if it goes wrong, it *really* goes wrong with Paul. I can't stand by and watch something go wrong but on the other hand I don't like arguing and scrapping all day. Basically, there is a generation difference between us.

It became obvious to me that the thing to do was for me to take the Parker-Majestic work down to Cross Road and run that part on my own. Kits could be sent down from Deedmore Road and assembled in clean conditions. It was a perfect solution.

Acquisition of Gulson Plating

Rolls-Royce, the well-known engineering company, was a major customer of Eaves and Washbourne. Towards the end of 1970 it became increasingly obvious to both the business world and the Government that Rolls-Royce faced a major cash crisis, owing to substantial investment in the development of a new engine, the RB211. As a result of the failure to raise additional working capital from either private or public funds, share dealings were suspended and a receiver appointed in February 1971.

On the day of the crash, Rolls-Royce owed Eaves and Washbourne £39,000, of which £9000 worth of components had been despatched by lorry the previous evening. The lorry had broken down on its way to Shrewsbury, much to Paul's relief. Paul telephoned the company.

PAUL: 'Our lorry hasn't arrived, has it?'
ROLLS-ROYCE: 'Hold on ... Oh, hard luck mate, we've just towed it through the gates!'

Although extremely serious, the Rolls-Royce debt was counterbalanced by the previous quarter's profit of £38,000, enabling the company to continue without raising additional working capital. In the event, Eaves and Washbourne continued to supply Rolls-Royce, since the receiver paid within thirty days, whereas prior to the crash four months' credit had been taken.

Two years later, in June 1973, Eaves and Washbourne received a pleasant surprise from Rolls-Royce in the form of a cheque for £20,000, and, says Paul, 'we wondered what to do with it'. Around the same time, a friend, Norman Haynes, manager of a small electro-plating company complained to him, 'I am that browned off, have you got a job at your place?'

Paul was sympathetic:

The bloke who ran the place hadn't a clue. he was a typical British owner – a Conservative councillor, who gets to the firm about 10.00 a.m., writes a few orders, pays the wages, goes and gets drunk at lunchtime and spends the afternoon in the Conservative Club. Then he blames Harold Wilson, the workers, the Labour Party and the TUC for not making a profit – typical British firm. I was sure that we could do better and since some of our jobs had to be sent out for electro-plating, such an acquisition would increase efficiency in the rest of the business as well as being a profitable sideline – just like Albion Heat.

The company had two sites, one of which was leased and used for all the electro-plating whilst the other was owned by the company and used for aluminium anodising. When approached, the owner indicated a willingness to sell the electro-plating side of the business. He wanted £21,000 and payment for the stock, which was valued at about £4000. Norman Haynes valued the plant at £16,000, which meant that they would be paying an extra £5000 for the lease of the premises ($3\frac{1}{2}$ years remaining, at £500 per year for 5000 square feet) and goodwill. The previous year had shown a turnover of £16,000 and no profit.

Paul was eager to go ahead: 'It would mean that we would be completely self-sufficient, no longer having to get things heat-treated and plated outside. I thought we could make £4000 profit in the first year.'

Stan, on the other hand, was violently against it: 'It went against the grain. It would mean that we would be in direct competition with a bloke I had been sailing with for twenty years, and it wasn't even as though we needed it.'

EXHIBIT 1B.1   Consolidated profit and loss account, (£), 1968–72

	1968	1969	1970	1971	1972
Turnover	192,851	209,650	313,524	335,625	233,623
Trading profit for the year	8,789	11,439	38,747	52,083	10,035
after charging					
directors' remuneration	6,900	10,000	13,160	7,374	10,692
auditors' remuneration	367	367	432	422	480
depreciation	8,295	10,420	11,139	8,701	9,016
amortisation of leasehold					
premises	–	–	–	1,379	325
hire of equipment	–	–	–	279	183
bank interest	5,182	3,776	3,473	2,028	1,907
short-term loan interest	638	912	590	335	29
and after crediting					
rents received	–	–	–	3,133	3,122
interest received	89	35	48	83	1,145
Provision for doubtful debt – Rolls-Royce Ltd	–	–	–	37,934	(5,628)
Profit before taxation	8,789	11,439	38,747	14,149	15,663
Taxation	(206)	7,150	14,700	7,839	5,225
Profit after taxation	8,995	4,289	24,047	6,310	10,438

EXHIBIT 1B.2   Consolidated balance sheet, (£), 1968—72

	1968	1969	1970	1971	1972
Fixed assets					
Property	2,783	1,969	8,151	325	—
Plant, fixtures and motor vehicles	42,724	41,995	40,719	41,756	41,580
	45,507	43,694	48,870	42,505	41,580
Goodwill arising on consolidation	13,435	13,435	13,434	14,974	14,974
Investment in associated company	—	—	3,000	3,000	3,000
Current assets					
Stock and work in progress	24,679	27,175	27,443	21,112	32,829
Debtors	43,262	54,248	89,832	88,601	69,158
Investment grants receivable	8,531	1,949	3,165	1,016	373
Cash — building society	16	1,020	408	7,127	33,023
— bank	2,443	318	180	280	151
Total assets	137,873	142,109	186,332	178,615	195,614
Less current liabilities					
Creditors	35,361	37,889	47,128	51,759	60,413
Due to associated company	—	—	—	660	788
Bank overdraft	42,393	30,348	33,690	17,283	28,491
Taxation	5,690	7,636	21,685	21,310	10,925
Directors' current account	2,030	—	—	6,631	2,588
	85,474	85,873	102,503	97,643	103,204
Net assets	52,399	56,236	83,829	80,972	92,410
Financed by					
share capital	10,000	10,000	10,000	10,000	10,000
reserves	36,689	40,493	64,705	70,792	74,410
tax equalisation	—	—	—	—	8,000
directors' loan	5,710	5,743	9,124	—	—
	52,399	56,236	83,829	80,792	92,410

CASE C

This case concentrates on the industrial-relations aspects of the business in response to external changes in the form of the end of an old-established payment system, the Coventry Toolroom Rate, and the rapid increase in the rate of inflation.

The company had always been non-unionised, a situation management preferred. With regard to unionisation Paul Washbourne commented,

> I wouldn't mind if it didn't alter our relationship, but I would hate to be in the situation where if a man wanted a job which was out in the yard, he wouldn't find a trolley and get it himself. This is the sort of thing you get with non-mobility of labour and it can substantially constrain your flexibility. We have enough trouble getting the work out as it is. It isn't because we pay them high wages – I know companies in this town that pay more than us and are no bigger than us, but which have terrible union problems – I think it is one's attitude to people that makes all the difference.

The Coventry Toolroom Rate

Since 1941 an agreement had existed – the Coventry Toolroom Agreement – to which all engineering companies in Coventry had subscribed (Exhibit 1C.1). This ensured that the rates in the area were far higher than in the rest of the country.

In the summer of 1971, when the rate stood at about £1 per hour, the agreement lapsed. Paul reports,

> I said to the lads, we are now going to have to negotiate our own pay rises, so I am suggesting to you that I pay an extra 10 per cent plus a bit on your holiday pay, for the next twelve months. They thought it was great, because in the past they had rises of 1p per hour every couple of months, which mounted up over the year, but here I was giving them 10p per hour in one go.

They agreed that in the first year the retail price index would be used as the guideline for determining wages instead of the toolroom rate, and that each month the wage rate would be adjusted according to the latest data available. In the event, this arrangement only lasted for one year, because the following year the Government introduced a statutory incomes policy which limited the amount of all wage increases.

Negotiations had always been conducted on an *ad hoc* basis between Terry Hutchinson, the works manager, and the chargehands (see Exhibit 1C.2 for the number of employees). No formal meetings were called, although, says Paul, '...there was one bloke in the place who was a keen union man, but a very fair one and if you satisfied him you knew everyone else would be happy. Although not a chargehand he was really the informal shop steward.'

At the same time a meeting of the Coventry Employers Federation was called which represented small companies in the area. Paul Washbourne was invited, although Eaves and Washbourne was not a member. Paul remarks,

> At that time Eaves and Washbourne were the only company to have reacted positively to the termination of the Toolroom Rate. All the rest were of the attitude that they were not liable to give any rises for at least twelve months – and they had

no intention of doing so. Within a very short space of time most were paying more than me and a lot of them had strikes, lock-outs and no end of trouble. Now that to me is typical of British management. And from that day onwards I never joined the employers federations, because, if that's the way they run their organisation, I just don't want to know.

The change of wage structure

Towards the end of 1972, business had become very brisk, necessitating a substantial amount of overtime for direct labour. Whilst this was a very happy state of affairs for the company, it created unrest amongst the chargehands, who complained that they were expected to take responsibility and work overtime without any extra pay. Direct labour worked ten to twelve hours a week of overtime,* thus giving them an extra £15 and eliminating any differential (about 10p per hour plus full holiday pay) between themselves and the chargehands. In order to avoid any conflict and to encourage the 'right sort of person' to take on the job of chargehand, a profit-sharing scheme was introduced during the summer of 1973. Twenty per cent of company profits, after depreciation but before corporation tax, would be divided among fourteen people: the three directors, the works manager, the chief draughtsman, the chief inspector, the process-planner, the accountant and six chargehands. Management felt that this would provide a good bonus whilst not being enough seriously to affect cash flow or the amount of capital retained in the business for future investment. Every three months the group would meet to discuss the performance of the previous quarter, and future targets and priorities for customers and products ('Maximum output for us means maximum customer satisfaction' – Paul). Paul and Terry both felt that this had proved very satisfactory: 'We don't have to chase them any more, they chase us!' (Terry).

The formalisation of negotiations

The high rate of inflation soon made annual wage reviews inadequate, and so, in July 1974, Paul suggested a new formula upon which to base the direct labour rates for the next twelve months: an immediate rise with the proviso that as soon as the cost of living increased by more than 7 per cent they would be given the percentage increase. In other words, they would maintain a 5 per cent real increase for the next twelve months. Despite this offer, Paul was asked in October 1974 whether he would object to a meeting being called in the works canteen to form a representative committee of three, for future wage negotiations. 'I was worried to death. It was the first time anything like this had ever happened. I began to see "Reds under the bed". Obviously I couldn't deny the request, but I did try to infiltrate one of the cleaners into the meeting – unsuccessfully.'

The committee, which when formed included the original 'informal shop steward', announced that they were not satisfied with the agreement previously negotiated. Their

---

*The overtime rate was time plus one-third of Consolidated Time Rate (CTR) for the first two hours worked on weekdays. Any overtime above this or any weekend work was paid at time plus one-half of CRT. For example, if the Eaves and Washbourne rate was £1.70 and CTR £1, a man working eleven hours on Monday would earn 11 × £1.70 + 2 × £0.33 + 1 × £0.50 = £19.86.

17

research on other firms in the area had shown that many were paying £1.50 per hour for a forty-hour week, while they were only getting £1.37 per hour. This was despite the fact that

(1) about half the labour force in Eaves and Washbourne were also getting a merit payment of 5p per hour (an anomaly from the past); and
(2) firms in the area tied their holiday pay to the Consolidated Time Rate (CTR), the minimum engineers' rate for the whole country. Whilst all paid more than CTR during normal working time, most only paid the minimum rate (75p per hour) for holidays. Eaves and Washbourne paid the full rate for holidays. (Normal holidays were five weeks plus two days at Easter and one day for New Year.)

One member of the committee remarked that it was all very well relying on the cost-of-living index, but other firms were giving regular pay rises: '... how do we know how much the cost of living will increase? We want £1.46 per hour for the next year inclusive of the merit payment.'

EXHIBIT 1C.1   Coventry Toolroom Agreement, January 1941

Memorandum of Agreement between the Coventry and District Engineering Employers'
Association and the Amalgamated Engineering Union (Coventry District).

CONDITION OF EMPLOYMENT OF SKILLED TOOLROOM OPERATIVES IN THE COVENTRY TOOLROOMS OF FEDERATED FIRMS

(1) This agreement is SUPPLEMENTAL to the National Agreement made between the
Engineering and Allied Employers' National Federation and the Amalgamated Engineering
Union and dated 4 June 1940.

(2) IT IS AGREED that in relation to the skilled operators employed by Federated
Firms in their Coventry Toolrooms or skilled men who are transferred from production
to toolmaking work in Coventry Toolrooms of Federated Firms (all of which are
hereinafter referred to as 'the skilled Toolroom Operatives') the following provisions
shall apply during wartime emergency in lieu of the terms of the National Agreement
aforesaid:

(i)   The skilled Toolroom Operatives are to be paid on a district basis in lieu of the
        establishment basis as specified in the said National Agreement.
(ii)   The district basis of payment to the skilled Toolroom Operative shall be the
        weighted average of the inclusive earnings during the normal workingweek of 47
        hours of the skilled production workers employed by the Federated Members of
        the Association having Toolroom Operatives in their employ over the period of the
        month next but two preceding the month of payment – that is to say the weighted
        average of the inclusive earnings of the skilled production workers as aforesaid
        during the month of October 1940 shall be taken as the basis of payment of the
        skilled Toolroom Operatives for January 1941, the month of November 1940 for
        February 1941, and so on.
(iii)   For all purposes of the said National Agreement and of this Agreement the
        expression 'skilled production workers' shall mean skilled fitters, skilled turners and
        skilled machinists only.
(iv)   Any adjustment that may be necessary in the remuneration of skilled Toolroom
        Operatives under this Agreement shall start to accrue as from the commencement
        of the week which begins on or after the 28 December 1940; the first pay to
        skilled Toolroom Operatives under this agreement to be made on 10 January 1941
        or on the usual pay day of the individual firms in that week.
(v)   Except as hereinbefore otherwise provided, the terms of the said National
        Agreement shall apply and operate in relation to skilled Toolroom Operatives
        employed in the Coventry Toolrooms of Federated Firms.

DATED this 7th day of January 1941.
SIGNED on behalf of:

The COVENTRY AND DISTRICT ENGINEERING EMPLOYERS' ASSOCIATION
        J Shaw, President   J Varley, Secretary

AMALGAMATED ENGINEERING UNION (COVENTRY DISTRICT)
        W H Stokes, Divisional Organiser   C Taylor, District Sec.

EXHIBIT 1C.2   Average number of employees in 1974

Management   15
Indirect labour   15
Skilled labour   35
Semi-skilled labour   31

Note: There were nine operatives permanently on
night shift.

EXHIBIT 1C.3   Index of retail prices
                (monthly average)

Year	Index
1962	101.6
1963	103.6
1964	107.0
1965	112.1
1966	116.5
1967	119.4
1968	125.0
1969	131.8
1970	140.2
1971	153.4
1972	164.3

*Source: Annual Abstract of
Statistics*, published by the Central
Statistical office.

EXHIBIT 1C.4   Index of retail prices
                (quarterly average)

Year	Quarter	Index
1971	1	149.0
	2	153.3
	3	155.5
	4	158.1
1972	1	160.3
	2	163.7
	3	166.4
	4	170.2
1973	1	172.3
	2	177.9

Source: Annual Abstract of Statistics,
published by the Central Statistical Office.

CASE D

This case deals with the career of Paul Washbourne and poses the question of his future and that of the company.

During his childhood, Paul had no real contact with the factory. Originally his father had wanted to be a journalist, and he became an engineer only as a second choice. He was determined that the same should not happen to his children. Paul was encouraged to study, and read French and German at Oxford. At the time that Dr Blythe came on the scene, Paul had met and married a girl in Germany and was preparing to settle down on the Continent. Within three days his whole career was turned upside down.

When Blythe left I had burned my boats and was stuck with it, having left Adcock and Shipley, which was in the field I wanted to pursue. I started working on the shop floor to learn about engineering, doing a bit of fitting and turning. In those days the chap in charge of progress [production control] was paid half as much as a bloke on a lathe and yet he was running the business – typically British. It is the old business of if you pay peanuts you get monkeys. He had no formal education, was very conscientious but had neither the authority nor ability to run the place. So I was thrown into the hot seat because he had a heart attack. Although I had no real training in this field, my native intelligence plus the fact that I had had a good education meant that I made a reasonable job of it.

When the new Training Bill came out in 1964 we were not big enough to start our own scheme, so we went into the local group's scheme – Warwickshire Training Services. One day in 1971 I went out to the pub for a drink with one of their staff, who asked me why I didn't go in for more formal management training. 'Big-head,' I said, 'I don't need any bloody management training. It's all a load of eye-wash – all these professors telling us how to run firms.' The usual argument of '. . . if they can do it so well, why the bloody hell don't they have a go. Anyway, I don't need you to tell me how to get it out faster, I need you to tell me how to sell more.' He said, 'I've got just the course for you – it is a series of four weekends run by the Aston Small Business Centre on marketing, production control, finance control and personnel and it only costs £15 per weekend, full board.' How could I refuse? I came back from the first weekend on marketing absolutely shattered, because I realised that I knew nothing about running a business and it was about time I learnt. All the basic questions: 'Where are you going?', 'What is your management structure?', 'What are your production and sales forecasts?' – none of these things meant anything to me or to anyone else in the business. It is incredible how naive we were at the time. No one ever thought of how much money we would make in the next twelve months or what machines we were going to invest in. It was just a day-to-day thing of whatever landed on your desk you would do and preferably four of you would all do the same job – four doing production control, four ringing Rolls-Royce, etc. The investment programme depended almost entirely on the mood of my father at the time he was approached – usually by one of the blokes from the shop floor.

As a result of the marketing course I decided that we ought to have someone in charge of sales. Cliff, who had been hired as an assistant to my father, was made sales manager. My father was put in charge of commercial aspects (quoting, operation sheets and production planning) and I looked after the shop floor with Stan Eaves. Even that small amount of formalisation made quite a difference.

The financial-control course was yet another salutary experience: I realised that not a single person in the place could read a balance sheet. No-one had heard of marginal costing. Words can't express the inability of the management of the company to do any of the things they should have been doing.

The same applied on the personnel side. If they were intelligent they would go to Stan, because he would always give them a rise and if they went to my Dad he would never give them one — with thirty-five employees we had thirty-five wage structures. No-one ever thought of making sure things were fair and properly organised and so I started yearly negotiations. To be fair, we were lucky in Coventry at that time, because the Toolroom Rate still applied and did a lot of the work for us, but it was lucky that I did begin to formalise some structure because shortly after that the Toolroom Rate finished and we had at least something to start with. [See Case C.]

As a result of this I was absolutely sold on training and a year later I decided that all my top people should have at least a week on various aspects of the business: the inspector went on a quality-control course and Terry on three courses on motivation, production control and financial control, to give him an overall idea of the business.

At the time of writing the case, Paul Washbourne was asked to describe the organisation structure (see Exhibit 1D.1).

I am an MD in fact, but production director in name. Brian Griffiths is in charge of sales and planning. I am in charge of external grinding, fitting, turning, capstan and quality control. Terry is in charge of milling, the slideway grinder, the radial drill, painting, the fitters and Stan's section. As far as customers are concerned, I deal entirely with Rolls-Royce and Terry does the rest, except for a few odd ones I know personally — so we don't really need a salesman.

Terry is thirty-two years of age and has spent all his working life with Eaves and Washbourne, having started at fifteen as an apprentice. When asked to comment on the running of the company he said,

Over the last two years we have really got organised; now all the requests for jobs come from the two of us down here [Paul and Terry share an office on the shop floor] and our main problem for the future is maintaining the performance we have had over the last two years. The acquisition of Gulson Plating was a great success. Norman Haynes was put in complete charge of profitability and in 1975 sales were £32,000 with £2000 profit. Eaves and Washbourne only account for about 10 per cent of their turnover.

Asked to comment about the future, Paul Washbourne remarked,

Apart from myself, Terry is the only person in the factory with any management potential and I ought to get him to gradually take over the areas which I control, but then what would I do? I would get depressed if I could not have the sense of achievement of getting something out of the door. Ideally I would like to leave here and return to Germany where I could use my language training, but who would run the company? Dad should retire, but the company only started a pension scheme fairly recently and he is worried about his future income. Stan would rather stay at Cross Road until he is fifty-five and then retire. Even then his children would still only be teenagers and not ready for such responsibility, always assuming that they wanted it.

22

EXHIBIT 1D.1   Organisation structure

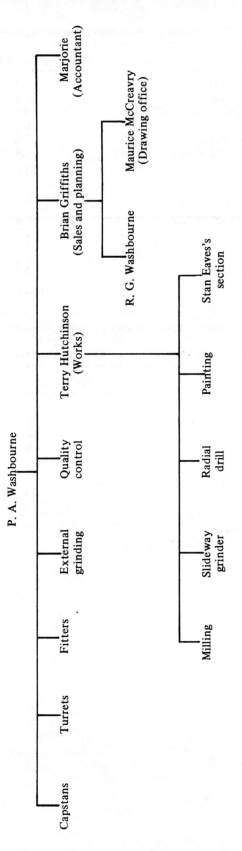

EXHIBIT 1D.2   Eaves and Washbourne products, sales analysis

Customer	Percentage of turnover
s/c Crosfield Electronics	40.3
s/c Rolls-Royce	27.8
s/c Kingsbury	5.8
s/c York	5.1
s/c Brush Electrics	1.0
s/c Colledge and Morley	0.4
	80.4

plus

s/c Broaching Machines	8.4
Cutter tools	1.2
Jigs	0.5
Quickset	0.4
Miscellaneous	9.1
	100.0

Note: s/c indicates sub-contract work to customer specification.

Parker-Majestic PRODUCTS (about 35 per cent of total turnover)

Product	Percentage of turnover
Spindles	51.7*
Spindles reconditioned	0.1
Machines	43.6†
Machines serviced	0.1
Spares	1.5
Miscellaneous	3.0
	100.0

*Five customers.
†30–50 customers, two-thirds repeat orders.

EXHIBIT 1D.3 Consolidated profit and loss account (£), 1973−4 (year ending 31 October)

		1973		1974
Turnover		435,103		671,634
Trading Profit for the year		45,151		49,723
after charging				
directors' remuneration	27,008		21,700	
auditors' remuneration	570		795	
depreciation	11,774		20,601	
amortisation of leasehold premises	—		1,500	
hire of equipment	370		844	
bank interest	3,180		5,230	
medium-term loan interest	2,561		2,743	
mortgage interest	5,536		6,942	
and after crediting				
rents received	12,285		15,249	
interest received	1,100		549	
Provision for doubtful debt recovered, Rolls-Royce Ltd		17,108		15,198
Net profit before taxation		62,259		64,921
Taxation (based on profits for the year at 47% 1973, 52% 1974)	23,200		18,675	
Transfer to taxation equalisation	6,600		21,915	
		29,800		40,590
Net profit after taxation		32,459		24,331

EXHIBIT 1D.4   Consolidated balance sheet (£), 1973–4 (year ending 31 October)

	1973		1974	
Fixed assets: freehold premises, plant, fixtures and motor vehicles		123,559		156,112
Goodwill arising on consolidation		14,974		15,724
Investment in associated company		3,000		3,000
Current assets				
Stock and work in progress	49,756		63,862	
Debtors and pre-payments	166,370		184,766	
Cash at building society	11,097		390	
Cash at bank	362		396	
		227,585		249,414
Total assets		369,118		424,250
Less current liabilities				
Creditors	87,067		134,931	
Amount due to associated company	1,722		2,609	
Bank overdraft	42,947		6,005	
Medium-term bank loan	18,574		15,250	
Tax	27,431		36,759	
Directors' current account	5,122		(8,721)	
		182,863		186,833
Net assets		186,255		237,417
Financed by				
share capital		10,000		10,000
reserves		104,469		128,800
tax equalisation		17,000		43,865
mortgage		54,786		54,752
		186,255		237,417

CASE E

By the summer of 1975 Paul Washbourne was desperate to leave Eaves and
Washbourne. He found the pressure of his responsibilities in running the company too
great and his family life began to suffer as he became more and more disturbed and
upset by the 'trap' in which he found himself. On one of the courses he had attended a
year previously he had met David Norburn and Sue Birley from the London Business
School and they had become friends. When they became aware of the extent of his
anxiety, David and Sue suggested that he explore the possibility of employing a
managing director from outside the firm and that he approach an ex-student of theirs,
Don Ellwood.

The meeting between Don and Paul was a great success: they took an immediate
liking to each other and were eager to pursue matters further. But Ron and Stan were
horrified. Not only did they feel betrayed by Paul's decision to leave the company, but
also they were not interested in employing someone from outside the family. Desperate
for a solution, Ron had a brainwave: what about Uncle Wally? Uncle Wally (Ron's
brother) had just retired from managing a division of a large engineering company,
Ransome and Rapier, and he was delighted to be asked to help in Eaves and
Washbourne.

For the first three or four months, everyone was happy. Paul, in particular, had found
someone to talk to, to encourage him and to share some of the burden. But within a year
it had become very clear that it was really only a short-term solution and that longer-
term measures had to be taken if the company was to survive and grow so that, at the
very least, Ron could retire with peace of mind. Ron and Stan approached Paul: 'Do
you think Don would still be interested?

Don Ellwood joined Eaves and Washbourne on 1 November 1976. This case outlines
his thoughts seven days later.

What is your background to date?

I left University with a degree in metallurgy and joined the Steel Company of Wales
as a graduate trainee. After two years I was put in charge of the metallurgy quality-
control inspection side of a mill turning out 30,000 tons of steel. From that I became
assistant to the guy running the works. Then came nationalisation and it became
more and more difficult to get anything done. I was spending at least 60 per cent of
my time negotiating with the unions and all to no avail. I suppose I would have done
OK in the company but it would have taken a very long time and so after looking at
various possibilities I applied for the two-year M.Sc. course at London and was
accepted.

On leaving the Business School I decided to try for a marketing job in a small
business since, I had interest but no experience in either of these fields, and I joined a
small company in Ross-on-Wye, called Woodville Rubber, as business-development
manager. Within six months of my joining we had all but lost two of our major
customers and our order book had been slashed in half. The sales manager was
sacked and I became the potential sacrificial lamb as the new sales manager.
However, I am pleased to be able to say that when I left the order book was at its
highest ever, *and* we were exporting 50 per cent of our sales. But the marketing
director was relatively young and there didn't seem to be any real possibilities

for further advancement for at least five or six years – far too long for me to wait.

I had been in contact with Paul a year ago but it all came to nothing when Uncle Wally took charge. Then about two months ago Paul wrote to me. He said that they were all being driven to distraction again, Wally hadn't been the answer and was I still interested?'

In what ways did you find the company different from your expectations?

I had always worked in companies where the availability of information was important. In Eaves and Washbournes I don't even know what the order book is, what is the forward demand on the factories or whether we are running at a profit! Actually I *can* say that we are making a profit, because our outgoings over the past three months were less than sales, but there is no financial-control system to give monthly forecast results. Obviously there are *systems*, because the bills are getting paid and the money chased in and, as we have just completed our annual stock-take, I hope to have some idea of the last year's profit fairly soon.

The second major surprise was a greater lack of direction than I had thought. There are so many sides to the business, so many bits and pieces that I don't know how the receptionist in the office manages: there is Eaves and Washbourne, Associated Machine Tools, Albion Heating, Gulson Plating and Helispur (a gear-cutting company we are operating within the factory) and yet the turnover is only £$\frac{1}{4}$ million! But, quite where it is all going, no-one has really bothered to think, and this is one of the reasons why I have accepted the challenge. After all, the company *appears* to be making money. It has a diverse but good product range, all in widely different markets, but none of which have ever been marketed before. Sales always came by word of mouth. It really is a business-policy strategy problem with great potential. Mind you, there is a peculiar family set-up, but I took the job because I got on well with Paul and because, as you can see, the organisation was ripe for change.

What do you consider to be the risks that you personally are taking and what is your time scale?

Well, I have had a reasonable track record to date and so the downside risk is minimal. I can always find a job elsewhere as a sales manager. Also, at thirty I am still young and I would really like to try and sort something out of this situation and also see if I can run a small business. If I couldn't do that then I certainly couldn't run a bigger business!

Regarding the time scale, it rather depends how things develop. If I was successful I would want to stay and expand the company, although by that time my objectives and those of the Eaves and the Washbournes may be different. To date they have had none – except to provide the daily bread.

What do you see as the advantages and disadvantages of working in a family business?

I can't answer that in general terms, but certainly working for this family has one big advantage. At the moment I am answerable to the board, but that doesn't meet and so I can really do my own thing. I have had no mandate from the family. On the negative side, they do not like taking any risks at all. As far as I can see, their objectives have always been to provide themselves with a living and to avoid disaster. However, although I am never going to be able to change their personalities, I think that, with sucess, I can modify their attitudes.

The other problem is what they are going to do in the future. At the moment Paul is involved in every decision, and, whereas that is understandable, it is not workable in the long term. I don't think that he should have a day-to-day involvement in the factory. He has an outward flair and personality which would make him an excellent European salesman, and I hope to move him in that direction.

I think that Stan is pleased that I have joined, because in the last week he has come forward with a lot of new ideas, including two propositions for buying other companies: a welding company costing about £10,000 and a gear-cutting company costing about £750,000. I think he is throwing ideas around now because in the past he never had much change from the others.

Nevertheless, he seems to be very happy at Cross Road and I am not going to disturb the set-up for the time being, although I will be pressurising him for information on, for example, how many hours it takes him to build a machine. In the long term I will be developing plans to use more of the space at Cross Road.

For the past week, Ron has been worrying a great deal about two problems. Firstly, I am not an engineer and can't do the things that he does, such as looking at a job and working out how to do it. Secondly, although Walter actually left before I arrived, he is continuing to act for us with a major client who is near his home in Norfolk. Since I have not been allowed to meet him or even speak to him, such an arrangement clearly cannot continue and Ron is faced with telling his brother that he doesn't want him. Whereas I can't help directly with either of these, one of my major aims in the next months will be to make decisions which will show a tangible benefit to the company and so give Ron some peace of mind.

What are your future industrial relations plans?

I have not as yet had a chance to get involved on this side, although I have begun to get to know the chargehands. As in the rest of the company, everything is informal. For example, we lease a lot of our property around the company but there are no leases: everything is done by arrangement. It is the same with the wages, and at present there are no problems over this because we pay more than the local rate. But of necessity it must become more structured, although it doesn't matter whether or not we eventually have a union shop, because the people on the shop floor are fully committed to the company. I intend to continue their involvement in our growth and to foster their pride in their work. After all, they are doing some very difficult work very well, especially with the limitations of the machines with which they have to work.

I think they see me as a stabilising influence in the company. For example, in the past it was not unusual for someone to be told 'sorry, there is no work for you this week', and, although it was all conducted on a very friendly basis, it did trade a lot on the workers' loyalty. I think that they see in me a more positive marketing approach which will give them a more even flow of work and thus better job security.

Who is the boss?

That is very difficult to answer. To date I have kept a low profile and not striven to be the dominating influence. Probably the people at Deedmore Road view Ron, the owner, as the boss, particularly as many of them have been with him for twenty years. They respect him a great deal as an engineer but they can see that he is not well and I hope that I can be seen as taking some of the load from him.

Paul has his own charisma and the shop floor regard him with affection and respect. Will I be able to transfer some of their loyalty to me? It is early days but I hope so. At the moment I am just getting my feet under the table, although, whilst the actual mechanics have yet to be established, regarding overall policy I am the boss.

What are your future plans for the company?

I have two short-term objectives. First, I want to develop an organisation capable of coping with the work it is acquiring, so that our customers do not become disenchanted: a distinct possibility if things had been left much longer. Second, I want to give peace of mind to the Washbourne family and the only way I can do this is by bringing in more orders. Setting up control systems or improving inspection procedures do not give tangible results.

In the long term, it is easy to split the firm in two. Paul will be responsible for marketing our range of machine tools and I will be responsible for the factory and for running the sub-contracting service side of the business. This should make my job of bringing in more orders relatively easy: Eaves and Washbourne are very good!

How do you think that the customers will react to you?

If my experience this week is anything to go by, I think that most are relieved that something has at last happened. Many of them have been with the company for many years and so have been involved in all the family traumas. Also, they could see that the company badly needed additional management strength.

Do you want shares in the business?

We have discussed this and there is an option for ownership in the future, but it will require me to buy out one of the partners and neither Ron nor Stan would be happy for me to do that until I have proved myself. The trouble is that the more successful I am the more expensive it becomes! Nevertheless, I think it is reasonable. After all, I wouldn't want to own shares if I was unsuccessful. We did discuss the possibility of issuing new shares but they didn't want to do this because it would upset the balance of power.

How do you see your relationship with Paul working out?

This could be a problem in the future. At the moment he doesn't want the responsibility of the whole organisation, but if things go well he may try to dominate me. If this does happen a lot will depend on our personal relationship and how much I am getting out of the job. Mind you, I do have an ally in Carla, his wife. Since she began to get involved in the company eighteen months ago she has become a very valuable asset, for two reasons. First, she has taken responsibility for all the necessary activities which Paul considered to be peripheral, such as insurance, welfare, improving working conditions and the company image. Second, as a result of all that she hears from other members of the company; she is sometimes the voice of sanity in family arguments. She is definitely to be encouraged!

At the moment both Paul and I are united in our determination to succeed, but if we do I could have problems in tempering his enthusiasm in the future. he is already talking about 'being the Rolls-Royce of the machine-tool trade'! I will go along with some of that because I think we can develop our reputation for skill and quality but in small, specialised sectors. I want to define a market, get it and most important make some money.

On 8 January 1977, at the firm's annual dinner–dance, Ron Washbourne announced his retirement and Don was faced with considering the question of ownership far earlier than he had anticipated.

2 Seed Oysters (UK) Ltd

DAVID NORBURN AND SUE BIRLEY

CASE A: PART 1

In June 1973, Airfix Industries Ltd, a large UK toy company, was approached by a small company, Seed Oysters (UK) Ltd, with a request for venture capital. This was caused by the cancellation of an overdraft facility, owing to the insolvency of its principal shareholder. The company urgently sought new finance (1) to cover immediate cash needs whilst financing initial sales; and (2) for a general operating reserve, especially during the winter, when few sales would be made. This was the first time that the members of the board of Airfix had heard of the company and its directors.

The company

Initial work on oyster-hatching had been started ten years previously, at Conway in North Wales, by the Government White Fish Authority (WFA), and by 1971 the development of a commercial hatchery had become a viable proposition. However, the WFA had been constrained in its actions by the need to show that any company with which it was involved operated in such a way that it supported the general development of the UK fish industry. Its problem was eventually solved when Ian Doré of Doré Consultants Ltd, specialising in the fisheries industries, expressed an interest in setting up a company to grow and sell oysters. Seed Oysters (UK) Ltd was eventually incorporated on 1 May 1972, to rear and grow seed molluscs, from the egg stage, for sale to oyster farmers in the UK and abroad. The new company was financed jointly by the Fishmongers Company, an old-established City institution, and private investment. The agreement which was negotiated between the company and the WFA included the secondment of the WFA's scientific and technical staff from Conway for a period of up to three years. In return, Seed Oysters gave undertakings to give precedence to UK customers (the agreed terms of reference included the statement that 'the seed shall be primarily available for sale to the British industry at proper commercial prices') and to allow the WFA to train UK interests in hatchery and oyster-growing techniques. After further development work, the new hatchery at Brynsiencyn, Anglesey, was formally opened by Earl Cairns of the Fishmongers Company on 14 March 1973, and started its rearing activities from that date.

The oyster: product characteristics

The Pacific or Japanese oyster (*Crassostrea gigas*) was first successfully hatched in Britain at the Conway station in 1965. Conditions required a carefully controlled temperature and the circulation of sterilised sea water to produce a seed of 5 mm in two to three months. After planting out, Pacific oysters reached a marketable size after approximately eighteen months, as against which the traditional European oyster (*Ostrea edulis*) needs four to five years to grow and is much more susceptible to disease.

The oyster is an unusual mollusc in that it can change sex regularly throughout its life. Indeed, the female European oyster often sheds its ora into the mantle cavity and can become a complete male while still carrying its own embryos. In the case of the Pacific oyster, the young are usually male and it is only after the first spawning season that the number of each sex becomes almost equal. Oysters spawn as soon as the water temperature is high enough and at such times are highly prolific – one reason for their reputation as an aphrodisiac.

The average female, whose productive life can be as long as forty years, releases as many as 70 million eggs in a single spawning. The European oyster is unique in that, unlike the Pacific oyster, it retains its young until tiny shells are developed, and it is their presence that in the summer months gives the European oyster a gritty taste and limits the 'season' for it to those months with an 'r' in the name.

Despite such a large birth rate, few oysters grow to a harvestable size. To begin with, many of the females' eggs are not fertilised by male-oyster sperm after they have been discharged into the water. Not only that, but large numbers are eaten by fish during the early period of their lives when they swim free in the water. Then, large numbers of the spat (young fertilised oyster seed) fail to find an object to which they can attach themselves, and die desperately trying to adhere to sand or mud. But, worse, once they do find something to hold on to, their troubles really begin: storms bury them alive in sand; the avian oyster-catcher is waiting at low tide for his dinner; there are scores of diseases which decimate their ranks; drills bore into their shells to scrape out the meat; the conch pushes open the shell; snails siphon their life blood through stylets that pierce their body wall; starfish pull the bivalves apart with their feet; crabs crack their shells; 'dive bomber' gulls drop then on rocks; worms squirm inside them and eat their host; drum fish and skates crush the bivalves with their teeth; mussels defecate on them and smother them; the slipper limpet can suffocate whole beds of oysters, and jingle shells take up squatters' rights in old oyster shells, the wombs on which the young oyster spats grow. Through all this the peace-loving oyster is incapable of attacking its enemies and, indeed, once settled on the ocean floor it is incapable of movement.

The oyster farm

The traditional method of growing oysters was to collect the seeds from the sea on culch, normally an old oyster shell, to which they adhered. This was then replaced in the sea, and once the mollusc had grown to a marketable size it was chipped off and sold. Because of the hazards already described and because many grew on top of one another and were killed during harvesting, there were always enormous losses. The use of hatchery seed meant that the operation could be made much more reliable, and less labour-intensive.

The hatchery process is a form of batch production and follows the sequence outlined below.

Parent stock kept at 20°C, causing shedding of eggs
↓
Eggs fertilised by stirring with sperms   ½ hour
↓
Fertilised eggs kept in holding bins at 19°C   3 weeks
↓
Transferred to settling tanks when a microscopic
examination shows readiness
↓
Spat stripped from settling discs and transferred to
batch bubblers   3 weeks
↓
Transfer to floating filter trays as growth continues
↓
Use larger trays as seed grows to 5, 10 or 15mm   2–4 months
↓
Dispatch to buyer
↓
Set out in bags on foreshore
↓
Harvest in eighteen months (for Pacific oyster)

The market

In 1973 the growing of oysters in the UK was a small-scale, undeveloped occupation, industrial output totalling 200–300 tons per annum. By contrast, in France annual output was 60,000 tons and it was estimated that this was some 20,000 tons under primary demand. Further, throughout the rest of Europe there were indications that the markets for oysters were growing, at a time when supplies were dwindling, as coastal waters became polluted. The French preferred the nobbly shelled Pacific oyster, which was usually sold at a minimum size of around 50 grams (a size which could be reached in twelve to eighteen months) and at a price of 6–8 francs per kilogram. (There was an 18 per cent import duty on edible-sized Pacific oysters, which was to be reduced by 20 per cent on 1 April 1973 and each subsequent year until the completion of the Common Market interim period, after which no tariffs would apply.) Thus the UK grower could expect to sell his oysters for between £24 and £45 per thousand.

The quality of the Pacific oysters grown in the UK had been favourably received by French buyers, since these oysters usually had a much larger meat content than similar ones grown in France. By contrast, not only was the UK home market much smaller, but also the British palate preferred the more attractive, smooth-shelled European oyster, the more difficult and more expensive to grow. Whereas in the seventeenth and eighteenth centuries, when the home market was at its height, oysters were so cheap that it used to be felt that 'poverty and oysters go together', in the twentieth century in Britain oysters have reached the status of a 'luxury' food.

Seed Oysters (UK) Ltd

By the spring of 1973, it had been demonstrated to the satisfaction of the scientists working on the project in North Wales that the small-scale laboratory methods could be developed to a point where procedures and requirements for the successful hatching and rearing of young oysters were sufficiently understood and documented. Thus, working on the assumption that the first seed bed would be laid in April 1973, Ian Doré, managing director of Seed Oysters (UK), presented to the shareholders his first estimates for the financing of the project. These estimates, summarised in Exhibit 2A.1, were available for the directors of Airfix to study.

By June 1973, when it became apparent that the private funds (see Exhibit 2A.2, section 6) would no longer be available, the company was operating profitably and Mr Doré fully expected to show an operating surplus at the end of the first full financial year. He began to search for alternative finance. Exhibit 2A.2 is the proposal which he submitted to the board of Airfix.

One of the main constraints put upon the company by the WFA was the requirement to sell to the undeveloped and thus unprofitable UK markets. In order to reach wider markets rapidly, Mr Doré proposed to form a second, independent company, Gwynedd Oysters Ltd, which would buy seed oysters from Seed Oysters (UK) to grow and market internationally. Exhibit 2A.3 is his outline of this scheme, also submitted to Airfix.

Availability of water

The growth rate of oysters in different water around the UK varies enormously, and, after the supply of seed, the second requirement prior to establishing growing enterprises is a suitable area for growing the seed. Considerable variation can be recorded within distances of 40 or 50 yards apart, and it is essential that any area proposed for growing oysters should have trials laid before money is spent on the establishment of a full size bed.

A number of trials have been undertaken by the White Fish Authority experimental mollusc unit in Conway, and considerable experience has been built up of suitable water on the East coast of England and West Coast of Scotland and Wales. The sites proposed in this outline have all been tested and offer *prima facie* excellent growth prospects.

The cost of growing hatchery seeds

Detailed costings for the proposed beds are given in Table 1. In very broad terms the average costings for a normal oyster bed of 2 million harvested oysters per annum can be expected to be as follows:—

Cost of seed from hatchery	approximately	£6.00 per 1,000
Allowance for mortality	approximately	£1.50 per 1,000
Costs of growing including capital costs and operating costs	approximately	£10.00 per 1,000
TOTAL		£17.50 per 1,000
Price to be expected		£25–£40.00 per 1,000

Site

We have available, under lease, 16 acres of tested and suitable water at Bangor in the Menai Straits and the provisional (free) use of part of the Inland Sea. We are also in the process of negotiating permission to use a large strip of excellent water in the Straits, under lease from Aethy Rural District Council. All these sites are located close to the Seed Oysters (UK) Ltd hatchery at Brynsiencyn, which will ensure ready availability of technical advice and assistance.

Risks

A. *Diseases and pests.* North-west Wales is free of oyster pests and diseases, and movement of oysters from infected areas is prohibited under the Molluscan (Control of Deposit) Order which has been effectively enforced to date. The possibility of the spread of disease or pest into the area, however, can never be ruled out entirely.

B. *Predators.* Mainly starfish, crabs and birds. The cultivation techniques to be used largely eliminate losses from predators. Human predation (poaching) can be prevented by ensuring attendance at the bed at low water.

C. *Natural and man-made disasters.* Neither predictable nor quantifiable. However, it is apparently likely that if four, five or more beds of the type proposed here are established, some insurance will be possible against natural disasters such as hurricanes. Man-made problems (e.g. chemical dumping near the bed) would specifically be insurable.

Table 1 Oyster growing: estimated costs (£)

Months:	2	4	6	8	10	12	14	16	18	20	22	24	
Capital equipment													
Bags	2,500												2,500
Trestles	1,200												1,200
Pens	300												300
Vehicle	1,500												1,500
Boat[a]	3,500												3,500
Cleansing system	1,000	2,000	2,000	3,000									8,000
Investigation and set-up	5,000												5,000
Experimental work[b]	500	500	500	500	500	500	500	500	500	500	500	500	6,000
	15,500	2,500	2,500	3,500	500	500	500	500	500	500	500	500	28,000
Seed[c]	8,000	5,800					8,000	5,800					27,600
	23,500	8,300	2,500	3,500	500	500	8,500	6,300	500	500	500	500	55,600
Operating expenses													
Consumables (ropes, etc)	–	100	100	100	100	100	100	100	100	100	100	100	1,100
Rents, etc.	200	–	–	200	–	–	300	–	–	300	–	–	1,000
Operation of vehicle and boat	400	300	300	350	350	300	350	350	300	350	350	300	4,000
Management, admin., insurance, etc.	667	667	666	667	667	666	667	667	666	667	667	666	8,000
Wages (3 men)	1,000	1,000	1,000	1,000	1,000	1,000	1,000	1,000	1,000	1,000	1,000	1,000	12,000
Total each 2 months	2,267	2,067	2,066	2,317	2,117	2,066	2,417	2,117	2,066	2,417	2,117	2,066	26,100
Cumulative total	2,267	4,334	6,400	8,717	10,834	12,900	15,317	17,434	19,500	21,917	24,034	26,100	

Net of WFA grant.

Notes

[a] *Vessel*: small boat equipped with hand dredges or escalator. WFA grant of 25% will be payable on vessel. If operation can be moved to Aethy, a vessel will probably not be needed.

[b] *Experimental work*: needed in the following directions –

(1) Search for suitable water, involving experimental lays, followed by negotiations with institutions, landowners etc.

(2) Experiments with growing techniques. While the methods now proposed are satisfactory, they should be capable of substantial improvement as the technology is in a very early stage of development. This work would be carried out in close conjunctions with the WFA and MAFF [Ministry of Agriculture, Fisheries and Food].

(3) Work on handling, packing, transporting and marketing. It is considered that this work should be written off as a capital expense.

[c] *Seed*: assuming purchase of 2.4 million seed to permit harvest of 1.8 million. This allows a very considerable margin for losses.

Table 2   Oyster growing: revenue estimates (£)

Months:	2	4	6	8	10	12	14	16	18	20	22	24
A. Average price £25 per 1,000												
1. 25% mortality — leaves 1.8 million harvestable – total revenue £45,000												
(a) slow growth									20,000	25,000		
(b) medium growth						10,000	10,000		20,500	25,000		
(c) fast growth				4,500								
2. 15% mortality — leaves 2.04 million harvestable – total revenue £51,000												
(a) slow growth									23,000	28,000		
(b) medium growth						11,000	12,000		22,900	28,000		
(c) fast growth				5,100								
B. Average price £30 per 1,000												
1. 25% mortality — leaves 1.8 million harvestable – total revenue £54,000												
(a) slow growth									24,000	30,000		
(b) medium growth						12,000	12,000		24,600	30,000		
(c) fast growth				5,400								
2. 15% mortality — leaves 2.04 million harvestable – total revenue £61,200												
(a) slow growth									27,200	34,000		
(b) medium growth						13,600	13,600		27,900	34,000		
(c) fast growth				6,100								
C. Average price £35 per 1,000												
1. 25% mortality — leaves 1.8 million harvestable – total revenue £63,000												
(b) medium growth						14,000	14,000			35,000		
2. 15% mortality — leaves 2.04 million harvestable – total revenue £71,400												
(b) medium growth						15,900	15,900			39,600		
D. Average price £40 per 1,000												
1. 25% mortality — leaves 1.8 million harvestable – total revenue £72,000												
(b) medium growth						16,000	16,000			40,000		
2. 15% mortality — leaves 2.04 million harvestable – total revenue £81,600												
(b) medium growth						18,100	18,200			45,300		
E. Average price £45 per 1,000												
2. 15% mortality — leaves 2.04 million harvestable – total revenue £91,800												
(b) medium growth						20,400	20,400			51,000		

Notes

1. 'Mortality' covers all losses.

2. Slow growth: harvestable month 18–20 (i.e. 2 full summers, harvested 2nd winter following planting).
   Medium growth: planted April, left 1 year, then harvested – 50% following summer, 50% following winter.
   Fast growth: planted April, 10% harvestable December, 50% following summer, 40% following winter.

3. (a) DTI grant and loan assistance is probably not available.
   (b) As project will be located in a Development area, free depreciation would be allowed; capital items can therefore be treated effectively as current expenditure.
   (c) Excluding interest charges.

Table 3   Net revenue after duty and transport (£ per 1,000)

Size (grams)	6 Fr.	Price per kg 7 Fr.	8 Fr.
60	25	29.08	
65	29.08	34.13	
70	31.18	36.60	41.96
75		39.46	45.25

Table 4   Accounts forecast after two years (£)

Profit and loss a/c	Out	In
Operating expenses (2 years)	26,100	
Finance costs (2 years)	8,000	
	34,100	
Revenue: A.1.a. (worst estimate)		45,000
Profit (loss) A.1.a.		10,900
Revenue C.2.b. (likely estimate)		71,400
Profit C.2.b.		37,300
Revenue E.2.b.		91,800
Profit E.2.b. (best estimate)		57,700

Table 5   Estimated cash flow (£)

Months:	2	4	6	8	10	12	14	16	18	20	22	24	Totals
Outflows													
Capital outflows	23,500	8,300	2,500	3,500	500	500	8,500	6,300	500	500	500	500	55,600
Operational outflows	2,267	2,067	2,066	2,317	2,117	2,066	2,417	2,117	2,006	2,417	2,117	2,066	26,100
Cumulative outflows	25,767	36,134	40,700	46,517	49,134	51,700	62,617	71,034	73,600	76,517	79,134	81,700	81,700
Inflows													
A.1.a. (worst estimate)									20,000	25,000			
									(53,600)	(31,517)	(34,134)	(36,700)	
C.2.b. (medium estimate)						15,900	15,900			39,600			
						(35,800)	(30,817)	(39,234)	(41,800)	(5,117)	(7,734)	(10,300)	
E.2.b. (best estimate)						20,400	20,400			51,000			
						(31,300)	(21,817)	(30,234)	(32,800)	(15,283)	(12,666)	(10,100)	

SEED OYSTERS (UK) LIMITED

1. *Background and history*

In an attempt to revive the dying UK oyster industry, the White Fish Authority, a Government/industry statutory body, undertook research into hatching and raising of baby oysters (seed) in artificially controlled environment. This work was successful, and Seed Oysters (UK) Ltd. is partly designed to demonstrate that the techniques developed by the WFA are viable on a commercial scale.

There is a considerable shortage of oyster seed, both in UK and particularly in France; further, the considerable labour savings possible by using seed from a hatchery rather than naturally caught add to the basic demand for supplies.

The market for seed is eventually dependent on the markets for edible oysters. Although consumption in the UK is under 200 tons p.a., the French eat over 60,000 tons a year, and peak consumption has been as high as 100,000 tons. This is at prices similar to UK levels, and against a background of falling output due to pollution, disease and labour problems in the traditional oyster growing areas.

Based on this analysis, a group of investors set up Seed Oysters (UK) with the intention of firstly selling seed to France and UK; secondly, expanding the growing industry in the UK in order to produce oysters to sell to France for consumption; and thirdly, to see if the market in the UK could be expanded through availability of supplies. The Company was formed a year ago, capital was pledged on 14 July 1972, and hatchery construction started August. The first sales were made in April this year, and production is now approaching capacity.

The hatchery's designed output is 20 million seed a year, of *Crassostrea gigas*, which is a fast growing Pacific species which reaches maturity in two years, compared with the 4 to 7 years of the native oysters, or less than 2 per cent of the French market.

2. *Capital structure and ownership*

The company is capitalised as follows:

	£
Ordinary share capital (authorised and issued)	30,000
Loan from Department of Trade and Industry	40,000
Loan from Fishmongers' Company	14,000
Loan from International Fishery and Ocean Services	20,000
Total	104,000

In addition, the company is required to have an overdraft facility of at least £15,000, as part of the terms of the loan from DTI.

DTI have lent under the Local Employment Acts, and have a debenture giving first floating charge over all the assets. The loan is at 6¾ per cent, repayable 1974–78, with a one year moratorium on interest payment. The Fishmongers' Company loan is at 5 per cent, repayable after 1978, and the loan from IFOS is at 12 per cent (variable with commercial rates) also repayable after 1978.

Ownership of the equity is as follows:

Fishmongers' Company	6,000
International Fishery and Ocean Services Limited	10,000
Offton Investments Ltd.	2,000
North British Bank	2,000
A. Kennaway	2,000
I. Doré	1,000
W. Wallace	1,000
I. Boyer-Millar	1,000
G. Syme-Thompson	1,400
Various small holdings totalling	3,600
Total	30,000

41

There is a shareholders' agreement which supplements the articles which controls the transfer of shares. However, over the last two weeks, control of IFOS and of Offton Investments Ltd has been obtained by another company called Gwynedd Oysters Limited, which is controlled by I. Doré, A. Kennaway and W. Wallace. This gives Gwynedd effective control of Seed Oysters.

3. Gwynedd Oysters Limited

This company has just been formed, for the purpose of growing oysters purchased as seed from Seed Oysters (UK) Ltd, to edible size for sale on European and UK markets. Technical Development Capital Ltd, a subsidiary of ICFC [Industrial and Commercial Finance Corporation], is providing approximately 35 per cent of the funds, including £7,000 of £20,000 share capital.

Although Gwynedd will have a substantial stake in Seed Oysters, it will not formally control it, and it would not be good for Seed Oysters' sales prospects if the company were to be too obviously controlled by one of its major customers. Also, the transfer provisions of the shareholders' agreement would make it virtually impossible for Seed Oysters to become a subsidiary of Gwynedd.

4. Current commercial position of Seed Oysters

Both output and sales so far are well up to forecast. Orders could be taken for delivery within the next two months which would be perhaps three times possible output. On the basis of orders booked for delivery to the end of July, of seed which is now growing in the hatchery, sales by that date should total £24,343 to UK customers, and £12,250 to France. This includes all outstanding invoices to 20 June, and excludes all deliveries that have been paid for, to 20 June. In addition, orders which are unlikely to be delivered until August total £16,000, and a further delivery worth £8,000 should be made to France during July.

Payments will of course follow deliveries. Details are set out in Table 1.

5. Current financial position of Seed Oysters

The attached balance sheet and profit and loss account for the period up to mid June shows a strong position. However, in terms of cash availability the company now needs to utilise overdraft facilities to complete outstanding payments while waiting for revenue from sales. A current cash statement is contained in Table 2.

6. Overdraft

It was originally envisaged that the final piece of required financing would be in the form of overdraft facilities, provided by the Bank of Scotland, Haymarket, London, SW1, and arrangements were confirmed both directly and with the bank through Department of Trade and Industry.

However, the largest shareholder in Seed Oysters is International Fishery and Ocean Services Limited (IFOS), and this company, which nominated four Directors, has run into financial trouble with a subsidiary company called IFOS Trawlers Limited, which was involved in a venture to catch fish off Argentina, and which lost considerable sums of money. Bank of Scotland is in an exposed position regarding IFOS Trawlers, and has cancelled overdraft facilities previously negotiated for Seed Oysters on the grounds of the connection of the two companies through common Directors and a large shareholding.

It is not possible to solve the problem of the common Directors until the Seed Oysters AGM on 23 July, but the shareholding is now separated from IFOS Trawlers, since IFOS is now owned by Gwynedd, and the loss-making subsidiaries have been sold, given away, or are in the process of being liquidated.

The need is to replace this overdraft facility so that the company can continue to meet its targets.

Table 1   20 June 1973: outstanding payments and orders for delivery June—July (£)

United Kingdom

Outstanding invoices   Total   1,322.80

Magowan	100
Duchy of Cornwall Oyster Farms	1,000
Holman	200
Macaulay	60
Thain	420
Poole Oyster Co. (Fitch Lovell)	8,000
Teck oyster	1,400
clams	2,000
Western Aquaculture	4,000
Irish Sea Fisheries Board	40
Gwynedd Oyster Co.	6,000

Total by end of July   23,220

Total 24,342.80

France

(Note: payment from France likely to be delayed 2 months.)
Outstanding invoices

Insurance claim (stolen shipment)	1,250
Shipment end May	4,000
Shipment 20 June	7,000

Further orders, for shipment July   8,000

Total expected due for payment by end of July   44,592.80

Later shipments

Normal policy is not to confirm orders until the oysters are settled and thus known to be available, barring accidents. However, we have customers whose requirements we expect to be able to fill August/September as follows:

Gwynedd Oysters (Aug)	10,000
Western Aquaculture (Sep)	12,000
Tokoroa Oyster Co. (Aug)	1,200
France (Aug and Sep)	8,000

Table 2   Cash position of Seed Oysters (UK) Ltd (£)

31 May 1973

Current account	1,889
Deposit account	500
Petty cash	34
Total cash	2,423
Debtors	
Trade	2,048
VAT	141
Insurance claim not yet approved[a]	1,250
Total credit items	5,862
Creditors	23,917
Net balance: deficit of	18,055
Current cash shortfall	21,494

Forecast to 31 August 1973

Negative current cash balance	21,494
Operational costs to 31 August	4,000
Loan interest	350
Electricity costs not billed	600
Staff production bonus	900
Final IFOS payment	2,000
Management costs	2,000
Contingency reserve	2,000
Total outflow to 31 August	33,344
Revenue to 31 August	44,592
Net inflow predicted	11,248
Less additional capital items	5,500
Net credit balance	5,748

[a]This is a claim for seed stolen in transit. It has not been included in the accounts because it has not formally been accepted by the insurance company.

44

Note on French customers

The French importers are organised in a cartel, the member of which who deals with us being La Marée-Bardou SA, of Arcachon. ECGD [Export Credit Guarantee Department] have approved this customer for £10,000 outstanding.

We are concluding negotiations with Bardou for a joint venure which involves his providing 'nursery facilities' in France to grow seed from very small up to good marketable size. This has two advantages to us: the seed grows faster in France, and by clearing it from the hatchery much earlier the capacity of the hatchery is greatly increased, since the pressure on both food supplies and space inside the hatchery is obviously greater as the oysters get larger. The agreement outlined is that our contribution would be to wait for payment until the seed is sold (which we would have to do if we grew it ourselves) to the grower from the importer; and to contribute one third of the cost of running the nursery (which, since in French water artificial feed is not required, is cheaper than growing it to saleable size ourselves). The deliveries listed above are on the basis of our providing 1 million seed a month for such a facility, which is their basic requirement.

A similar proposal has been presented by another French group which is outside the cartel, and which might in the end be more beneficial, though perhaps more risky.

Medium term forecasts

The following factors are considered important.

(a) Sales will be minimal between mid-November and mid-March in the UK, though, depending on temperatures, the French should be able to take seed again in mid-January.
(b) Depending on the cash situation, we intend to overwinter in our own nursery facilities as much seed as possible, since sales of large seed in March fetch very high prices.
(c) On the basis of present performance, we expect the hatchery to exceed its design performance of 20 million seed next year. In addition by more intensive use of nursery facilities, we expect to be able to push total output to over 40 million, giving revenue as follows:

	£
10 million at £8.00 per thousand	80,000
10 million at £4.00 per thousand	40,000
20 million to other nurseries, average price	
of £2.00 per thousand	40,000
Total revenue for season	160,000

(d) Running costs are forecast as follows:

		per annum (£)
General expenses		10,000
Salaries		
Present Seed Oysters staff		4,800
Present WFA staff		17,000
Management and administration		8,000
Interest charges		
IFOS	2,250	
Fishmongers	700	
DTI	2,700	
		5,650
		45,450

(e) The first £5,000 repayment of DTI loan will be due in July 1974, and thereafter at 6-monthly intervals.
(f) An allowance of £7,500 for new capital expenditure yearly is considered necessary.

Outline cash flow based on the above is attached [Table 3].

Table 3   Predicted cash flows (£) to 31 August

		1973					1974			
	At 31 May	June	July	Aug	Sep/Oct	Nov/Dec	Jan/Feb	Mar/Apr	May/June	July/Aug
		1-month periods			*2-month periods*					
Net position (see Table 2)	(21,494)									
Operating costs		1,330	1,340	1,330	2,100	2,100	2,400	2,400	2,900	2,900
Loan interest										
Fishmongers			350				350			350
IFOS						2,250				
DTI							1,350			1,350
Loan repayment (DTI)										5,000
Electricity costs				600	1,330	1,330	1,330	1,330	1,330	1,340
Staff bonus				900						
Final IFOS payment				2,000						2,000
Management costs			1,000	1,000						
Contingencies				2,000			3,000			
Capital items				5,500				4,500		
Outflows for period	(21,494)	1,330	2,690	13,330	3,430	5,680	10,440	8,230	4,230	14,940
Projected inflows			(24,000)	20,592	40,000	15,000	10,000	35,000	30,000	35,000
Net cash flows	(21,494)	(22,824)	(1,514)	5,748	42,318	51,638	51,198	77,968	103,738	123,798

Notes

Additional allowance will be required in accounts for payments to WFA for staff: £10,000 to August 1973 and £17,000 for year 1973–74.
These payments need not be made until 1975.
Starting position assumes financing for creditors, and full repayment by end of financial year.

Table 4   Profit and loss account (£) for period 1 June 1972
(inception) to 31 May 1973

Sales invoiced	530
UK	2,048
Export	2,578
Expenses	
Office, printing and stationery	466
Legal and professional	94
Travel and subsistence: home	4,454
overseas	1,969
Sundry expenses	66
Telephone	75
Bank charges	56
Management fees	6,000
Loan interest Fishmongers' Company	308
Repairs	1,104
Wages: management and trainees	2,120
hatchery staff	1,211
Advertising	191
Consultancy fees	3,600
Accounting fees	250
Chemicals	844
Motor expenses	292
Oil fuel	298
Canteen	38
Rates	16
Packaging	138
Formation expenses	942
	24,532
Loss for period on operations	21,954
Stock[a]	10,000
Net loss for period	11,954

[a]Valuation of stock: Seed living in hatchery at date of
accounts valued at £20,000 in terms of orders received for
those animals. It has been entered at 50 per cent of this
valuation.

Table 5   Balance sheet (£) as at 31 May 1973

Share capital, authorised and issued		30,000	Current assets			
Loans			Trade debtors	2,043		
Fishmongers' Company	14,000		VAT repayable	141		2,189
Departmentment of Trade and Industry	40,000		Petty cash	34		
IFOS Investments	20,000	74,000	Current account	1,889		
			Deposit account	500		4,612
Deposits on orders		57	Fixed assets			
Creditors		23,917	Property	84,390		
		127,974	Office equipment	351		
			Hatchery equipment	14,971		
			VW double cab pick-up	1,440		
			Tractor	100		
			Trial and special equipment		156	101,408
			Stock			10,000
			Loss for period			11,954
						127,974

48

EXHIBIT 2A.3   Proposal for formation of new marketing company: Gwynedd
Oysters Ltd

*OUTLINES FOR GENERAL PLAN FOR DEVELOPMENT IN OYSTER/SHELLFISH
INDUSTRY*

A. *Assumptions*

1. The supply of seed from Seed Oysters (UK) Ltd hatchery is reliable up to a figure of
20 million a year.
     So far, the hatchery has reached its expectations, and has demonstrably overcome
some of the problems that have faced other hatcheries in the past. The snags here
include:

(a) There is still no sign that there will be other viable hatcheries. Scottish Sea Farms
has managed to produce 1.7 million seed so far, which have been delivered this
year, but their prospects for further output do not look too good. If they do not
perform adequately this year, it seems probable that they will give up the venture.
The other three are never likely to be successful, in my opinion, because of site
and personnel problems.
(b) The market for seed is many times larger than Seed Oysters (UK) can hope to
supply on its own. With the right arrangements in France (see later) we could
probably sell up to 100 million seed a year.
(c) The market for seed in the UK (which Seed Oysters has special obligations to
supply) is also much larger than expected, excluding any demand we are creating
through our own growing activities.

These problems all point to expanding capacity for producing seed. See later.
2. There is a substantial market for oysters in the shell.
     The French in 1971 ate 60,000 tons of oysters, while the British ate 171 tons.
There are approximately 20,000 oysters to the ton, so that the entire production of
the hatchery, if grown under the best conditions to edible size, would produce 1,000
tons of oysters. There should not be any problem in selling such small numbers in
France; other European markets are also available, including Germany, Holland and
Sweden. The prospects of selling many more oysters in the shell in the UK must also
be recalled: it is generally believed in the the industry that demand has fallen off from
the early-century levels (perhaps 10,000 tons a year) because of the high prices.
However, the reactions we have had to proposals to supply oysters on a regular basis
lead me to believe that the fall in demand is due more to the lack of supplies, which
makes them an unaccustomed food, than to the price, which in any case can be cut. I
have no doubts of our ability to sell at least five million in the shell to UK outlets a
year, initially.
3. There seem to be good prospects of developing markets for processed oysters, mainly
in the UK, which are worth exploring.
     The WFA work on processed Gigas [Pacific oyster] has created a great deal of
interest, and we have verbal offer from THF [Trust House Forte] to take 5 million
frozen and frozen breaded oysters at $3\frac{1}{2}$p each for trials. It seems likely that oysters
could compete most directly with scampi, which is now apparently peaking out in
terms of market acceptance, and has been downgraded by the frequent production of
substitute and inferior products.
     If the market were to develop in the way that the early trials indicate (and we must
remember that 96 per cent of all new products never get off the ground commercially)
my guess is that the market in the UK could take 10,000 tons a year. At an average of
10 grams per meat, this is 1,000 million oysters.
     The problem here would be securing supplies at this rate.

B. *Proposals*

MARKET STRATEGY

1. As in most businesses, it is important to be at the consumer end of the market, and
this strategy is basic to the following.

49

2. The relationship between the fresh (shell) markets for oysters and the processed market is fairly remote:

   (a) the same basic raw material is used.

   (b) the development of a large market for processed oysters would probably help to develop a snobbier market for shell oysters over the top, simply by creating awareness (see 2 above).

3. It is vital to create and sustain a quality reputation.
4. If a generic market term like scampi could be created for our exclusive use, this would be most valuable.
5. The marketing of shell and processed oysters should be kept separate through different companies.

COMMERCIAL STRATEGY

6. Establish enterprises for growing oysters in the UK, for sale both here and in Europe, in the shell. Gwynedd is the first, and we have built into the capitalisation room for finding further areas for growing, and the opportunities for funding. We might aim at producing as soon as possible 10 million oysters a year, and then think about development from that point.

7. Meanwhile, start to test the processed market by importing oysters from Japan, and processing them and packing them under our own label. This should be done by a subsidiary, rather than by Gwynedd itself, in case of problems. I would propose to acquire a small Billingsgate business, and use that as the vehicle. Since the distribution of oysters will inevitably lead on to other 'exotic' seafoods, this firm could be the basic vehicle to operate in this market also. Detailed plans for this are being drawn up, but I estimate that the costs would be as follows:

	£
Purchase of suitable company	10,000
Initial purchase of oysters	10,000
Processing and distribution costs	2,000
Promotion costs (incl. packaging etc)	2,000

Returns would be fairly rapid, and as the company purchased would have some sort of cash flow, which could probably be improved with a little effort, so that if we were able to invest £25,000 in the venture, returns ought to be good, and if we fail to sell processed oysters, there will be a basic business to fall back on, and it will be possible to cut the costs fairly early on.

8. Although my intention would be that Gwynedd should market its fresh oysters direct to consumer points in the UK (mainly caterers) it would obviously be useful to have direct access through our own Billingsgate dealer for the disposal of surplus or exceptional supplies, and would also let us buy in supplies discreetly if this is necessary.

9. If we can control Seed Oysters (UK), then we can be assured of supplies of seed for Gwynedd. However, this leaves out the prospects of selling seed elsewhere, which we see as a profitable undertaking. We must therefore give thought to expanding hatchery capacity, initially by at least 20 million a year. I would guess that, using our experience with Seed Oysters, an investment of £200,000 would enable us to produce 50 million or more seed a year, starting from scratch, and give returns on capital of perhaps 30 to 40 per cent.

10. However, there are other ways of increasing the output of the hatchery, using the technique as it stands, without making large investments. The French importers have offered to us a deal which, with some modifications, would be very valuable. They have the facilities, largely provided by ourselves over the last 9 months, to take small seed and grow it rapidly to a size where it is sellable at very high prices to French growers. Our hatchery investment problem is the space and feeding costs required at the later stages of the seed growth: we can produce very large numbers up to say three weeks after settlement, but thereafter we have to progressively kill them to avoid overfilling our available space and good supplies. The French therefore offer a way of

sending this 'surplus' output away before it becomes an embarrassment, and, in return for a proportion of the costs, being able to sell it as large seed in one or two months' time. I estimate that this would increase our present hatchery capacity by 50 per cent, with virtually no increase in costs. Such a deal is not feasible under the present 'industry assisting' regime, however.

11. For rather greater cost (in that we would have to put up the capital ourselves, rather than letting the French do it for us) we may be able to find such nursery sites in the UK. If in fact it turns out to be possible, by using nurseries, to send all the seed from the hatchery at 3–4 weeks after settlement as standard practice (instead of 2–3 months), then for the cost of about £4,000 in re-equipment, I would guess that the hatchery capacity would be increased to maybe 60 million. Nursery facilities could be built on the site or nearby for this number at a cost estimated now of £75,000, but I have no doubt that cheaper sites are available to develop in this way, since at Brynsiencyn the distance from low water mark makes pumping expensive and requires the use of large storage tanks. If it were possible to find a tidally filled tank (as in France) the cost would be cut by more than half.

12. Following on from above, the cost of starting growing beds is, on the lines of Gwynedd, £50,000 for 2 million p.a. harvestable. We will have to consider doing franchise or part ownership deals with other people, since the capital required for all this is getting out of our own range. Also oyster beds need supervision at odd hours, and we might get better results if people are looking after their own investment rather than looking after ours.

13. Overall, it seems to me to be important that we, as first priority work towards securing our market position, so that we are equivalent to Youngs in scampi or Heinz in baked beans. A lot of the rest will flow from this.

Summary

We should

(a) draw up alternative ways of expanding the capacity of our group for hatching oysters, and decide soon on whether we want to build another hatchery, or want to invest in various nursery facilities to give us the same result.

(b) acquire a suitable Billingsgate dealer for trading in frozen oysters imported from the Far East.

(c) start work on the marketing programme for frozen oysters, so that we are prepared once we have proved our initial trials.

(d) start looking for further sites to grow oysters, with the immediate intention of forming four more enterprises similar to basic Gwynedd.

Capital requirement for this would be very approximately as follows:

	£
Oyster growing	200,000
Hatchery expansion up to	200,000
marketing of frozen oysters	25,000
and, if this is successful, we will need production facilities	70,000

Each aspect of this should be examined separately, within the overall plan, which in production terms would be:

— hatchery production of 50 to 100 million;
— grow for shell trade 10 to 20 million;
— import for processed trade what the market will bear, but with the objective of becoming absolutely dominant in marketing. Once we have this sort of organisation in being, we can begin to think of selling other shellfish through it.

I. Doré
17 June 1973

CASE A: PART 2

As a result of the approach to the board of Airfix Industries Ltd made in June by Ian Doré and described in part 1, Adrian Kloeden was asked to conduct a further, independent analysis and report back before a final decision was made. Adrian had joined Airfix in July as a roving trouble-shooter, having just gained an M.Sc. from the London Business School. The rest of this case consists of a summary of the notes which he made in preparing his analysis.

Notes on Seed Oysters (UK) Ltd and Gwynedd Oysters Ltd

General comments

It is envisaged by Mr Doré that 60 million seed oysters will be produced by Seed Oysters (UK) Ltd; that 2 million table oysters and some clams will be produced by Gwynedd Oysters Ltd; and that seven consignments of imported oysters from Japan will be sold. The profit before tax resulting from this operation is approximately £284,000 for the period July 1973 to August 1974 (Exhibit 2A.6). The cash flow for this is given in Exhibit 2A.4.

Sensitivity analyses were undertaken to determine the effects on production of only 20 million seed oysters, sales of only one consignment of imported oysters, and no sales of table oysters in the period. The profits for each of these events taken independently and in total are shown in Exhibit 2A.6; the cash flows in Exhibit 2A.5. The worst profit is £50,100 before tax, which represents a loss of £20,400 by Gwynedd Oysters and a profit of £70,500 for Seed Oysters (UK).

Seed-oyster production is only assured at 20 million, although new techniques and facilities will be introduced to produce 60 million. No orders have yet been placed for imported oysters, although this may be resolved shortly. Also it is possible that table oysters will grow more slowly than expected and mature in the 1974–5 period. However, it is unlikely that these events will occur simultaneously, so the profit before tax will probably lie between £50,100 and £284,000 for 1973–4.

Data supplied for the analyses are tentative and will be subject to modification throughout the period. For example, Mr Doré considers that the budget selling price for table oysters is based on a minimum price.

Imports of Mitsubishi oysters will give a net cash flow of £140,000, for which Mitsubishi will require letters of credit once the credibility of the company is established. These imports have one purpose: to improve oysters as a scampi replacement in the long term. Trust Houses Forte kitchen testing has already been undertaken and a taste testing should be completed in the next few days. If successful, orders for the entire quantity imported from Japan would be forthcoming.

Sales of seed to French growers spreads the risk. Small seeds are to be provided and costs and revenues of growing in France are to be shared. The French market for seed is allegedly undersupplied by 400 million per annum.

Research is being conducted to improve methods. The WFA will provide information on new developments free of charge.

Possible problem areas

BUSINESS RISK OF THE OPERATION
1. 20 million seed oysters are believed to be reasonably assured. However,

an additional 20 million are not. In the case of only 20 million being produced, annual revenue would fall by £40,000. Mr Doré has quoted the case of one hatchery which was unable to supply seeds for which orders had been accepted.
2. The Pacific oyster has not been grown commercially in this country before. This venture depends upon the rapid growth and survival of the Pacific oyster, so a failure could be serious. Insurance has not yet been finalised to cover risks caused by natural and man-made disasters. Furthermore, Mr Doré says that 'the possibility of the spread of disease or pest into the area cannot be ruled out entirely'. A disaster to seed production would cause a loss of six to eight weeks' production and 15–20 per cent of seed turnover.

FINANCING

Airfix has been asked to contribute £80,000 to the venture. Mr Doré would like this incorporated into the capital structure of Gwynedd Oysters Ltd, but he has no specific proposals as to how this would be effected. He is generally keen to minimise equity financing because he, Mr Wallace and Mr Kennaway wish to retain control. He feels that Airfix would receive approximately 40 per cent of the equity of Gwynedd by a new issue. This would account for £13,000 of the £80,000. The remainder would enter the capital structure as long-term debt. He sees the future as Seed Oysters (UK) Ltd becoming a subsidiary of Gwynedd Oysters Ltd. Thus Airfix Industries would only exercise control of Seed Oysters (UK) Ltd through its holding in Gwynedd Oysters Ltd.

REQUIREMENT FOR ADDITIONAL FUNDS

Mr Doré plans that Gwynedd Oysters should acquire the equity of Seed Oysters (UK) Ltd not already controlled either directly or indirectly by him. This would require an additional £28,000 of loan capital plus £14,000 to repay the Fishmongers' Company loan. Further, he believes that North British Bank will finance a £20,000 loan to buy out the loan and equity capital held by the Fishmongers' Company. He is not certain where the remaining £22,000 will come from. This purchase of the uncontrolled equity of Seed Oysters (UK) Ltd assumes, of course, that the shareholders are prepared to sell.

It is not certain the £80,000 will cover the net cumulative cash shortfall of about £75,000 expected in August and September. This £75,000 may underestimate the proposed capital expenditure for the table-oyster production facilities.

FINANCIAL RISK

The high gearing of Gwynedd Oysters Ltd, could result in the following capital structure, although this is not yet certain.

Equity	£	Debt	
Kennaway ⎫		Kennaway ⎫	
Doré ⎬	12,000	Doré ⎬	20,000
Wallace ⎭		Wallace ⎭	
ICFC	19,000	Airfix	67,000
Airfix	13,000	North British Bank	20,000
		ICFC	10,000
	32,000		117,000

If revenue was not up to expectations, the high cost of fixed charges (interest) could be acutely embarrassing.

In the light of this risk, Airfix may wish to ask a high rate of interest for its loan capital. In the event of a break-up, assets (which are not yet completely specified) would not go far.

MARKETING

Sales are mainly directed at France. This could lead to several problems.

 (i) The ECGD has only approved the customer for fresh oysters for £10,000 outstanding.
(ii) Mr Doré recognises that the current marketing outlets for France would be unsatisfactory for larger sales, but is unable to say how he would plan to overcome possible resistance by the French.

EXHIBIT 2A.4 Cash flows (£) for the basic proposal

	1973						1974							
	July	Aug	Sep	Oct	Nov	Dec	Jan	Feb	Mar	Apr	May	June	July	Aug
Cash outflows														
Seed Oysters (UK) Ltd														
Seed production	2,700	13,300		3,400		5,700		10,400		8,200		4,200		14,900
WFA staff					2,000	2,000	2,000	2,000	2,000	2,000	2,000	2,000	2,000	2,000
Capital equipment				13,000				25,000	25,000	25,000				
Total outflow	2,700	13,300		16,400	2,000	7,700	2,000	37,400	27,000	35,200	2,000	6,200	2,000	16,900
Gwynedd Oysters Ltd														
Capital and operating	25,500													
Operating		3,000	3,000	3,000	3,000	3,000	3,000	3,000	3,000	3,000	3,000	3,000	3,000	3,000
Imported oysters		50,000							50,000	50,000	50,000	50,000	50,000	50,000
Total outflow	25,500	53,000	3,000	3,000	3,000	3,000	3,000	3,000	53,000	53,000	53,000	53,000	53,000	53,000
Total cash outflow	28,200	66,300	3,000	19,400	5,000	10,700	5,000	40,400	80,000	88,200	55,000	59,200	55,000	69,900
Cash inflows														
Seed Oysters (UK) Ltd														
40 million seed	24,000	20,000		40,000		15,000		10,000		35,000		30,000		35,000
60 million seed				2,000	2,000	2,000			2,000	2,000	2,000	2,000	5,000	5,000
Total inflow	24,000	20,000		42,000	2,000	17,000		10,000	2,000	37,000	2,000	32,000	5,000	40,000
Gwynedd Oysters Ltd														
Clams						3,000								5,000
Oysters													4,000	36,000
Imported oysters				70,000					70,000	70,000	70,000	70,000	70,000	70,000
Total inflow				70,000		3,000			70,000	70,000	70,000	70,000	74,000	111,000
Total cash inflow	24,000	20,000		112,000	2,000	20,000		10,000	72,000	107,000	72,000	102,000	79,000	151,000
Net flow for the period	(4,200)	(46,300)	(3,000)	92,600	(3,000)	9,300	(5,000)	(30,400)	(8,000)	19,800	17,000	42,800	24,000	81,100
Cumulative flow[a]	(27,200)	(73,500)	(76,500)	16,100	13,100	22,400	17,400	(13,000)	(21,000)	1,200	18,200	61,000	85,000	166,100

[a] Base −£23,000

EXHIBIT 2A.5 Cash flows (£) for variations of the basic proposal

	1973						1974							
	July	Aug	Sep	Oct	Nov	Dec	Jan	Feb	Mar	Apr	May	June	July	Aug

(1) 20 million seed oysters, 2 million table oysters, 7 consignments imported

	July	Aug	Sep	Oct	Nov	Dec	Jan	Feb	Mar	Apr	May	June	July	Aug
Total outflow	28,200	66,300	3,000	19,400	5,000	10,700	5,000	40,400	80,000	88,200	55,000	59,200	55,000	69,900
Total inflow	17,500	14,600		101,500		14,000		7,300	70,000	95,600	70,000	92,000	74,000	136,600
Net flow for period[a]	(10,700)	(51,700)	(3,000)	82,100	(5,000)	3,300	(5,000)	(33,100)	(10,000)	7,400	15,000	32,800	2,900	66,700
Cumulative flow[a]	(33,700)	(85,400)	(88,400)	6,300	1,300	4,600	(400)	(33,500)	(43,500)	(36,100)	(21,100)	11,700	40,700	107,400

(2) 60 million seed oysters, 2 million table oysters, 1 consignment imported

	July	Aug	Sep	Oct	Nov	Dec	Jan	Feb	Mar	Apr	May	June	July	Aug
Total outflow	28,200	66,300	3,000	19,400	5,000	10,700	5,000	40,400	30,000	38,200	5,000	9,200	5,000	19,900
Total inflow	24,000	20,000		112,000	2,000	20,000		10,000	2,000	37,000	2,000	32,000	9,000	81,000
Net flow for period[a]	(4,200)	(46,300)	(3,000)	92,600	(3,000)	9,300	(5,000)	(30,400)	(28,000)	(1,200)	(3,000)	(22,800)	4,000	61,100
Cumulative flow[a]	(27,200)	(73,500)	(76,500)	61,100	13,100	22,400	17,400	(13,000)	(41,000)	(42,200)	(45,200)	(22,400)	(18,400)	42,700

(3) 60 million seed oysters, no table oysters, 7 consignments imported

	July	Aug	Sep	Oct	Nov	Dec	Jan	Feb	Mar	Apr	May	June	July	Aug
Total outflow	28,200	66,300	3,000	19,400	5,000	10,700	5,000	40,400	80,000	88,200	55,000	59,200	55,000	69,900
Total inflow	24,000	20,000		112,000	2,000	20,000		10,000	72,000	107,000	72,000	102,000	79,000	115,000
Net flow for period[a]	(4,200)	(46,300)	(3,000)	92,600	(3,000)	9,300	(5,000)	(30,400)	(8,000)	19,800	17,000	42,800	24,000	45,100
Cumulative flow[a]	(27,200)	(73,500)	(76,500)	16,100	13,100	22,400	17,400	(13,000)	(21,000)	1,200	18,200	61,000	8,500	130,100

(4) 20 million seed oysters, no table oysters, 1 consignment imported

	July	Aug	Sep	Oct	Nov	Dec	Jan	Feb	Mar	Apr	May	June	July	Aug
Total outflow	28,200	66,300	3,000	19,400	5,000	10,700	5,000	40,000	30,000	38,200	5,000	9,200	5,000	19,900
Total inflow	17,500	14,600		101,500		14,000		7,300		24,500		22,000	4,000	40,500
Net flow for period[a]	(10,700)	(51,700)	(3,000)	82,100	(5,000)	3,300	(5,000)	(33,100)	(30,000)	(13,700)	(5,000)	(12,800)	(1,000)	20,600
Cumulative flow[a]	(33,700)	(85,400)	(88,400)	(6,300)	(11,300)	(8,000)	(13,000)	(46,100)	(76,100)	(89,800)	(94,800)	(82,000)	(8,300)	(62,400)

[a] Base – £23,000

EXHIBIT 2A.6   Estimated profit and loss accounts to 31 August 1974 (£)

	Proposition				
	1	2	3	4	5
Sales					
Seed oysters	233,000	155,100	233,000	233,000	155,100
Imported oysters	490,000	490,000	70,000	490,000	70,000
Table oysters/clams	48,000	48,000	48,000	12,000	12,000
Total	771,000	693,100	351,000	735,000	237,100
Cost of sales					
Seed oysters	77,800	77,800	77,800	77,800	77,800
Imported oysters	350,000	350,000	50,000	350,000	50,000
Table oysters/clams	42,000	42,000	42,000	42,000	42,000
Total	469,800	469,800	169,800	469,800	169,800
Depreciation					
Seed oysters	3,400	3,400	3,400	3,400	3,400
Imported oysters					
Table oysters/clams	5,400	5,400	5,400	5,400	5,400
Total	8,800	8,800	8,800	8,800	8,800
Profit before interest and tax					
Seed oysters	151,800	73,900	151,800	151,800	73,900
Imported oysters	140,000	140,000	20,000	140,000	20,000
Table oysters/clams	600	600	600	(35,400)	(35,400)
Total	292,400	214,500	172,400	256,400	58,500
Interest					
Seed oysters	3,400	3,400	3,400	3,400	3,400
Imported oysters	5,000	5,000	5,000	5,000	5,000
Table oysters/clams					
Total	8,400	8,400	8,400	8,400	8,400
Profit before tax					
Seed Oysters (UK) Ltd	148,400	70,500	148,400	148,400	70,500
Gwynedd Oysters Ltd	135,600	135,600	15,600	99,600	(20,400)
Total	284,000	206,100	164,000	248,000	50,100
Propositions					
(a) Seed oysters (million)	60	20	60	60	20
(b) Table oysters (million)	2	2	2	0	0
(c) Imported oysters (consignments)	7	7	1	7	1

(a) Seed Oysters (UK) Ltd; (b)/(c) Gwynedd Oysters Ltd.

EXHIBIT 2A.7   Scheme for oyster-industry development venture (proposed by Mr Doré)

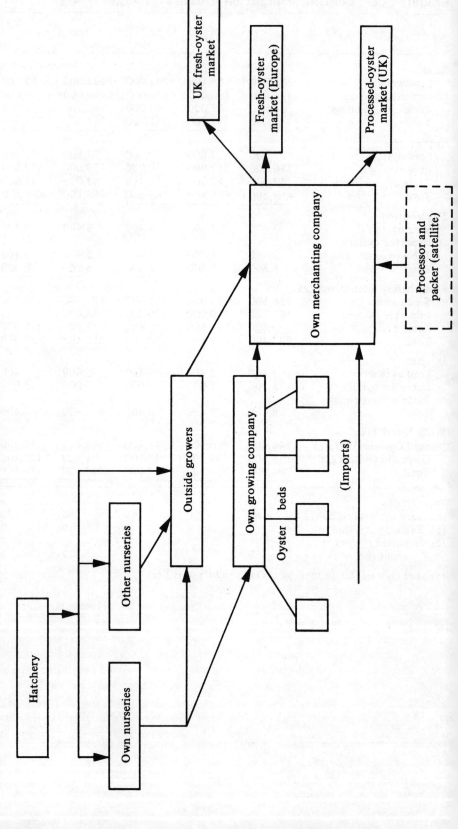

CASE B

The Board of Airfix Industries Ltd declined to offer to participate in Seed Oysters (UK) Ltd (see Case A), for two major reasons. First, the venture was too small, relative to the size of Airfix Industries, to be viewed as a serious diversification; and, secondly, it was completely outside their knowledge and thus skills. However, the chairman, Ralph Ehrmann, and a fellow director, Quintin Hoare, felt that the opportunity had great potential and decided to investigate further in a private capacity. After taking advice, they offered to acquire a controlling interest in Gwynedd, but only after Seed Oysters had become a wholly owned subsidiary. Legal negotiations took some time and it was not until January 1974 that they were eventually finalised. Meanwhile, the potential investors helped the company to raise a bank loan of £32,000 to help with cash difficulties. This case describes the next eighteen months of trading to the point in the summer of 1975 when, with the company continuing to generate a negative cash flow, Ralph and Quintin decided to review its future.

The sequence of events

Ralph and Quintin had no intention of becoming involved in the management of the business, as Ian Doré would continue as managing director, with Jim Knowles as manager of the hatchery, and technical assistance being provided by the WFA. Indeed, without the help, and in particular the staff, of the WFA, Seed Oysters would not have been able to carry on at all. (The terms of the agreement of 13 July 1972 between the two organisations allowed termination by either side with one month's notice.)
In a note to Ralph Ehrmann Ian Doré wrote,

In July 1973, when it became clear that we would be injecting new cash into the business, the WFA appeared to be reluctant to continue our arrangement. It should be borne in mind that the main benefit to the WFA was that having reached a point in its oyster research where the R and D Committee had indicated that it could not be taken further in the light of there being no commercial interest, our appearance on the scene with clear expressions of interest meant that the team could be kept together, and further work undertaken. Richardson, the team leader, was a most imaginative scientist and had expanded the WFA research role both extensively and qualitatively to a point which, when the Government commenced to scrap the WFA by moving it to Edinburgh in March 1973, it was one of the leading bodies in the world. The Edinburgh move was particularly unfavourable for us in that Richardson and other friends left the WFA, and their replacements worked hard to put their own mark on matters with the result that arrangements entered into by the old guard automatically come in for criticism.

After long-drawn-out negotiations, the WFA eventually withdrew from the scene and its staff transferred to the payroll of Seed Oysters. However, this, plus previous rumours of acquisition, had seriously disturbed the staff and resulted in very low morale.
By June 1974, sales had not reached anticipated levels and Ralph and Quintin had to provide a further injection of cash. In September 1974 Ian Doré resigned as managing director, reduced his shareholding to 5 per cent and became sales director. In February 1975, with sales remaining depressed, he resigned from the company. Jeni Glanfield

from the Gwynedd sales office in London took over short-term responsibility for sales, whilst Ian Richardson, now managing director of a consulting company, Fisheries Development Ltd, was asked to look at the company 'to provide a sales, technical and managerial appraisal'.

The sales in March, April and May were very encouraging, but by June they had slumped to their former low level and yet again the company faced cash-flow problems owing to lack of sales. In August, Fisheries Development reported a number of new, large orders for seed but yet another disaster: owing to a number of production problems, the seed was not available.

Marketing

Whilst the oyster was very popular on the Continent (see Case A), the market in the UK was very undeveloped. In fact, very little was known about it by either food manufacturers, restaurateurs or members of the public, and recipes were usually limited to oyster soup or fresh oysters as the first course of a meal. However, the newly acquired ability to produce the quick-growing Pacific oyster, plus advances in freezing techniques, meant that many more could be available for sale. The WFA launched a campaign to promote the oyster, which was now available frozen on the shell or '…in a crisp, golden crumb, individually frozen at the moment of perfection. Simply deep-fat fry while still frozen at 350°C for two and a half minutes until golden, or shallow fry in butter.' The leaflet put out by the WFA emphasised the flexibility of the product, with recipes for oysters meunière, oysters merinbula, oyster avocado, oyster soup, tomato oyster bisque, oyster au gratin, oyster bay chowder, oyster noodle casserole, oyster vol-au-vents, curried oyster vol-au-vents, oyster kebabs, steak with oysters, devilled oysters, oyster and kidney toast, and oysters like snail.

But this was merely a drop in the ocean, as Jeni Glanfield discovered:

> There were no funds to hand for a major publicity campaign (which I estimate could cost up to £1 million) to promote the eating of oysters by the British public. Mr Doré and his associates had attempted, as I understand, to publicise frozen oysters by holding promotional evenings and gatherings in hotels and pubs, as well as participating in some catering fairs. The price to retailers and wholesalers was established at around £1.10 per lb, selling to the public at £1.35 per lb. [Break-even was estimated to be between 56p and 70p per lb.]
>
> It was my understanding, following 20 January, when I assumed responsibility for sales of frozen oysters, that I should attempt to ascertain the potential markets for both breaded oysters and quick-frozen oyster meats. I was given to understand that Seed Oysters (UK) Ltd had a viable future, in that there was a demand and a market for seed and table oysters. However, Miss Jones at Brynsiencyn had told me that there were 32,160 lbs of breaded oysters and 23,800 lbs of oyster meats already in cold store, and I therefore decided to attempt to sell these as quickly as possible at the highest price I could obtain.

Exhibit 2B.1 is an extract from a report from Jeni Glanfield to the board of Gwynedd Oysters on 24 February 1975, which details the initial results of her work.

Meanwhile, towards the end of January, Jacqueline Giles of Fisheries Development was commissioned to carry out an assessment of the marketing possibilities in North West Spain. The following are extracts from her report.

The initial purpose of the tour of the Galician oyster growing area was to endeavour to secure firm orders for the surplus of 1974 and proposed 1975 Edulis [European oyster] production from the Seed Oysters (UK) Ltd. hatchery. [The oyster was either sold from the hatchery as seed to other oyster farms at sizes ranging from 2 mm to 50 mm or transferred to the Gwynedd oyster beds in the sea at Brynsiencyn to be grown for sale at full size.]

Galicia had previously been visited on a number of occasions in 1974 by two representatives of Seed Oysters (UK) Ltd, but during my visit it soon became apparent that these representatives had failed to fully understand the nature of the requirements of this important potential market. This failure was most significant since Seed Oysters (UK) Ltd was only in a position to offer seed for sale which was too small for the market. For this reason I was only able to obtain one firm order. The Galician grower requires seed of 35–40 mm which meets the requirements of the traditional rope culture technique and not 2–6 mm and 8–15 mm offered by Seed Oysters (UK).

The Market. I estimate that the present [1975–6] market for seed oysters in the five rias of the Galician coast is between 50 million and 55 million oysters, and that by 1978, following present expansion trends, it could attain a potential of between 90 million and 110 million. The Spanish government is operating a development programme which is helping the scientific sector of the industry to improve, but the programme is unlikely to achieve significant results, because the local growers, who are very independent in nature, are withholding their collaboration, and they are slow to respond to directions from Madrid.

Hatcheries in North West France are the traditional suppliers to the Spanish market, taking as much as 90 per cent of the total sales. However, the outbreak of abba disease, traced to imported French seed, badly affected the Spanish growers last year and forced the Spanish Government to impose restrictions on the import of French seed. This restriction has now been lifted as no alternative source of supply of Edulis of the right size is available, and it would have meant the total closure of the industry.

There are a number of hatcheries in North West Spain, but only one is producing small quantities of seed for supply to the local market. A further hatchery has recently started and a third is at the drawing board stage. It will, therefore, probably be 2–3 years before the national hatcheries will be in a position to supply any significant quantity of seed to the local growers.

Another factor which influences the situation and makes it vital for the Spanish industry to become self-sufficient within the shortest possible time is the fact that the French hatcheries are turning to the Gigas [Pacific oyster] and I think that from 1976 onwards the production of Edulis seed will be limited. The oyster Gigas is not grown in Spain, and its introduction to, and acceptance by, traditional growers and consumers is likely to be slow.

Seed specification to meet the traditional market. For the traditional culture method the following specification is necessary for the seed:–

(a) Edulis oyster seed of 35–40 mm (10 gms. per unit weight) for immediate use on the rope culture system.
(b) A proven quality oyster which has shown from trials that growth rate is rapid, and the rate of mortality is minimal.

61

(c) Competitive price.

(d) Documentary evidence that the seed has been inspected before leaving the United Kingdom and a written guarantee from the Ministry of Agriculture, Food and Fisheries [*sic*] certifying that the seed is disease free.

It is quite obvious that if seed had been produced by the Seed Oysters (UK) Ltd hatchery six months ago to meet the above specification, the sales potential in North West Spain would have been increased and the purpose of the most recent trip could have been realised to a far greater extent.

As a guide on prices one Spanish grower quoted the buying price of French seed of 35–40 mm at 10.5 francs per kilo (35 units to kilo) this year, i.e. approximately 3p per seed oyster.

Nevertheless, the contacts made during the visit have expressed a great deal of interest in buying seed. Bearing in mind the difficulty of breaking into a new market made resistant by fear of infected seed, and the natural reluctance of growers to buy seed of unaccustomed size, it is heartening to see that growers are prepared to place orders, but these will be for trial purpose initially. A rapid and positive response to these growers who have shown interest is necessary to make up for the previous failure of the company to appreciate this market.

Interest was expressed by a number of companies in the possibility of entering into some form of on-going association with Seed Oysters (UK) Ltd. One suggestion put forward, which could well provide an answer to some of the problems of Seed Oysters (UK) Ltd, would be that the Spanish associate would purchase seed of the small size and grow it on until it conformed in size to local market requirements. Given that the Spanish associate has the right facilities and technical know-how to handle the small 2–5 mm seed and the on-growing period in the rich Spanish rias is shorter than in North Wales, the possibility could be interesting for the longer term supplying of this important market.

Production

Problems at Seed Oysters (UK) had not been confined to sales alone, since although there had been no real capacity problems the oysters had experienced a high mortality rate during 1974. For example, a total of 1,250,000 Pacific oysters had been despatched to Loch Sunart to hold against future Scottish orders and to take pressure off the site in Wales, but despite this the production of 10–12 mm oysters only reached 6,774,000, of which only some 3,535,000 (48 per cent) survived. (Exhibit 2B.2 shows the production and survival rates of all the Pacific oysters.) Jim Knowles felt that this performance was explained by:

(1) the bad results at Loch Sunart, due to poor weather conditions and possibly lack of attention;

(2) the mild winter, which, as the temperature did not drop low enough to prevent the oyster from continuing to respire, caused a loss of condition and the failure of the weaker part of the population; and

(3) a tendency for the stronger part of the population to be sieved off and dispatched, against orders, leaving the weaker part behind for overwintering at Brynsiencyn.

Exhibits 2B.3 and 2B.4 show the stock in hand and projected production for both Pacific and European oysters for 1975.

Costs

On the basis of a breakdown of total costs (see Exhibit 2B.5), Jim Knowles prepared his estimate of future costs. The following is his report.

The cost of producing 3–4 mm seed when 15 million are produced (Gigas or Edulis) is £4.30/1,000 and when 17 million are produced £3.79/1,000.

On the costs of the 10–12 mm size (sold at £8/1,000) the production costs come to £7.48/1,000 whilst for the 15 mm size (sold at £10/1,000) the cost is £7.73/1,000.

At this stage there is a split between the species. For Edulis, growing on to 40 mm size will cost £9.06/1,000 and these should be saleable at £17/1,000 in Spain. It will take, however, a full eighteen months (two summers) to reach this size at Brynsiencyn. There is no ready known market for 40 mm Gigas. However, in eighteen months 2,000,000 of the survivors of the 10,000,000 15 mm size should come to saleable size, followed by a further 3,000,000 over the next 6 months, giving a likely income of £185,000. Points about this are:

(1) an average income of 4p is assumed, since at least three quarters of this number would need to be grown on elsewhere and payment made to those outside growers of 4p each.
(2) selling price would be at 6.5p each.
(3) make-up of the £185,000 would be:–

$$
\begin{array}{rr}
 & \pounds \\
1{,}500{,}000 \ @ \ 6.5p = & 97{,}500 \\
3{,}500{,}000 \ @ \ 2.5p = & \underline{87{,}500} \\
 & 185{,}000 \\
\end{array}
$$

(4) ways of doing this are discussed below.

It appears that the best way to reduce the price is to increase production, assuming that a sale can be made of the produce.

Within the hatchery, it is possible that the production of 3–4 mm. Gigas and/or Edulis can be increased up to 20 m p.a. This would require an additional cost of £2,600 for new equipment. Existing services and staff could cope, but only small savings could be made in the costs listed herewith [Exhibit 2B.5], approximately £1,000 in all, and this is likely to be swallowed up in price increases. Cost/unit at this size would drop, therefore, to £3.23/1,000.

On the next sizes a further cost of £4,000 would be incurred on new equipment to cope with handling the larger number of small oysters being put down on the beach during the summer months. The existing stage could cope with this increased workload.

On this basis costs for the 10–12 mm size would be

$$\pounds 30{,}650/\pounds 14{,}000 + \pounds 3.23 = \pounds 5.23/1{,}000$$

and for the 15 mm size

$$\pounds 2.45 + 3.23 = \pounds 5.68/1{,}000$$

In the summary, the following points would need to be put into action for obtaining 20 m 3–4 mm p.a.:

63

		£
1.	8 extra larval tanks and associated fittings (no difficulties)	1600
2.	Extra filter press and pump	400
3.	Algae need to be grown in outside greenhouse from April to October (known to be possible from work in 1974). Savings of £800 p.a. in electricity possible, but mainly allows a greater production of algae. Extra equipment	600
		2600

(Note. The above assumes that production is not interrupted by unexpected hazards, such as disease, water pollution etc. and that all existing hatchery staff will be maintained.)

For the growing-on of the 3–4 mm size to 10–12 mm a further cost of £4,000 would need to be incurred (non-recurring annually). This is for the production of small mesh bags to hold the excess production during the summer months. The advantage of the small mesh bags would be to save about £500 of electricity per annum and, more important, to allow production to expand.

Regarding table oysters, we have at present 8,500 Gigas which are being sold at a steady rate at 8p each (carriage extra). I estimate that for up to 500,000 no extra costs would be required for the handling or ground preparation. For the sales, however, an increase in 'phone charges might be expected of a further £50/quarter, together with postal charges of an extra £100 p.a. The price for selling this quantity would drop to 7p each. There will be available for buying in, up to 60,000 Gigas locally this summer.

For the production of an extra 1,000,000, a cost of £1,000 for ground clearance would be required plus £1,000 for extra cleansing facilities. No further staff or labour would be needed except for a van and a driver which would cost a further £1,000 if we used J. Cresswell as delivery/sales. Running costs for the van might total a further £1,000 p.a. Sale price for 1,000,000 is likely to be 6.5p each.

On the increase up to growing 5,000,000 Gigas some market research would need to be undertaken and no real costs can be sensibly arrived at. From a production viewpoint the figure is possible using other local growing areas as mentioned above. An improvement in handling would be needed, however, and it is likely that an extra cost of £10,000 (non-recurring) would be required. Extra casual labour at spring tides would also be needed (Bangor students?) say at an annual cost of £500.

EXHIBIT 2B.1   Results of Jeni Glanfield's investigations

Sea Products International of Birmingham made enquiry for two tons of frozen meat and subsequently ordered 50 cases @ 65p per lb. on understanding that they might well order more. Terms net payment within 21 days of order (17.2.75) ex Bristol. Total value of order £1,300.

Seafare Frozen Foods of Sevenoaks have been visited by myself and are possibly interested in breaded oysters in 1 lb poly bags for sale into retail trade. Took samples of both breaded and frozen meats.

Clouston International have asked for quotation on 1 ton and 10 ton lots for export to France. Quoted 75p/lb frozen.

Affish asked for quotation for 1 ton per week frozen meats for export to USA. Quoted 75p/lb.

Clayton Love, Dublin asked for quotation for 5, 10 and 20 ton lots frozen meats. Quotation given 85p/lb CIF Dublin.

Associated Fisheries, Hull. Mr Jackson visited, quoted 80p/lb on ton lots breaded and frozen. Sample to be sent. JMG [Jeni Glanfield] to discuss further.

Finnbar Sea Foods, Hull. Sample breaded sent. Deliver bulk to freezer companies, wholesalers, etc. Was displeased with breaded. Will come to London to discuss subject with JMG and any other person who is willing to attend. INSTRUCTIVE.

Alpino Restaurants. Visited, left sample. May market frozen in coquilles and on shell throughout their chain of bistros and restaurants. Quoted 70p/lb.

British Caledonian Airways interested in breaded for flight menus. Left sample. Quoted 90p/lb.

Frinor of Grimsby interested in ton lots frozen and breaded. Quoted 80p/lb delivered Grimsby. Sample to be delivered.

Bejam are opening new freezer centre opposite Harrods in Knightsbridge. Sample to be given and discussion to follow.

British Transport Hotels still considering.

B. & A. Britton, Leyton to be visited.

Qantas have oysters on Australian flight menus. Will write after contacting Australian Head Office.

Post House Manchester, replied to Terry Roberts' circular and have breaded oysters on their menu every weekend. So far have ordered three cases in three weeks.

Guernsey Sea Farms express great interest in marketing frozen oysters in the Channel Islands and believe that they have a good potential market. We are, however, encountering difficulties in sending the oysters from England to the Islands. Peter Duport can only find cold storage space for 30 cases breaded and 8 cases IQF and I have yet to find a means of delivering these. However, contact is being maintained and I hope that between us we shall find a solution.

Flying Goose Limited, who sell everything from breaded scampi and prawns to scallops and lobster tails, are not interested in oysters: they say maybe in 1976.

Wheelers have never encountered 'this type of oyster', but the Chairman said he would be willing to talk to me.

London Hilton − no interest.

Alveston Kitchens − no interest.

Shellfish Soundings. Shellfish newsletter in USA. Request placed with them for us to advertise. No reply received yet.

Fisheries Development will do nothing until they receive up-to-date health certificate. Mr Knowles informs that the inspection is under way.

Severnside. Mr Jackson held meeting with Mr Selby on 20 February. I understand they show no great interest in marketing frozen oysters. Since their finances are known to be somewhat shaky, this would not be surprising.

Chequers Hotel of Barnstaple is opening in April and we should contact them then. They have received a sample.

Gael Seafoods of Glasgow are no longer interested in selling our oysters. Jeremy Cresswell from Brynsiencyn is taking over Scotland and will use Gael's stock of oysters at the Union Cold Store to sell from. It should not be forgotten that these will have Gael labels on.

EXHIBIT 2B.2   Pacific oyster (*Crassostrea gigas*): production and survivals

Size (mm)	Production (thousands) 1973	1974	Mean survivals (%)
0.44	16,000	20,000	50
3—4	10,000	7,000	79
10—12	6,100	6,770	55
15+	4,100	3,530	

Notes to Exhibit 2B.3 on p. 67

[a] Subject to count currently in progress.
[b] List of buyers, prices, delivery dates available.
[c] Anticipated purchase based on past demand. Raises question of whether a contract should be signed for supply of 2,000 per month over four months.

General notes

1. Sales of frozen oysters, approximately £3,800 to date, are excluded.
2. *Options* — Immediate sale: 'confirmed revenue' £17,600 — 'available for sale' £10,566 = £28,166.
   Delayed sale as seed: £30,300.
   Confirmed sale of seed, plus on-growing with delayed return to July—Sep 1975: £57,700.
   Needs revised terms of trade, including penalty clause.

EXHIBIT 2B.3   Pacific oyster (*Crassostrea gigas*): stocks and sales

	Actual numbers in stock, or, after April, projected production	Firm orders[b]	Confirmed revenue (£)	Available for sale No.	Available for sale Value (£)	Stock unsold brought forward No.	Stock unsold brought forward Value (£)	Stock unsold, therefore laid for on-growing No.	Value (£)
(November 1974 to March 1975 inclusive: sales 350,000, value £3,500 – mostly 15mm; table oysters £212)									
April 1975									
3–4mm (£3/1000)									
10–12mm (£8/1000)	1,250,000[a]	544,000 / 282,000 for May	5,150	424,000	3,816 (at £9/1000)				
15mm (£10/1000)									
Table	8,500 saleable May–Sep / 2,000 saleable Apr	2,000[c]	160[c]						
May									
3–4mm	300,000	130,000 (170,000 for June)	390						
10–12mm		282,000 from April	2,600			382,000 from Apr	3,820	300,000 (to June–Aug 1976)	24,000 (at 8p each)
Table		2,000[c]	160[c]						
June									
3–4mm	1,600,000	300,000 / 1,300,000 for July	900						
10–12mm		150,000 from May	1,080 / 7.20						
Table	4,250	2,000[c]	160[c]	2,000					
July									
3–4mm	150,000	950,000 from June		150,000	450				
10–12mm				150,000	1,200				
Table	2,000	2,000	160[c]						
August									
10–12mm						135,000 from July	1,080		
Table						140,000 from July			
September									
10–12mm						130,000 from July	1,500	70,000 (to July 1976 and after)	5,600
15mm								65,000 (to July–Sep 1976)	5,400
October									
3–4mm	1,700,000			1,700,000	5,100		5,100		5,100
	4,700,000 +350,000		17,600		10,566		7,600 +5,100 = 12,700	Approx 35,000 recoverable July–Sep 1976	

EXHIBIT 2B.4   Continued

(Actual sales November 1974 to March 1975: 53,000 15mm, value £530)

	Available for sale	Stock brought forward		Stock laid down for on-growing	
		No.	Value	No.	Value
April 1975					
3–4mm £3/1,000					
10–12mm £8/1,000	435,000 reserved				
15mm £10/1,000	for May sale				
30–40mm					
Table (5½p each)					
May					
3–4mm					
10–12mm	15,000 maximum				
15mm					
June				Assumes growing on to	
3–4mm	1,200,000			30mm for Spain at Brynsiencin	
July					
3–4mm	2,000,000				
10–12mm		400,000 from June	3,200	320,000 (to June–July 1976)	5,540 (30–40mm)
August					
3–4mm		550,000 from June	4,400	1,080,000 (to June–July 1976)	18,360 (30–40mm)
10–12mm^c		800,000 from July	6,400		
Sept					
10–12mm^c		400,000 from Aug	3,200	240,000 } (to July	14,080 (30–40mm)
		800,000 from July	6,400	640,000 } 1976 +)	
October					
10–12mm^c		800,000 from Aug	6,400^d	480,000 (to June–July 1976)	8,160 (30–40mm)
March 1976					
10–12mm^c		300,000 from Aug	2,400	180,000 } (to June–	3,060 } (30–40mm)
		675,000 from Sep	6,750	600,000 } July 1976)	10,020 }
					66,280

Notes

aShould the order be refused and oysters grown on to sell at 10p.
bSale to Lintell no advantage unless extra commission of approximately £8000 agreed – otherwise better to sell to Keresen for £20,000 less
10 per cent. The Spanish alternative (for instance, Rejogo or Ribas) would require £2000 to hold at Brynsiencin and depends on the conclusion of an
agreement by Jacqueline Giles.
cAssuming grown on at Brynsiencin.
dNot earmarked for Keresen.

EXHIBIT 2B.4   European oyster (*Ostrea edulis*): stock and sales

(Actual sales November 1974 to March 1975: 53,000 15mm, value £530)

	Actual stock	Firm orders	Confirmed Revenue (£)	Possible orders No.	Revenue (£)
April 1975					
3–4mm £3/1,000				3,000 Rejogo	
10–12mm £8/1,000 }				3,000 Bruzon	} Free trials
15mm £10/1,000 }				9,000 Torre	
30–40mm	450,000				
Table (5½p each)	6,000	Free sample to Spain			
	4,500	Teck[a]	247		
May					
3–4mm	100,000	10,000 Baldegos	30		
		100,000 W. Aquaculture	300		
10–12mm		4,000 Baldegos	34 {from 435,000	200,000 Ribas	1,600
		100,000 Calway	800 {brought	100,000 Bruzon	800
		8,000 BIM	80		
15mm		4,000 Ministry of Agriculture,	40 {forward		
		Fisheries and Food			
June					
3–4mm	1,200,000				
July					
3–4mm	2,000,000			2,500,000	} 7,500
10–12mm				Lintell[b]	or
August					20,400
3–4mm	2,400,000			2,500,000	
10–12mm[c]				Keresen	
September					
10–12mm[c]					
October					
10–12mm[c]					
March 1976					
10–12mm[c]	7,500,000		1,531		8,700 or
	+ 483,000				21,800

EXHIBIT 2B.5   Forecast costs for 1975 (according to
                Jim Knowles)

	£
Salaries	
Works	
Secretarial	
Canteen (see below)	51,650
Management	
Directors	
Oil: 52 weeks/3 x £115	2,000
Electricity: £1000 x 4	4,000
Telephone: £150 x 4	600
Insurance	2,000
Motor	800
Travel	1,000
Depreciation	3,000
Maintenance	3,000
Chemicals	250
Other materials	1,700
Postage and stationery	300
Carriage	200
Audit	1,000
Accountancy	1,800
Legal	100
Interest	
DTI: £40,000 x 7%	2,800
WFA: £13,000 x 9%	1,170
Bank: £165,000 x 14% (this applies to frozen	
breaded oysters also — £40,500)	23,100
General expenses	300
Sales expenses, consultancy and travel	6,000
Rates	150
Canteen	1,200
	108,120

EXHIBIT 2B.6   Gwynedd Oysters Ltd: consolidated profit and loss account (£)

	6 months to 30 Apr 1975		14 months to 31 Oct 1974	
Sales		11,829		24,527
Cost of sales	23,492		18,414	
Stock losses	16,717		29,806	
		40,209		48,220
Gross loss		23,380		23,693
Expenses	20,375		41,639	
Interest payable	11,858		15,192	
Formation expenses	—		12,230	
Miscellaneous income	—		1,766	
		32,233		67,295
Loss for the period		60,613		90,988

EXHIBIT 2B.7   Gwynedd Oysters Ltd: consolidated balance sheet (£)

	6 months to 30 Apr 1975		14 months to 31 Oct 1974	
Employment of funds				
Fixed assets	127,267		127,267	
Less depreciation	18,570		13,849	
		108,873		113,418
Current assets				
Stocks	34,268		48,398	
Debtors	10,563		6,799	
Cash	3,741		12	
		48,572		55,209
Current liabilities				
Bank overdrafts	–		111,797	
Creditors and accruals	24,476		30,903	
Net current assets		24,096		(87,491)
Net assets		132,969		25,927
Sources of funds				
Share capital		25,334		25,334
Share premium		46,666		46,666
Profit and loss deficit	151,601		90,988	
Goodwill	29,276		29,276	
		(180,877)		(120,264)
		(108,877)		(48,264)
Loans				
Unsecured loan stock 1974–8	20,000		20,000	
DTI	40,000		40,000	
WFA	11,846		14,191	
Bank	170,000		–	
		241,846		74,191
		132,969		25,927

3 M. D. Benedict Ltd

SUE BIRLEY

CASE

M. D. Benedict Ltd, was incorporated 2 June 1971 to carry on business as closed-circuit television (CCTV) specialists. The directors and founders of the company were Ali Cameron and Chris Quarton, who held equal shares in it. By January 1974 the company had an order book for £100,000 but was in serious need of working capital to fund further growth. (See Exhibit 3.1 for a complete list of events.)

The set-up

Ali Cameron took a thick sandwich course in physics at Imperial College, London, in the early 1960s under the sponsorship of GEC. During the course he developed an interest in TV video systems, which was deepened when he joined the BBC as a trainee engineer. Working in television, both at the BBC and later at London Weekend, he gained valuable experience, and, when the latter achieved a complete *volte-face* in production and programme terms, following a palace revolution, he became a freelance engineer, working mainly for a small company, Studio 99 Video Ltd. It was there that he met Chris Quarton, who, after a stormy career at school, university and in the army, had discovered that his major asset was an ability to sell. Both Chris and Ali felt that the potential in the CCTV and video market was enormous and that this was not recognised, and thus exploited, by the management of Studio 99. Eventually a major rift between the employees resulted in Chris being fired and in April 1971 he and Ali formed their own company. Asked why they decided to join together, Chris remarked that their technical skills were complementary and that each felt the 'requirement to become more of an individual'. Each needed the other if they were to satisfy their goals, because their individual knowledge was not enough. Both agreed that their long-term aim for the company was the provision of a complete service to the customer – both equipment and films, packaged with a consultancy service. The initial step was to form Visual Impact Ltd, which was to become the film-making arm of the business. Unfortunately, filming required a large capital outlay for studio facilities and equipment, and so for a time the concept was shelved. Instead the pair decided to capitalise on their main asset – a good reputation in the trade both with suppliers and customers – and formed M. D. Benedict Ltd to buy and sell video systems. Whilst Chris and Ali owned both companies, M. D. Benedict and Visual Impact remained separate entities.

Reflecting on the formation of the business, Chris felt that Visual Impact reflected Ali's interests much more than his own. 'I viewed it merely as a vehicle to get the ball rolling. It was purely a stepping-stone to more lucrative and enjoyable areas – the selling of the total package.'

The market

The video cassette was a logical extension of the sound cassette, but despite this it was only in 1969 that the first system was demonstrated by EVR (then a consortium of CBS, ICI and CIBA-Geigy). Thus, this part of industry was no more than two years old when M. D. Benedict began, and, in marketing terms, had then hardly started. At that time it was felt that there were two roads along which the technology could develop.

1. Prepared films to be shown on video receivers or systems. These could be training films to be used in schools or universities, allowing the student to learn at his own pace, or strategically placed in museums, video films could replace the guided tour. Whilst such films required special video receivers, it was clear that one future development in the field would be the conversion of home television sets to accept video cassettes, thus allowing the viewer to play television programmes as easily as audio recorders. Further, there was no reason why this should not extend to the recording of broadcast programmes on video tapes.
2. The outdoors or field use whereby a system of cameras would allow constant surveillance of many points by one undetected individual. The possibilities here were countless – covering, for example, process control in industry, security surveillance in stores, and traffic control. The cameras and receivers were available, but not necessarily manufactured by the same company and therefore not always compatible. There was a need for specialist consultant engineers to design and set-up systems to customer requirements. Further, the customer needed to be taught how and when to use them. M. D. Benedict would provide missionary salesmen with technical back-up.

The first six months

As a result of the many contacts which both Ali and Chris had made, the business soon flourished. They set up CCTV systems for a number of academic institutions, including the London Business School, Luton College and London University, and were responsible for installing an automatic-cycling public-display system in HMS *Belfast*, a large warship moored on the Thames in London and open to the public. In the latter case, M. D. Benedict was not responsible for the films (software) but was responsible for the equipment (hardware) and the consultancy back-up to support a smooth running of the system. Including a set of automatic slide-change systems and some tape and sound systems, the invoice to HMS *Belfast* was £8000, giving the company a comfortable 30 per cent margin. This was the mark-up on most equipment; the engineers' time was priced, says Ali, 'according to the job'.

The re-forming of Visual Impact Ltd

Melvin Kirner had also worked at Studio 99 with Ali and Chris but in January 1971 had emigrated to New Zealand. In November 1971, on the death of his father, he returned to England and, being at a loose end, contacted Ali. He had a varied background, having been a laboratory technician in an electronics engineering company, a process manager in quality control at J. Lyons, and finally a salesman at Studio 99. Having always been interested in films, he soon became very involved in developing video-tapes for schoolchildren. 'In those days,' he said, 'you had to spend a

73

lot of time showing the customer the capabilities of a CCTV system.' In New Zealand, he had worked for a large advertising agency, where he had rapidly gained experience directing films. Chris and Ali's concept of, as he put it, 'a complete service to the communications industry, including films, video systems, artwork, printing, sound-recording', appealed to him, and as he had no other immediate plans he agreed to revive and run Visual Impact. On 12 January 1972 he was appointed to the boards of M. D. Benedict and Visual Impact.

From its incorporation M. D. Benedict had traded from a bedroom in Ali's house. With the rapid expansion of orders, Ali and Chris decided to employ two salesmen, two engineers and a secretary, and this, along with the revival of Visual Impact and the need for a workshop and storage facilities, necessitated a search for larger premises. In March 1972 they took out a lease on premises at 8 St Dunstans Road, Feltham, Middlesex (named Benedict House), for a period of five years at an annual rent of £3600. Despite the fact that the first year's trading would show a turnover of £50,000, the extremely rapid expansion resulted in the company's having problems regarding cash flow and capital. As a result of negotiations on their behalf with a secondary bank, London and County (A & D) Ltd, a discounting facility (a cash 'loan' on the security of invoiced debts) was arranged in April 1972. With cash problems eased, the company was poised to capitalise upon its now established reputation and to fund the development of Visual Impact.

The rise and fall of Visual Impact

The daily running of Visual Impact was the responsibility of Melvin, although he did not consider himself to be responsible for major decisions. These were taken collectively by the board, which had now expanded to include Ken Bowers, the company accountant.

Although the original intention was to produce video films, it soon became evident that customer knowledge of such systems was limited, even in the educational world. The resultant risks involved in making video films without a sponsor or a guaranteed customer was considered too high and the group decided to concentrate upon larger projects, such as films for television. In the event, it became involved in a few small jobs for companies such as Walt Disney. Ali reports, 'This was work that I operated and, it is fair to say, very profitably. I never had a margin of less than 50 per cent.' However, the first major project was for a film proposed and to be set up by the agency Telebureau, which was to be responsible for the programme design, the script and selling. Called *Tradition for Hire*, it was to feature the dress-hire company Moss Bros in a look at the style of dress in the UK, and was to be aimed at the American television market. To assist Melvin, who was to direct the film, Mike Prince joined the group as producer, although his primary expertise was seen to be in the marketing of Visual Impact's services. As a member of the Visual Impact board, he provided the bank guarantees, secured by shares, which formed the only working capital. Mike also worked for ATV Birmingham as an announcer and it was felt that he would be a valuable addition, being able to contribute both knowledge and contacts. The group also hired a researcher to work full-time on the Moss Bros film. The total cost was estimated by Melvin at about £5500. This he says 'was too low, but workable; the estimate should have been between £7000 and £8000, but everyone in the unit was keen to do it'. Moss Bros contributed £4500 in return for which it was to share the profits with Visual Impact.

Halfway through filming, Mike Prince was put on a nine-to-five, five-days-a-week schedule by ATV and was thus virtually eliminated. In January 1973, finding the clash of personalities too great under the prevailing structure, Melvin resigned, leaving Visual Impact with no tangible assets other than an incomplete film, a VAT rebate, and a debt to M. D. Benedict of £10,900 (the final cost of the film, excluding profits, was in excess of £15,000). Investigating the situation, Ali decided that the best strategy would be to invest a further £2000, in order to finish the film and then sell it in order to generate cash as soon as possible. Melvin eventually finished it on a freelance basis, but before it could be sold a creditor applied for liquidation and in November 1973 the company was wound up.

The three full-time directors describe what happend:–

ALI: Melvin had been making films in New Zealand and as a result had come back with a lot of grandiose ideas, although in fact he had only been a director in the second and third division of film making. As a result, he was unable to run the company profitably. After Mike Prince left, he ran wild, and, when about £6000 or £7000 had been spent, I took over the production. There was the basis for a film but it wasn't quite right: it was very loose and ethereal. Unfortunately I am basically a director rather than a producer and I found it impossible to give advice without taking over completely. I couldn't say 'no' to a friend and so I found myself standing on the sidelines doing nothing. Stupid things happened, like a weekend shooting costing over £1000 because of the careless way it was handled. To be fair, some things were outside Melvin's control. For example, we had to pay an extra £700 processing costs, because copies were lost in the post.

My problem was one of firmness. I should have taken over, kicked Melvin out and done it myself. I know I could have done it more adequately and cheaply.

MELVIN: I was very unsure about this particular venture, but it was a job available and it saved me tramping the streets for the next month. I had got quite a lot of experience in directing films in a short time, but because I had learned my trade (directing films for video) from Ali, he was never very confident that I could do it alone.

The original concept for the group was a vital and necessary aim, although not possible initially, because cash constrained the amount of work which we could do ourselves. For example, printing and script-writing had to be sub-contracted.

Telebureau, with whom we didn't even have a proper contract, were very inexperienced in the area. They set-up location shots which we had to cancel because the script didn't arrive. In fact, it usually arrived in instalments and I never knew from one day to the next what I was going to be asked to direct. That meant that there was no real continuity, and editing was a nightmare. Sometimes we had forgotten the original purpose of a shot made seven or eight months previously!

I left because it eventually became obvious to me that the personalities of the people involved were such that it was impossible for the three of us to work together. Whereas any two could come to a compromise agreement, it was not possible for three (and so no-one ever took control of the company). We all had such very different values and life styles. I feel that it failed for a number of reasons. First, Telebureau was very inexperienced in the field. Second, I had no experience in casting or producing, only directing. Third, Mike's heart was not in the project because he couldn't stand the aggravation involved in the Moss Bros film; and, finally, Ali and I handled directing in completely different ways and Ali was unable to accept my ability.

CHRIS: I was never really interested in Visual Impact – it was a diaphanous object. It reflected Ali's personality rather than mine. I viewed it merely as a venture to get the ball rolling. It failed due to bad management on the part of myself, Ali, Melvin and Mike. I felt that there were too many directors in the company. I rocked the boat in the beginning by opposing the inclusion of Mike in the project, but that created a lot of bad feeling. I always felt that the Moss Bros film was badly conceived from a selling viewpoint, but even though I was aware of the increasing costs I allowed it to happen. I should have tried to stop it, but I would have met opposition and certainly upset Ali.

M. D. Benedict and the Spelthorne Engineering Company

'Benedicts', says Ali, 'was very successful throughout the summer of 1972 and we had grown to a staff of sixteen people. It wintered reasonably well and came out at the end of December with a target turnover for the next year of £200,000.'

The accounts for the period 1 June 1971 to 30 November 1972 show the following details:

	£
Turnover	60,904
Gross profit	18,419
Net profit	1,793
Directors' remuneration	nil

One of Ali's skills in installing CCTV systems was an ability to adapt the equipment available to new uses and very often this required the making of special parts. For example, cameras used outdoors needed a special housing to protect them from weather. Those placed permanently for security surveillance needed special tilt heads to hold them firmly in position. As a result a meeting through a mutual friend, Paul Stretton and Jerry Schofield had begun to make such parts for Ali. In the beginning, they worked on a part-time basis using their own garage as a workshop, but the work expanded fast. Although M. D. Benedict was their principal customer, they soon began to take on various prototype engineering jobs from other companies, and in March 1973, encouraged by Ali, Paul and Jerry formed their own company, Spelthorne Engineering, and began working full time: another example of Ali's philosophy for 'a corporate umbrella of interlocking companies.'

The management of M. D. Benedict

Ali explained that the responsibilities within M. D. Benedict were clearly defined. He was completely involved in the technical and engineering aspects and Chris in sales and finance (with advice from Ken Bowers, the company accountant). Commenting upon the company, one customer remarked that, whilst Ali gave a very good service personally, the engineers he employed were second rate. Also he seemed not to be aware of this and to leave them to their own devices without any control or direction. Further, relations between Ali and Chris had become strained. Sales were buoyant, forecasts optimistic, but there was no real tight control of cash – a crucial area, as 75 per cent of their business was with slow-paying industries. Ali felt that Chris did not pay enough attention to the financial aspects of the business: 'He only devoted one day a month to it.'

Paul Stretton remarked,

There was a large flow of ideas from Benedicts but little money to get anything off the ground. In fact there was a complete lack of organisation on the engineering side. The space in Benedict House was badly used, the staff weren't very well employed, nor were they of the same calibre as the image which they put forward.

Ali is a very good engineer but not a manager. He doesn't want to know anything about the financial side of the business, and unfortunately Chris, whilst he is a superb salesman, has a total lack of comprehension of costing. For example, for a five-camera channel system, costing was done in about five minutes at a meeting by people just suggesting various prices. The exercise should have taken a day!

I know that Ali wants to incorporate us into the group in the future but I feel very uneasy about it.'

[Ali remarks, 'We were aware that the need for the chief engineer to cover day-to-day management was not working and I felt that Paul's abilities could be applied to this effort.']

Cash problems

The discounting facility with London and County had solved the company's cash-flow shortage for a while and allowed it to expand its business. However, in May 1973 cash problems arose again. Rent for Benedict House was outstanding to the extent of £2000 and the landlord was exerting pressure on the company. Rather than lose the property, Chris and Ali, under an option clause contained in the lease, purchased the property plus the adjoining barn privately for £62,000, thus incurring a charge of £700 per month in mortgage fees. Benedict House was then leased to M. D. Benedict for £8500 per annum and the adjoining barn to Spelthorne Engineering. By July 1973 the cash situation had become critical and National Westminster, the company's bankers, would not inject any more capital into the venture. At the suggestion and recommendation of one of the company's suppliers, an account was opened with Barclays Bank, which advanced £20,000 on the basis of a charge on Benedict House, supported by the personal guarantees of Ali and Chris. With the injection of fresh working capital, expansion proceeded anew and in November 1973 they were again making good progress. Although the accounts showed a loss, turnover had increased by 40 per cent over the previous eighteen months trading.

For the year 1 December 1972 to 30 November 1973 the accounts showed:

	£
Turnover	102,744
Gross profit	23,903
Net profit	(944)
Directors' remuneration	nil

Unfortunately, in the same month, London and County collapsed, as a result of which the discounting facility became inoperable. At the same time, the inter-company debt due from Visual Impact was seen to be of no value. To fulfil existing orders, they had to find alternative funds for £100,000 of debts plus forward stock – but from where and on what basis?

POST MORTEM

By January 1974 the company was without any real cash funds. No money existed to restock supplies, and, despite the fact that orders were increasing, it could not satisfy them. It struggled along until March, when it managed to arrange further factoring facilities for debts with Martex, part of Minster Finance. Unfortunately, this did not work out as envisaged, and the company suffered further losses as suppliers refused to supply goods, leaving the company, now burdened with excessive overheads, unable to meet the orders then being placed.

In May 1974, having reviewed the situation, the directors decided to liquidate. At the last minute, they were approached by Mike Shaw, who, through his company Principality Finance, was considering setting up a group to make, sell, instal and hire CCTV systems. In return for finance, Benedict, with Ali as managing director, would be part of the new group. 'Mike viewed Chris as a wheeler-dealer who would never do what he was told, and he chose me,' says Ali, 'because, although I would be out of my depth, I would do what I was told.'

Three weeks later, on 24 May 1974, and before financial arrangements had been completed, Mike Shaw committed suicide. M. D. Benedict was finally put into the hands of a receiver. The principal asset was Benedict House, which had provided the basis for the directors' guarantees and by this time was valued at between £120,000 and £140,000. However, by the time it reached the market, the property balloon had burst and it reached only £68,000 in bids against a reserve of £90,000. The creditors petitioned for the bankruptcy of Chris and Ali.

ALI: Barclays played it supersafe all the time and wouldn't take any risks. After all, the fall of London and County was in no way our fault and they could have found us alternative sources of finance from one of their internal companies. It is self-evident that if you remove the ignition key from a car it will stop. I feel that there are three major reasons why the companies failed. One, London and County; two, the property valuation failed to support us (we could have recapitalised); and, three, we did not have the tight accounting procedure that we needed.

CHRIS: Our skills were complementary but we really needed a strong managing director to hold us together. I had got myself into an administrative position which was greater than I deserved. We were right to buy Benedict House, because it gave the company solid assets. I think the beginning of the end came after the collapse of London and County.

KEN BOWERS: In fact, the problems existed from the commencement of the venture and in particular the constitution of the company, which involved a partnership with the common-law right of veto to each partner. In incorporating the company, it was necessary to devise some form of corporate constitution that retained the balance of power, since without it neither would have been prepared to commence the venture. The device I used was to divide the capital into two classes of shares, each class having the right to appoint directors, and the regulations governing directors' meetings specifying that a voting favour was required by a director of each class before any resolution could be passed. At one stroke, therefore, I had retained the balance of power in the limited company that previously existed in the

78

partnership, and I also provided a situation where neither side could control the company in the manner envisaged by Chris. The question is, therefore, whether the need of the business to have a strong controller is capable of being compatible with the requirements of the proprietors individually not to be dominated by the other. My own view is that management by committee cannot work, particularly in a high-risk industry.

A report to the creditors, made on 26 June 1974, concludes by saying,

The company's directors attribute its failure to:–

1. Over-expansion of the company's business without the basic capital structure necessary to finance the length of time needed to produce orders.
2. The taking on of leasing and hire purchase agreements which the company could not afford.
3. High overheads not adequately provisioned for.
4. Bad management and high interest rates.

4 Cohen and Fowler

SUE BIRLEY

CASE A

During the spring of 1975, Cohen and Fowler, a small firm of solicitors, was faced wi the need to monitor and control its cash flow on a more formal basis than it had done the past. Two factors had contributed to the situation. First, the practice had recently moved premises, incurring a substantial increase in rental; and, secondly, three of its major clients had gone into liquidation as a result of the fall in the property market, leaving the firm with a large amount of fees owing and irrecoverable.

The formation of the practice

The practice had been formed in December 1971 by Sidney Cohen (36), an establishe commercial solicitor, who upon the dissolution of his previous partnership invited his colleague Jo Fowler (28) to join him. Having just qualified, Jo jumped at the offer: 'no only was it a marvellous opportunity for a newly qualified solicitor, but, also, Sidney was the first lawyer I met whom I really liked and respected'. At the time Harry Clark was an articled clerk to one of Sidney's previous partners, although he had been working with Sidney for three years: 'I was a bit of an ugly duckling. With a year to g on my articles I would have to transfer to another firm and I was fortunate that Sidne decided not to ditch me.'

During 1972 the practice flourished and towards the end of the year it became increasingly obvious that a decision had to be made with regard to future expansion. Whilst they were experienced in the commercial area, which paid well, the partners fel that litigation work was safer, as it was less susceptible to political vagaries. It was als a sevice which many commercial clients expected them to offer. Because they already had more litigation work than they could cope with, it was decided to employ an assistant solicitor with specialised experience in the field. The post was advertised in th national press and in law journals. Sidney explained that they were looking for someo who would fit in on a personal level, since they wished to continue the friendly atmosphere in the office, which extended to an efficient service for their clients.

A number of applicants were interviewed and in April 1973 Debbie Harris was appointed. Debbie (25) was an LL.B. from a provincial university and had completed her articles in a local solicitors' office, specialising in litigation. By 1972 she was married, had moved to London and was looking for a job which suited her training. Whilst the two partners agreed upon the appointment, Sidney had taken the lead as Jo had little experience in interviewing ('I would have employed them all!'). Reflecting up the decision, Sidney felt that Debbie 'had appropriate experience, was very personable and appeared to know what she was talking about, although her youth meant that she had limited experience. We were looking for someone who had not become entrenched in particular ways of running an office.'

During the last six months of his articles, Harry began to consider his future. No discussion had taken place with regard to his remaining in the practice, and, since he had only ever worked for Sidney, he felt that he should consider a change.

I interviewed four or five solicitors and was a bit pushy about it because I thought I was very good. My main ambitions at the time were to earn a lot of money and buy a flat and sports car – articled clerks earn very little [then £1000 per year]. Then I became engaged and simmered down, and Sidney and Jo asked me to stay. We agreed that I would be paid as an assistant solicitor for the rest of my articles with a view to becoming a partner in the near future. I was bowled over: I really thought I was the cat's whiskers. I didn't think too much about the future and the responsibilities of being a partner. What do I want now [three years later]? Bags of money and a load of job satisfaction. I have plighted my troth to the others. I can work with them and I trust them, a very important factor when you have a partnership with unlimited liability.

On 1 December 1973, both Harry and Debbie became full partners. Negotiations with Harry had been hard and took a long time. 'There seemed', said Sidney, 'to be no great hurry, as it was always agreed that he would join us and he was already receiving a share of the profits. However, by October it seemed sensible to finalise the situation and to include Debbie.'

The partners

Sidney had a quiet, restful personality which was felt immediately on entering his office, where he sat behind a large desk quietly smoking a pipe and listening. His opinion was greatly respected by clients, colleagues and in the profession, and in the practice he was often consulted for his legal opinion: he was the senior partner not only in age but also in stature. He had introduced most of the original clients to the practice and they were often friends or acquaintances of long standing. Nevertheless, he made sure that the other three were fully involved in all client matters; jobs were divided on the basis of expertise and not of age, status or personal relationships. The good name of Cohen and Fowler was of prime importance to him, and in defending this or any other person or matter which was close to him he was strong willed and loyal. Underneath the quiet exterior lay a stubborn streak.

Jo came from an originally working-class family which had been successful in business. He was an ambitious person and had completed his educational career by gaining a law degree. He had an urge to create and build something lasting and did not consider his life's work to be in the day-to-day routine of a solicitor's practice. He felt that such work could often be dealt with just as efficiently by unqualified, but supervised, staff, leaving him more time for grappling with the complex legal problems. He was not a rapid worker and often rivalled Harry in the number of hours he spent at work in the evenings, when he was able to dictate letters and bills undistracted. He needed pleasant, attractive surroundings both at work and at home, and his clothes had elegance and flair. Although he had a desk in his office, all his work was conducted from a round pine table: he disliked a barrier between himself and others. Initially he sometimes gave the impression of being whimsical and indecisive, but this was soon dispelled by his obvious competence as a solicitor, his enthusiasm and his social awareness and general empathy.

Harry was brought up in a provincial Jewish family. Although he had a powerful drive to succeed in his chosen career, his success had been more rapid than he had ever anticipated. He had a strong dislike of borrowing money and found heavy financial commitments worrying. He was an explosive, sometimes tactless character, moving through each day like a whirlwind and never leaving in the evening until he was cleared of the day's work. His office was full of files on the floor and desk and any other available surface, and even on the hottest day the windows were closed, the blinds drawn and a cloud of pipe smoke filled the room.

Clients who were at first deterred by the youth, sex and attractiveness of Debbie were soon reassured. Much of her litigation and divorce work involved meetings with clients, opponents and barristers and it is here that she excelled. She had a quick, active brain and an iron will and, whilst she was often quiet for long periods, her ability to summarise discussions and focus upon solutions was often startling. She lacked tolerance of incompetence and in her dealings with people was sometimes accused of being blunt and aggressive. She viewed administration as a necessary evil.

In spite of their very different personalities, there was a strong bond between the partners. They were united in a determination both to survive and to earn a reputation for competence and efficiency. On a professional level, they would regularly discuss cases and help each other with difficult legal and technical points, a process only made possible by their mutual regard. On a personal level, there were differences. In particular, Harry was very aware of having worked with Sidney before either of the other two. This, combined with strong male-chauvinist tendencies, made relations with Debbie sometimes a little strained. However, since neither found it particularly easy to keep their feelings to themselves, the air was often cleared by a short but sharp exchange. Relations between Harry and Jo were best illustrated at partners' meetings. Jo was constantly nagging at the others to improve the administration of the practice. At various times he had suggested introducing, for example, better duplicating equipment, a tape-typewriter and a computerised billing system. At such meetings, Harry and Jo dominated the discussions and, as each usually took extreme opposite views, often argued violently. Sidney would make occasional comments or remarks, but it was usually Debbie who brought matters to a conclusion. Exasperated by the other two, she would silence them with one remark, summarise the situation and suggest a solution. Usually this was adopted by the rest.

The change of premises

The premises which the new practice occupied were part of a large terraced building near Tottenham Court Road, London. The building was leased to two small firms and was in a relatively poor state of decoration. Cohen and Fowler occupied two floors of the building but were overcrowded, a situation made worse when Debbie joined the firm. 'We had', said Sidney, 'to create an office for her. There were books and papers everywhere, the typists could hardly move and the rooms were very dingy. We certainly were not giving our clients a very good impression.' Sidney and Jo began to search for new offices and eventually in the summer of 1973 a building nearby became vacant. Jo felt that it would be ideal. 'Whilst it wasn't very pretty, the layout was flexible and would have given us plenty of room to grow.' However, on consideration Sidney thought the rental of £10,000 per year as against the existing £3,500 was too high, and the matter was shelved.

A number of their major clients were in the property business, a market which had experienced boom conditions in 1972 and 1973. As a result, the practice continued to flourish and by the spring of 1974 it became obvious that a major move had to be made. All agreed that the time had come when either they improved both their image and their working conditions, or they would go rapidly downhill. In Debbie's words, 'It wasn't a matter of cost, we had to move. It was sink or swim.'

In April 1974 a period building nearby, which had just been renovated, became available for letting. It comprised four floors with space for about twelve offices. Whilst the annual rental was £16,000, the cost in the first year could be reduced by an £8000 premium received from selling the lease of the existing office and by letting the basement in the new office for £3000 per annum. They decided to move. Although they were greatly worried about their resultant financial state, they decided on a budget for furnishing and negotiated a bank loan of £5000, an amount which they felt they could afford. In June 1974 they moved into their new offices.

The management of the practice

Initially, Jo had done the book-keeping in his spare time, but when this became too onerous they employed a freelance book-keeper, who worked on an *ad hoc* basis in the evenings and weekends. It was soon apparent that this was an unsatisfactory arrangement and the partners decided to employ someone on a more regular basis, who would be available during office hours. Eleanor Roberts, an old friend of Jo, was at the time looking for part-time work. Although she had no formal qualifications or training, she had worked for solicitors as a book-keeper and was familiar with the attendant problems and procedures.* As this fitted their requirements, she was employed by the partners on a part-time basis (2½ days per week) in May 1974. Although she took an active part in financial administration, the main burden continued to rest on Sidney.

Whilst Sidney was the senior partner and stabilising influence, the practice was managed by consensus at regular weekly meetings of all four partners. However, as the workload grew, it became increasingly obvious that they had to consider questions of administration, which had previously been dealt with on a very *ad hoc* basis: 'Sidney looked after the money side and I ordered the light bulbs' (Jo). In particular, as the property slump began to bite and it 'became necessary to watch figures almost daily' (Sidney), the whole question of the billing procedure and the management of the practice came under review.

Usually jobs were assessed on completion (this could be as much as three years after the start of the job) on the basis of time spent multiplied by the hourly charging rate, which at that time was quoted at £21 per hour. (The rate had been fixed by Sidney in 1973 on the basis of 1972 accounts.) This did not apply to all jobs, since in some cases, such as legal-aid work, fees were fixed. Whilst the partners did make notes of the time

---

* For example, the Law Society requires that all solicitors hold client money (pre-payments) in a separate bank account from practice money. Any gross negligence in this can lead to the practice being closed down and the solicitors 'struck-off', and in cases of persistent lack of care the firm would receive a severe reprimand. It is therefore important to ensure that all cheques are drawn from the correct account at all times.

spent in client meetings, they were less careful about such things as telephone calls, which could often take as long as half an hour, or time spent in the office preparing documents. In fact, letters were charged at a standard rate of £2 each, whatever the length or complexity. This situation was made worse by the fact that all the partners disliked preparing bills, a job which they were compelled to do themselves because of the paucity of data. Often they would put off the task until conscience or cash flow forced their hand (some clients did not receive a bill till six or nine months after completion). In assessing the amount they tended to make rough calculations from the files and then adjust them 'according to what the client would stand and we felt it was worth' (Sidney). Usually this meant that commercial and conveyancing jobs were charged at higher than £21 per hour and litigation at a lower rate (the Law Society does safeguard the client by 'taxing' procedure, whereby any bill can be independently assessed). In fact Debbbie refused to charge more than £15 on most of her work which she viewed as a service to clients. Also, in such matters as divorce, she felt that many of them could not afford a higher rate. Already the size of the bill was often a serious shock for many.

In January 1975 Sidney began to review the charging rate, which he felt was too low. Whilst he was able to forecast costs for 1975 (Exhibit 4A.1), he was in great difficulty in forecasting revenue, as he had no idea of either the number of jobs or the time spent on each type of work. Previously he had used a formula given in a booklet published by the Law Society, which suggested that solicitors spent about four hours per day on directly chargeable matters. However, he felt that this was unhelpful, since the partners often worked for long hours both in the evenings and weekend. The time sheets (see Exhibit 4A.2) were unhelpful, because they were incomplete – in fact, Harry never used them at all – but with them Sidney was able to glean some idea of the division of work (see Exhibits 4A.3–4). Should he try to impose a more formal and regular billing system and, if so, how? Further, should they adopt one charging rate or a differential pricing system?

EXHIBIT 4A.1   Fixed costs (£): [a]estimates
                for 1975

Accountants	850
Computer	2,400
Gestetner	500
United Linen	80
Library	1,000
Motor	6,000
Insurance stamps	1,750
Office cleaning	1,000
Office leasing	350
Office maintenance	600
Partners' insurance	1,600
Salaries[b]	15,000
Postage	2,000
Stationery	4,000
Telephone	2,800
Subscriptions	200
Gas	400
Temps	1,000
Rent	16,000
Rates	2,000
	59,530

[a]This excludes electricity, Diners Club, miscellaneous expenses.
[b]Of four secretaries, one office junior, one telephonist, one articled clerk and Eleanor Roberts.

EXHIBIT 4A.2   Time sheet

PERSONNEL/   WORK TYPE/

CLIENT/

MATTER/

COMPUTER NUMBER/

DATE	TIME	CUMULATIVE TOTAL	DATE	TIME	CUMULATIVE TOTAL
			C/F		C/F

CLOSING ANALYSIS

PROFIT COSTS: £   p
CONCESSION/FULL RATE
TOTAL TIME (INCORPORATING
ADDITIONALS):   Hours   mins.

HOURLY RETURN   £   p

TOTAL C/F

EXHIBIT 4A.3   Individual subjective assessments of the proportion of time each partner spends on litigation, conveyancing and commercial business

	Litigation	Conveyancing	Commercial
Sidney's assessment			
Sidney	25	41	33
Jo	25	75	–
Harry	25	50	25
Debbie	100	–	–
Average	44	41	15
Jo's assessment			
Sidney	25	50	25
Jo	27	55	18
Harry	20	70	10
Debbie	100	–	–
Average	43	44	13
Harry's assessment			
Sidney	15	30	55
Jo	25	50	25
Harry	20	65	15
Debbie	100	–	–
Average	40	26	24
Debbie's assessment			
Sidney	25	15	60
Jo	40	50	10
Harry	10	70	20
Debbie	100	–	–
Average	44	34	22

EXHIBIT 4A.4   Jo Fowler's analysis of thirty client matters

1. Proportion of time spent on

commercial conveyancing	18%
domestic conveyancing	55%
litigation	27%

2. Hourly return (£) achieved on

commercial conveyancing	18
domestic conveyancing	19
litigation	
High Court	15
divorce	16[a]
personal injury	17
landlord and tenant	20
magistrates' Court	8
tribunal	2.76
wills	11.11

[a] Without legal aid.

EXHIBIT 4A.5   Revenue account (£) 1972 and 1973 (year ending
                30 November)

	1972	1973
Fees receivable	28,690	59,632
Bank deposit interest	255	792
	28,945	60,424
Salaries	10,419	10,198
Rent	1,763	3,150
Rates and water	676	646
Light and heat	113	194
Telephone	813	1,163
Insurance	387	629
Postage	669	751
Stationery, law books, advertising	1,589	1,751
Motor and travelling expenses	1,542	2,851
Miscellaneous expenses	1,535	1,470
Computer service	446	1,685
Hire of equipment	227	375
Repairs and renewals	636	394
Cleaning	228	407
Bank charges and interest	79	1,105
Hire-purchase interest	84	182
Legal charges	242	788
Accountancy	525	3,154
Depreciation on motor vehicles	454	1,026
Depreciation on fixtures and fittings	497	943
Profit before taxation and partners' drawings	6,021	27,562

EXHIBIT 4A.6 Balance sheet (£) 1972 and 1973 (year ending 30 November)

	1972			1973		
	Cost	Depreciation	Total	Cost	Depreciation	Total
Fixed assets						
Premium on lease	2,750	–	2,750	2,750	–	2,750
Fixtures, fittings	3,297	497	2,800	4,240	1,440	2,800
Library	266	–	266	730	–	730
Motor vehicles	1,804	454	1,350	4,560	1,480	1,480
	8,117	951	7,166	12,280	2,920	9,360
			7,166			9,360
Clients' bank account		364,620			140,604	
Less liabilities to clients		364,620			140,604	
			–			–
Current assets						
Work in progress and disbursements		8,396			19,577	
Pre-payments		–			555	
Office bank account		1,430			6,132	
			9,826			26,264
Total assets			16,992			35,624
Current liabilities						
Sundry creditors and accruals		525			3,110	
Hire purchase less future interest		122			1,730	
Office bank overdraft		4,923			12,400	
Bank loan account		1,160			–	
			6,730			17,240
Net assets			10,262			18,384
Capital account						
Retained profits			10,262			18,384

CASE B

On the morning of Sunday, 23 March 1975, Sidney Cohen died suddenly. Severely shocked, the three remaining partners met to discuss the future, both short and long term. They were particularly concerned about financial matters, since as a result of the fall in the property market the practice had an overdraft of £12,000 and a loan account of £4000. Whilst they expected to recover £20,000 from the winding-up of one bankrupt client, who had gone into liquidation owing them approximately £36,000, they had paid neither rates (for which they had not been assessed) nor rent at the full rate since moving into the new premises. The full rent was payable from March 1975. Also, they had been unable to let the basement, although they had allowed a short occupation, which had proved unsatisfactory. Sidney had been in the process of negotiating future terms with the bank and had agreed in principle a £15,000 overdraft limit and a £5,000 loan account, but nothing had been finalised. Would the bank continue to support such a young group of people? The only current financial information which they had was an estimate of the cash flow for the previous five months from a system which he had recently instituted. (See Exhibit 4B.2.)

The partners also faced a further problem. The practice was insured against death to the extent of £10,000 per partner, an amount which had seemed more than adequate in 1973. However, Sidney had held 40 per cent of the equity and this would have to be valued and paid to his estate. Would the insurance be enough?

EXHIBIT 4B.1   Revenue account for the year ended
30 November 1974 (£)

Fees receivable	94,510
Profit on sale of lease	6,250
Bank deposit interest	93
	100,853
Salaries	14,760
Rent	4,305
Rates and water	2,649
Light and heating	383
Telephone	1,926
Insurance	1,052
Postage	1,120
Stationery, law books	3,185
Motor and travelling expenses	3,984
Miscellaneous expenses	1,971
Computer service	2,182
Hire of equipment	302
Repairs and renewals	1,329
Cleaning	589
Bank charges and interest	2,354
Hire-purchase interest	214
Accountancy	1,300
Bad debts written off	36,749
Depreciation on Motor vehicles	604
Depreciation on fixtures and fittings	1,400
	82,358
Profit before taxation	18,495

EXHIBIT 4B.2   Cash flow (£), December 1974 to April 1975

	Dec	Jan	Feb	Mar	Apr	Cumulative
Cash in						
Gross fees received	5,180	4,659	14,530	918	4,279	29,566
Transfers[a]	4,158	4,675	2,818	3,059	1,955	16,665
Bank interest	–	–	–	1,031	–	1,031
	9,338	9,334	17,348	6,008	6,234	47,262
Cash out						
Accountant fees	–	–	787	–	–	787
Bank charges	–	–	–	–	829	829
Computer service	150	236	200	191	81	858
Diners Club	12	–	84	–	146	242
Electricity	–	–	–	–	–	–
Gas	–	–	–	–	–	–
Gestetner	18	51	30	20	20	139
HM Land Registry	–	–	–	22	3	25
Library	20	80	47	17	23	187
Luncheon vouchers	–	–	–	–	91	91
Miscellaneous expenses	204	211	64	154	191	824
Miscellaneous office sundries	38	44	53	145	87	367
Motor account	615	202	435	(472)	139	919
Motor vehicles	91	112	–	590	182	975
National Insurance	–	–	91	113	37	241
Office cleaning service	–	–	76	–	–	76
Office insurance	–	–	–	–	31	31
Office leasing	–	63	2	14	52	131
Office maintenance	16	–	62	87	80	245
Partner insurance	56	–	87	69	56	268
PAYE income tax	757	–	620	–	278	1,655
Petty-cash account	53	79	(8)	(44)	(20)	60
Postage	69	69	70	135	141	484
Rates	–	–	–	–	–	–
Rent	–	2,441	–	–	–	2,441
Salaries	1,076	791	745	645	966	4,224
Stationery	247	180	13	127	192	759
Subscriptions	4	13	–	14	10	41
Telephone	–	–	900	446	54	1,400
Temporary staff	43	59	96	114	–	312
Travel	143	181	62	27	28	441
United Linen	–	6	6	6	6	24
Write-offs and bad debts	9	53	418	44	65	589
Capital expenditure	41	15	60	10	–	126
Total fixed expenses	3,662	4,886	5,000	2,475	3,768	19,791
GROSS PROFIT	5,676	4,448	12,348	2,533	2,466	27,471
Less partners' drawings	1,345	1,345	1,345	935	1,930	6,900
Partners' income tax	–	500	700	1,500	–	2,700
CASH RETAINED	4,331	2,603	10,303	98	536	17,871

[a]Client pre-payments held in a separate account.

	Cost/ amount	Depreciation	Total
Fixed assets			
Premium on lease	8,741	–	8,741
Fixtures, fittings and equipment	7,006	2,840	4,166
Library	1,481	–	1,481
Motor vehicles	5,181	1,980	3,201
	22,409	4,820	17,589
Clients' bank account	138,500		
Less liabilities to clients	138,500		
			–
			17,589
Current assets			
Work in progress and disbursements	29,155		
Pre-payments and sundry debtors	521		
Office bank account	486		
Cash	10		
			30,172
Total assets			47,761
Current liabilities			
Accruals and sundry creditors	7,345		
Hire purchase *less* future interest	1,204		
Office bank overdraft	15,330		
Bank loan	5,000		
			28,879
Net assets			18,882
Capital account			
Retained profits			18,882

5 Stephenson, Turbridge and Bassett, Inc.

DAVID W. TURPIN

In December 1975, Richard Stephenson, chairman of Stephenson, Turbridge and Bassett, Inc., was pondering the performance and future of his London office. Although ST&B, a Texas-based engineering consulting firm, had been represented overseas since 1967, Stephenson had never defined the London operation, the key to ST&B's foreign activities, to his own satisfaction. Part of his problem was that his strong personal desire for an international presence resulted in his considering market position and presence one of the most important factors, if not the most important factor, in judging London office performance.

> [Said Stephenson,] I wish I knew what ought to be done about our London office. We're having a meeting in Houston in February to review London's 1975 performance and consider next year's activities and I just don't have a proper picture of it all.
>
> The question is, I'm afraid, probably much deeper than how much profit London makes. Unfortunately, I don't know how to look at the problem. I know I'm interested in how the head office in Houston can keep abreast of what's happening in London and where our European activities are headed.
>
> At the same time, though, a lot of our staff have been uncertain about our non-Texas operations and I know that a lot of seemingly unnecessary personal communications seem to be flowing between our various offices. I find it difficult to find any two people in the firm with the same view on anything.

The firm

ST&B defines its business as an engineering consultancy. The firm specialises in the planning and management of projects in the formative stages and in the preparation of economic evaluation and feasibility reports for oil and gas pipelines, oil refineries, chemical plants, natural-gas processing plants, synthetic gas and liquefied natural-gas facilities and related operations. The company also functions as independent engineers, but does not engage in plant construction, process licensing, equipment sales or equipment fabrication which might conflict with the interest of its clients.

The company evolved from the one-man office opened by Robert W. Bassett in Houston in 1948. He was joined in 1949 by Richard 'Chuck' Stephenson and Dr Peter Turbridge and the firm operated as a partnership until 1956, when it was incorporated. Shortly thereafter, Mr Bassett and Dr Turbridge sold their interest in the firm to the stockholders, all of whom were employees, and left ST&B.

In mid 1964, the Dallas office, with two consultants, was opened. Other offices followed later. The London office was opened with one consultant in early 1967, followed by the establishment of the Singapore office in 1970 and a government liaison office in Washington DC in 1971. A subsidiary was set up in Edmonton in 1971 in conjunction with a Canadian consulting firm.

Over the years the company has slowly moved away from purely technical undertakings towards those that involve economic evaluation of major activities and thorough knowledge of markets. This has come about as a result of a shift in the market for ST&B's services. When the firm was smaller, most of its customers tended to be small entrepreneurial petroleum operators. However, with growth and the emergence of more economic concentration in the petroleum and chemical industries, larger corporations joined the client list. This was particularly true outside the United States.

In 1975 ST&B's list of satisfied clients ranged from West Texas oil 'wildcatters' to major US and European industrial concerns, various governments and OPEC. One of the firm's current 'bread and butter' lines of business is in advising financial institutions on specific projects, and some of the most prestigious banks in the world have made loan commitments and joint ventures contingent on satisfactory project evaluations by ST&B.

Personnel and management

An ST&B company brochure states,

> The stature attained by Stephenson, Turbridge and Bassett, Inc. in the field of engineering and consulting and the respect it holds in today's industry are due primarily to the efforts of highly capable personnel. Their diverse experiences and backgrounds bring a wide range of discipline to bear on all projects or problems. Assignments are related to both domestic and overseas services and projects.
>
> In addition, the Stephenson, Turbridge and Bassett, Inc. staff includes 'back-up' personnel in technical and non-technical capacities. Located at our head office in Houston, the people are selected and utilized so that projects can be completed in an accurate, efficient and expedient manner.
>
> At various times our consultants have testified both in the courts and before regulatory agencies in the United States and Canada.

ST&B currently has twenty-six primary consultants: sixteen at the head office in Houston, three at the Dallas office, one each in Singapore and Washington, two in Edmonton and three in London. Virtually all of them are American or Canadian; twenty-three are engineers (most of them chemical engineers); and many of them have advanced degrees. The non-engineers are MBAs or economists. The majority of the consulting staff are young and all of them are well-paid, reflecting the very high calibre of staff at ST&B and the work they do. ST&B can afford to pay top salaries because its reputation and output allows it to command the highest fees in the world for its type of services.

Although it operates as a corporation, ST&B is entirely owned by its employees and perpetuation of employee ownership is provided by the company's charter. All the employees, including the thirty support personnel (secretaries, computer technicians, statisticians and draughtsmen) are shareholders in the company. The charter limits ownership of ST&B shares to current employees only and makes provision

94

for the repurchase of any shares belonging to an employee who leaves the organisation. The charter also stipulates that no employee may hold more than 10 per cent of the authorised shares of ST&B.

All employees are also participants in the bonus system administered at the end of the year. Bonus payments are based 40 per cent on length of service with the company and 60 per cent on performance as determined by the five-man Executive Committee. The opinion of the Executive Committee is important, as it is not unknown for one consultant to receive twice the bonus of an equivalent consultant. In some good years, consultants have increased their $30,000–$40,000 salaries by as much as 30 per cent with the year-end bonus.

Of the original three partners, only Richard Stephenson remains. His title is chairman, although he devotes only about one-third of his time to the firm, the rest of it going to his several outside petroleum interests and businesses. Three years before Turbridge and Bassett left, Alfred Siemend joined the firm as a staff engineer. The next year, 1954, a second young engineer, Bill Simms, was brought in. These three, Stephenson, Siemend and Simms, have provided direction to the firm over the years and, together with the heads of the Houston and Dallas offices, form the Executive Committee.

Although there are various formal operating and *ad hoc* committees within ST&B, the true authority rests almost exclusively with Stephenson, Siemend and Simms. As Stephenson has become less involved with the firm on a day-to-day basis, power has shifted into the hands of Alfred Siemend, whose personality is particularly well suited to providing strong direction to an unstructured group.

The organisational structure of the firm is as follows:

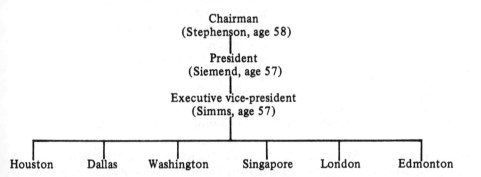

Stephenson, a native Texan, is well liked within ST&B. Tall, self-confident, personable and gregarious, he is easy for everyone to get along with, particularly clients. Within ST&B he has an almost paternal image.

Promoted to president in mid-1971, Siemend is quite a different person. His chief value to ST&B lies in his immense capacity for hard work, and he makes everyone near him work at the same gruelling pace. Without question, he is the company's super-salesman. He has continually ensured that as much as possible of the consultants' time is charged out to client projects. This has quite an effect on revenues and profits. In 1974, on revenues of $1.25 million, the firm made after-tax profits, before distributions, in excess of $300,000.

Siemend is not as popular in the firm as Stephenson. Although extremely good at getting business and satisfying clients, his aggressive, autocratic style and activities as

Stephenson's 'hatchet man' in the mid and late 1960s (when Stephenson was chairman and president and Siemend was executive vice-president) have engendered what one consultant described as 'ambivalent attitudes' towards him within the firm. The availability of a man such as Siemend to perform some of the less popular management functions during Stephenson's days as president certainly helped in maintaining Stephenson's image in the firm.

Looking to London

In 1967 ST&B went international and established a London office. Stephenson and Siemend had felt that ST&B's expertise at basic feasibility studies could be well applied in Europe from a European base.

Stephenson's statements at the time indicate a strong personal desire to expand the horizons of ST&B beyond what could be handled from Texas. He was of the opinion that the firm's reputation and experience in the large and sophisticated US petroleum and chemical industries would be directly transferable to overseas markets. The hoped-for expansion soon took real form as new business from Europe (including North Sea activities), Africa and the Middle East made its way to the company – both by way of the London office and directly to Houston. Stephenson maintains a strong interest in ST&B's international business and visits London on working holidays three or four times a year.

The business in London, although brisk, turned out to be educational for many associated with it, both in London and in Houston. Because London is a cosmopolitan city and because much contact work is done through entertaining, the office began to be perceived by some in Houston as indulging in a good deal of high living.

The independence of the few consultants in the London office and the perceived perks of overseas duty also fuelled uncertainty within the US offices, where apparent status and office politics played an important role, owing to the unstructured nature of the firm.

Also difficult to adjust to, for all concerned, were the local business customs of areas of the Middle East. To native Texans used to six or seven appointments a day, waiting the better part of a day outside the office of a government official was a new, sometimes uncomfortable approach to business.

A year and a half after the London office was opened, a second engineer was transferred from Houston, establishing a pattern of three-year 'tours of duty' in London with eighteen-month overlaps. In 1974 a 25-year-old American-trained British chemical engineer was hired by the London office to provide support in face of an increasing workload. Despite its expansion of business, the London office has never appeared to have the same contribution margin as the Canadian and Texan operations. Part of this has been due to the high overheads of the London activities and part of it has been a result of the irregular way in which its revenues ($275,000 in 1975) and costs have been allocated by Houston.

The following are excerpts from interviews during December 1975 with the three consultants in the London office. Brian Thompson (36), the titular manager of the branch, had been in London three years and was due to return to Houston in July or August 1976. Most of Brian's industrial experience had been in petroleum refining and chemical processing. He was the London office's specialist in refinery operations.

John Anderson (33) was the other transferee from Houston. He arrived in London in

96

August 1974. A Ph.D. in chemical engineering, his specialities are transportation and economic evaluation, in which areas he has had extensive experience in computer simulation.

Ian Graves (26) a British graduate of the Massachusetts Institute of Technology in chemical engineering, joined the London office right after John's arrival. Since starting with ST&B Ian has been heavily involved in economic feasibility studies of proposed refineries and pipeline systems.

Although all three have had successful prior careers in industry, they are easy going individuals. However, long hours and constant travel are not unknown to them.

BRIAN: I feel that we are uniquely placed to be a force in our business. Although we aren't a Bechtel or Kellogg [major US construction firms specialising in large projects overseas], we have a real good reputation and, with so many places wanting a national petroleum and chemical industry, they will need the kind of expertise we can provide – an expertise that is not readily available.

If I were a modern-day adventurer, I'd put all my money into an office in Riyadh and make my first million in about eight months. To someone in the petroleum-service area, the developing countries are really a wide open place. It's fun swinging deals in a place where half of the petroleum interests in the world are competing all out for the business.

I like being an engineering consultant as opposed to being a manager. We have a different kind of arrangement from a lot of consulting businesses. Each consultant doesn't have his own particular group of clients like accounting firms, for example. Back in Houston it is understood that each consultant contacts certain clients about once every six months. However, in Houston, because we have people teaming up on various projects a lot, no one is ever guaranteed to be working on a given project unless there is no one else qualified in a particularly rarefied area.

Over here we just try to see as many different people as we can in the industries that we deal with. Business can come from anywhere and the best way to ensure it comes to us is to keep our name in circulation. We benefit to some extent from our reputation back home. With so many oil-company executives in London coming from Texas, we're already fairly well known. At the same time, though, this isn't Texas, so we keep trying to meet new people to see what we can come up with.

The big thing within the firm is how much time a consultant bills out and how much new business he brings in, not how much profit he makes. Annual reviews are pretty much qualitative and the only time people look at the profits of one office or another is when an argument is pretty far gone. At that point, it becomes a contest to see who can juggle the figures the best. A full, realistic financial review of branch offices is only conducted every couple of years. That's when someone gets excited enough to get some kind of crisis management instituted in Houston. We don't conduct much of a review on our own except to see if we're approximating what passes for a budget. The problem is that things are so unpredictable that it's difficult to forecast what the situation within the office will be in six months.

We do set a budget here in London for expected expenses and a hoped-for revenue level and it is discussed and generally approved by the Executive Committee, but our performance isn't really judged strictly against. Alfred and Chuck want an international firm and want us to maintain our revenues and remain viable in our market. We all have our salary reviews on individual performance and the bonus decisions, but the office wouldn't be closed or cut back unless Alfred and Chuck decided that we hadn't been doing a good job.

Our treasurer in a nice guy, but he doesn't really know what's going on. Besides, even if he did, it wouldn't matter. Alfred and Chuck don't look just at the profit figures in assessing performance, but just about everyone else looks at nothing else and then they tend to make subjective evaluations on that one number.

People do complain in Houston because they think we're living the high life in London without sweating enough, meaning we're cutting down profits. There is no question that some aspects of living here are different and exciting; however, going out on business/social occasions four or five times a week after a full day gets old. The interesting thing, though, is that opposition in Houston is usually 'underground', because a lot of people there want their chance at a London tour. I imagine that most of them could live without coming here, but it is different here and a lot of folks at head office like the idea of the way they think we do business – assuming they get a chance to do some of the business.

You asked a while ago how we were viewed in Houston. One of the Houston consultants was over here several days ago working on a project. He told me that London was a big topic of conversation back home. Interestingly enough, it wasn't centred on any of us or our business dealings, but on Alfred and how much time he is spending in London and how much he isn't in Houston. Apparently, billings and the percentage of time billed out are down. Most people in Houston attribute this to Alfred's absence. No one can sell ST&B to a client like he does. The London billings, in contrast, are up this year and this office is so busy that we have several thousand dollars worth of seminars that we are supposed to give that we just don't have time for.

I know that there are people in Houston who honestly believe that there isn't a place for us over here among all the 'big boys'. [Most of the firms that ST&B regard as competition have London staffs several times larger and maintain other European and/or Middle East offices as well.] This office performance review meeting next month will certainly include a discussion of the future of the London office. I'm returning to Houston next summer and Ian has been offered a great position with Shell which he intends to accept. This will provide an opening for those who want to lobby for winding down or at least de-emphasising the London office.

My own feeling is that too many people who have input to that kind of long-range decision don't know enough about what we're doing here. That's strange actually, since London people and Houston people always seem to be talking to each other. Once a week, we even trade tape recordings of the 'Monday morning meeting' at the respective offices. [The tapes are mailed to the opposite offices and played at the meeting on the Monday following the recorded meeting.]

JOHN: The stated purpose of the move to London was to expand the scope of the firm and there is no question that that has happened. We can't compete head-to-head with someone like DSM [Dutch State Mines], for example, but we can provide supplementary services to some of their technical staff sections. Although their guy may have a mound of numbers and other information, we have a much better 'feel' for markets, because we're constantly in contact with a wide range of people. All their specialist may do is go to a couple of conventions a year. It's difficult for us to make any impact in places outside of Europe, though. Unless we have a particularly good contact, it's difficult to convince someone that we're as good as we say we are. To a lot of people good equates with successful, i.e. big.

Talking about money and budgets, it's difficult to figure out exactly what is going on here anyway. Anyone from Houston over in London on a 'reward trip' project will have his expenses, or some of them, charged against the London office. Alfred spends almost 50 per cent of his time over here on this joint venture [the firm is engaged in a major petroleum venture with several large European companies, the first undertaking of this kind for ST&B], which was his idea in the first place.

I don't think Alfred would want to lessen our operations here if for no other reason than he likes coming to London and flitting about Europe doing deals. This is not to say that he doesn't work, he just likes to play as hard as he works and London can be a great place to enjoy the sights. But he does work. In some ways, Alfred truly is a man of vision, but mostly he can just keep going and going. Where Bill Simms might catch you on your blind side, Alfred just keeps banging away until somebody working with him folds under the pressure. We've got what we call the 'Alfred effect'. Anybody here who winds up working with him on his visits takes on a whole new personality and doesn't smile much. Brian has the right idea. He has gotten pretty good at scheduling trips to the Middle East when Alfred comes to London. Of course, that doesn't help him much when Alfred thinks he ought to go to the Middle East too.

Every now and then, we get nasty letters, from the treasurer or someone who is a member of some operating committee that we might affect, complaining about how our expenses are too high and saying that we aren't bringing in enough business. For example, the most recent exchange, I'm sure, was motivated by office politics back in Houston, but we were the subject. We got a letter from Bill that was prompted by all of the money we have to spend on Alfred. Although it was sent to us, it was really Bill getting mad at Alfred for running all over the world. That sort of thing helps no one, except maybe Bill, who can let off steam with it. But it certainly didn't help our tempers here and it doesn't strengthen the position of the London office.

IAN: What do I think of ST&B? That is some question. In the main, I like the firm. Certainly the opportunities and education I have had here are nothing short of marvellous for me.

I have been involved in more aspects of the oil and gas business than I ever expected. I have learned a great deal and had some very high responsibility loads that I would not have had other places.

Without any doubt, the people here are some of the best in the field. Both John and Brian are tremendously multi-faceted and very smart. All of the people I have met from Houston are also extremely competent. The firm's good reputation is well deserved and it is nice to be attached to a reputation like that.

Unfortunately, I do not easily identify with the firm. Somehow, something is missing in the relationship. When I am talking about ST&B and say 'we', I don't feel as though I am referring to the whole company, and I own some of it through the shareholding scheme. All I actually feel I'm representing is the London Office. I have only been in the headquarters for $1\frac{1}{2}$ days. I find myself sometimes wondering what the 'real' business of ST&B is like.

It seems as though 50 per cent of the petroleum deals in the world have a Texan as one of the parties. I went to MIT and that provides me no insight at all into how

Texans operate. It's very frustrating for me, not having any real 'feel' for the business and no idea of where I am going as far as my career is concerned. I suppose that lack of any future reference point is one of the primary reasons why I am going to work for Shell in Holland. John and Brian spent a lot of time trying to convince me to stay, but I didn't come from Houston and I feel that this will work against me in the long run.

Alfred is a man who seems to turn up with a new facet to him every time he turns a corner. Personally, I find him a very contradictory character. He is not a great engineer, but one has to work with him for a while to realise that. He is very much a 'take charge' kind of person and things definitely quicken their pace when he comes to town.

I know Brian and John feel that he prematurely ages them, but I rather like him – although I must admit that I have not worked with him on many projects. There is no question, however, as to who is in charge of this company.

I think that Alfred is in many ways the typical folklore American executive. He always seems to be doing something related to business. Whenever he comes over from Houston, he walks in with massive position papers that he has written on the plane. It does not make the secretaries happy to have to type all of that in addition to their regular workload, but it gets a lot of ideas spread out for discussion and decision. Even when he goes out on his famous entertainment sprees it is usually with a client, banker or an oil executive and his wife in tow. At times I think he substitutes business travelling for hobbies. He is incredibly conversant about a large number of topics as a result of his travels. It makes him a difficult act to follow and no one in the firm can stay with him.

It is my opinion that half of the complaining about him by people in ST&B is nothing but envy. He has a capacity for work that few can match and he is in a position to combine work and play, as well as push the number crunching off on the others.

You might be interested in a bit of folklore from ST&B history. Every now and then, apparently, the employees all get together with a unique kind of authority. While he was away on a trip once, Alfred supposedly was fired by an Extraordinary General Meeting so that a particularly controversial contract could be cancelled. After the cancellation letter was written, Alfred was rehired and business went on as usual, all in the space of a few hours. My impression, though, is that such solidarity is relatively rare.

6 Regent Printers Ltd

SUE BIRLEY from material collected by DEREK ESSEN and WALTER MAUGHAN (London Business School Masters Programme 1975)

Regent Printers Ltd was formed in 1968 by two master printers, Alf and Bernie, and an accountant, Charles, and by 1974 sales had reached £279,600 and net profit £15,400. Early in 1975, prompted by a potential management crisis, the partners began to consider whether the method of growth and management style which they had previously adopted would be appropriate for the future long-term growth and development of the business, since they intended that Regent Printers should become publicly quoted by 1983.

Alf and Bernie, both in their late thirties and both time-served master printers, had a combined total of twenty years' experience in the industry, much of it in a family-run firm, Goal Press. Over the years, Alf had become more involved in the production work, whilst Bernie had concentrated upon selling. Charles had joined Goal Press on the rebound from a business failure which had left him doubting his own judgement. He was a qualified company secretary with a strong accountancy background, and had gained substantial experience in management both at home and in South Africa, culminating in the managing directorship of the printing subsidiary of a large corporation. It was this post from which he resigned in order to go into business with a partner. Very shortly afterwards he found himself with no business and an absconded partner.

Although neither had a share in the equity of Goal Press during their time with the company, Alf and Bernie had become convinced that the business was being milked of resources and profits by the family owners, who did not believe in sharing their prosperity with employees. They soon found a common link with Charles in this reaction, and a mutual respect and strong friendship developed between the three.

Matters came to a head when, feeling that without Bernie's knowledge of the local market Goal Press would probably collapse, the trio approached the family and asked for a share in the business, only to be met with a firm 'no'. As a result they decided to set up on their own in October 1969, taking advantage of the local phenomenon of a 'silly season' when printing capacity was very strained. Their total resources were £500, which they used to hire purchase a letterpress machine and a typesetter, and for working capital. Charles took another job in order to supply further cash until the business was viable enough to support the three of them.

Alf and Bernie were soon involved in both selling (by day) and producing (by day and by night), together with a small staff, in leased premises which were bigger than they actually needed, but which they acquired on quite advantageous terms. On weekends, Charles would do the company's accounts and occasionally commute to South London from his permanent job some miles away to help out with odd jobs. This also provided an opportunity to discuss the present and future of the business.

Throughout its growth, the company emphasised customer service, reflected in

101

particular by a very rapid turn-round of jobs. However, such an approach meant that overtime was almost a norm at Regent Printers, especially in view of the owners' attitude towards increasing capacity. In essence they refused to buy new equipment until their existing machines had been stretched to over 150 per cent of a forty-hour week. At that point they would take an opportunistic approach to purchasing, attending equipment auctions within a wide radius of London. Knowing first how much they would have to pay for specific equipment from alternative suppliers (only one of which was the manufacturer), and knowing what they were prepared to pay for a machine of given specifications, they had acquired very inexpensive fixed assets. This meant that they sometimes had to wait for bargains to be available, a fact which aggravated the overtime problem. However, Alf and Bernie had always maintained an active participation in the two unions represented in the company and as a consequence no grievances came as a surprise to them. Indeed, in the early days when they were very involved in production themselves, no man was asked to put in more hours than they did; in fact they both worked considerably longer than the others. Also, wages, overtime and benefits were well above union minima and had been from the start. In fact, after the first six months' accounts had been produced, a profit-sharing scheme was instituted (this practice was followed for all associated companies subsequently formed) – a very unusual phenomenon for the industry. The partners believed that as a result the employees were prepared to work long hours and took a pride in their company.

Very early in its development, the company was profitable (see Exhibit 6.4) and the partners began to consider how to expand sales. There were a number of alternative methods whereby such an expansion could be accomplished, only two of which were serious contenders. Bernie could begin to direct his full efforts to generating sales, either travelling in search of clients or concentrating his efforts in South London. Alternatively, a strong second man could be retained to sell the product and services of the company to customers other than those already covered by Regent Printers. For a variety of reasons, and as a good salesman (Donald) approached them, the partners chose the second alternative.

The way in which they set up the arrangement with Donald was unusual. They had always been of the opinion that the most efficient printing companies were small ones, an opinion strengthened by an article in *Business Week* which stated that the most profitable firms had fewer than twenty-five employees. They thus decided to incorporate this view into their growth. In November 1970, they formed a separate company, General Sales Ltd, gave 40 per cent of the equity to Donald and divided the remaining 60 per cent among themselves. Donald was appointed chief executive and, although he was responsible to the board of directors (Alf, Bernie and Charles), he was given considerable freedom in running the company. For example, he was not required to place orders with Regent Printers, although he preferred to do so whenever the type of job was appropriate and capacity available.

One year later, in December 1971, encouraged by the apparent success of General Sales Ltd, City Sales Ltd was formed. Again, this was in response to the increasing sales requirements of the company, and it followed from the realisation of a need for territorial expansion, the South London market having been saturated by Bernie and Donald. City Sales Ltd was incorporated to sell Regent Printers products to the Central London market, but this time its chief executive, Elroy, came from within Regent Printers rather than from outside. Elroy had a different approach to selling from Bernie and Donald, in that he believed in offering a complete range of stationery products to the customer, who was usually the print buyer for a company. Indeed, he had a particular advantage over his competitors, since he held the local monopoly on the supply of rubber stamps. Bernie and Donald, however, were more concerned with providing a product, printing, of quality appropriate to the customer's needs, as fast as possible and at a price which could therefore afford to be somewhat higher than competition.

One month earlier, in November 1971, Plate Makers Ltd had been established. This company was set up in response to a technological rather than sales need, and was incorporated to produce both the artwork and the plates for the lithographic process. Up to this point Regent Printers Ltd had either had to decline orders which required such processing or sub-contract the platemaking, at the cost of a slow-down in service. When Fitz approached them with his experience as a cameraman in this field, Alf, Bernie and Charles seized the opportunity to enter it. They gave him the same 60:40 per cent deal they had given Donald and Elroy. With an initial capital of £500, plus hire-purchase of equipment, they set him up in separate works nearby. The objective of the company was to produce the plates for the sales generated by Bernie at Regent Printers Ltd, Donald at General Sales Ltd, and Elroy at City Sales Ltd. The production process included artwork (which necessitated an art department as well as some client contact, to get things absolutely right) and a platemaking department, the two chief functions of which were photography and plate production from transparencies. Eventually the company evolved into a sales entity with its own clients as well as those provided by salesmen from the associated companies. As with the latter, it capitalised on the fact that it was not immediately identifiable with Regent Printers Ltd.

In November 1973, the group decided to try their management abilities in a field outside the printing industry. Since they were all interested in cars, and since Alf in particular had always been a keen amateur mechanic devoting much of his spare time to his current sports car, they decided to buy a small unprofitable garage. The garage, renamed Regent Motors Ltd, was located in a rural area, on a secondary road about ten miles away from their other works. It sold petrol, provided a breakdown and maintenance service and usually had about six to eight used cars for sale at all times. Giles, a life-long friend of Alf's who shared his interest in cars, offered to run the garage for them and they jumped at the chance. However, the acquisition of a loss-making concern was different from setting up a new company. Giles would be responsible for creating a profit, and so Alf, Bernie and Charles offered him the promise of future participation in the garage business if this was achieved over his first year's trading. But the promise was never activated and within four months Giles had left. The three partners felt that, in the event, whilst he may have been a good mechanic, he did not have sufficient management ability for the job.

Howard, the second chief executive of Regent Motors Ltd, came to the garage with a more detailed working experience of the industry, and it was felt that he would be the type of man for whom their approach to delegation would pay off. However, he was not given the same deal as Elroy, Donald and Fitz, since 'he was not the initiator – i.e. he did not have full responsibility or authority until the business was already nine months old and had incurred substantial losses'. Further, to take advantage of the tax loss, Regent Holdings (see below) had to have a minimum shareholding of 75 per cent. To facilitate matters, Regent Holdings took 80 per cent of Regent Motors and gave the remaining 20 per cent to Howard with an agreed 'working arrangement' that for future profits Howard's 20 per cent would rank 2:1, i.e. 40 per cent. In the event it was never really a profitable venture, and this, combined with the fact that Alf, Bernie and Charles regarded it as a hobby, meant that they continued to spend a disproportionate amount of their time on it. For example, on visiting Regent Printers, it was very noticeable that they received numerous telephone calls concerning the most minute matters, such as locating batteries and body parts for jobs in the works. All three of them were caught up in the process and gave every indication of enjoying it and being fulfilled by it. Indeed, every Saturday one of them helped out at the garage itself, normally starting at 7.30 a.m. and working through the day.

In January 1974, a reorganisation of the holdings of the three partners was undertaken and their privately held stocks in each of the subsidiaries were consolidated into Regent Holdings Ltd, of which they each owned one-third (see Exhibit 6.2). The only exception to this general rule was Regent Printers Ltd (of which they held dissimilar amounts at the time of this move) and it remained as a loosely associated company at the side of the main group. This manoeuvre was undertaken with three objectives in mind:

(1) to consolidate the investment position,
(2) to provide a central staff for services to group companies, and
(3) to act as a source of capital for present or future investments. (It is worth noting that, guided by its board and by Charles in particular, each company continued to produce its own accounts and no consolidation ever took place. The accounts shown in the appendix are a result of Derek Essen's efforts. All the cash was held in various accounts in one bank and adjusted according to need.)

In February 1974, Regent Holdings funded its first new investment by taking 60 per cent of Shopkeepers Ltd. This company was associated with City Sales Ltd, in that the remaining 40 per cent was held by Elroy. Shopkeepers Ltd was an entity set up to hold the stocks which Elroy used as extra inducement in selling print to his customers. (Stocks were sold to City Sales at the normal wholesale price. No discount was given.) It comprised a shop in a small arcade in South London, the company having its own commercial-stationery customers as well as a small retail trade. The rubber-stamp production was carried out in a small room at the back of the shop and the upper floor was used as offices by City Sales Ltd. The shop was manned by a second employee.

The last acquisition to date is that of Goal Press, the former employers of the partners. As can be seen from Exhibit 6.2, it differs from the five other companies in that it is 100 per cent owned, and owned *via* Regent Printers rather than Regent Holdings. The acquisition is better described as an expansion, and in itself was a violation of the company philosophy of a maximum of twenty-five employees per establishment. The transaction was extremely favourable to the purchasers, and Alf, Bernie and Charles felt that, even if the structure could not be worked out, the physical assets and the lease could be sold at a profit.

The growth strategy and organisation structure chosen at Regent Printers were not without their problems. As can be seen from Exhibit 6.1, when Regent Holdings was formed General Sales became a wholly owned subsidiary, although originally 40 per cent of the equity had been held by Donald. Donald had proved to be a very effective salesman and had expanded his own sales within the South London area dramatically. This he continued to do within General Sales and, as the company grew, he became more and more dissatisfied with the original deal. Matters finally came to a head when he declared that either he be given 60 per cent of the equity or he would prefer to leave. As the three felt that the increase would have been 'against the democratic principle of equity distribution' which they had established, they agreed to purchase his interest and he left the business. Thus the entire equity of General Sales Ltd reverted to Regent Printers Ltd, and, as orders continued to flow to the company unsolicited, the shell continued to be very profitable.

At the time of writing the case, Alf, Bernie and Charles were facing a similar problem at City Sales Ltd and Shopkeepers Ltd. As the business had grown Elroy had appeared increasingly to be under severe stress. He seemed unable to take even the simplest decision and would, for example, ask for advice upon the pricing of even the smallest jobs. Also, he had had a string of second salesmen working for him, all of whom left or were fired by him because he found them inadequate. With the start-up of Shopkeepers Ltd, the problem became acute, because, to fulfil his function in City Sales Ltd, he had to leave the shop in the hands of an employee. He appeared unable to do this and was spending more and more time at work to less and less apparent effect. This was particularly unfortunate since in the early days he had been very good at identifying, procreating and servicing ideas for customers and hence translating them into sales. For example, he had presented and promoted an idea for forms standardisation to a very large machinery-service company, which maintained a national unintegrated, independent dealer network for stationery. If City Sales had become the printer recommended to the dealers for their standard forms, Elroy would have been responsible for a vast increase in turnover. For this reason, and also because they had known him for some time and regarded him as part of their extended family, Alf, Bernie and Charles were loath to take any drastic action such as firing him. (Elroy had been at Goal Press with Alf, Bernie and Charles before Regent Printers was formed. He had been known to Alf and Bernie for some eight years before that and had spent all his working life in print sales.) Nevertheless, they knew that they had to resolve the problem quickly, before his health was seriously affected. Further, the incident had raised in their minds the question of whether the management style they had chosen was the right one for the future expansion of the business.

EXHIBIT 6.1   Performance of Regent Printers relative to the industry

| | Regent Printers | Industry (sample of 31 companies) | | |
		1st quartile	Average	3rd quartile
Operating profit/				
operating capital	38.7	7.1	11.3	14.3
Operating profit/				
net sales	19.2	4.6	7.0	9.0
Production cost (gross)/				
cost of output	69.6	79.4	82.1	83.9
Selling cost/cost of output	13.8	4.0	5.5	7.7
Administration cost/				
cost of output	14.6	8.7	10.8	11.8

Source: DPIF Management Ratios Scheme 1974.

EXHIBIT 6.2   Group structure

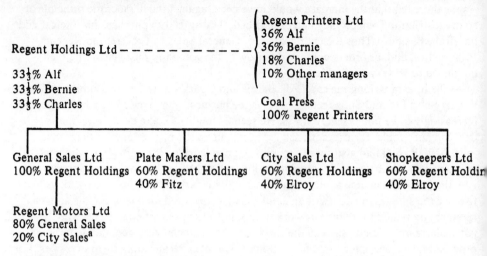

Regent Holdings Ltd — — — — — — — — — — {
    Regent Printers Ltd
    36% Alf
    36% Bernie
    18% Charles
    10% Other managers

33⅓% Alf
33⅓% Bernie
33⅓% Charles

    Goal Press
    100% Regent Printers

General Sales Ltd   Plate Makers Ltd   City Sales Ltd   Shopkeepers Ltd
100% Regent Holdings   60% Regent Holdings   60% Regent Holdings   60% Regent Holdir
                         40% Fitz   40% Elroy   40% Elroy

Regent Motors Ltd
80% General Sales
20% City Sales[a]

[a]Temporary financial arrangement to allow loss write-offs of Regent Motors to profits o
City Sales Limited.

The companies were incorporated or acquired in the following sequence:

(1) Regent Printers Ltd   Oct 1969
(2) General Sales Ltd   Nov 1970
(3) Plate Makers Ltd   Nov 1971
(4) City Sales Ltd   Dec 1971
(5) Regent Motors Ltd   Nov 1973
(6) Regent Holdings Ltd   Jan 1974
(7) Shopkeepers Ltd   Feb 1974
(8) Goal Press   Mar 1975

EXHIBIT 6.3 . Consolidated balance sheet (£), 1970–4 (year ending 30 September)

	1970	1971	1972	1973	1974
Share capital issued	100	200	61,000	6,100	6,600
Directors' loan account	5,300	9,500	8,500	23,900	28,800
Unappropriated profit	400	3,600	11,500	19,600	31,300
Net investment grant reserve	1,300	1,100	1,000	800	700
	7,100	14,500	27,100	50,400	67,400
Long-term liabilities					
United Dominions Trust loan	–	–	–	–	13,400
Hire purchase debt (net of interest)	5,900	8,700	17,200	15,400	15,900
Loans from associated companies	–	3,700	6,700	16,800	19,500
	5,900	12,400	23,900	32,200	48,800
Current liabilities					
Bank overdraft	200	2,300	7,600	15,400	27,400
Sundry creditors and accruals	6,900	12,500	15,500	15,000	22,000
VAT/purchase tax	2,000	2,000	2,100	3,500	2,600
Provision for corporation tax	–	200	600	2,100	5,700
	9,200	17,000	25,800	36,000	57,700
Total liabilities and net worth	22,200	44,000	76,800	118,600	173,900
Fixed assets					
Type and metal	100	200	900	2,400	2,200[a]
Plant and machinery	8,200	11,200	23,600	21,500	36,100[a]
Motor vehicles	500	1,400	3,800	7,700	6,100
Furniture and fixtures	100	200	700	1,100	2,100[a]
Land and buildings	–	–	800	19,600	23,500
Loans to associated companies[b]	–	3,700	6,700	16,800	19,500
Interest in subsidiary companies	–	–	–	–	300
	8,900	16,700	36,500	69,100	89,800
Current assets					
Stocks	800	600	700	4,000	19,100
Work in progress	700	1,100	1,800	3,700	6,600
Debtors and pre-payments (net of bad-debt provision)	10,400	24,100	30,100	39,200	54,800
Cash	–	500	6,600	1,800	3,600
Investment grant receivable	1,400	1,000	800	800	–
	13,300	27,300	40,000	49,500	84,100
Total assets	22,200	44,000	76,500	118,600	173,900

[a]Estimates of September 1974 *current value* of plant, machinery and fixtures and fittings, total £65,000. Metal and type was valued at £4,000.
[b]In practice, when a new company starts off, initial funding is helped by its being lent money for a period of time from a group company that is doing well and has a credit balance at the bank. This avoids (1) payment of interest for overdraft facilities for the new company, and (2) a 2 per cent surcharge payable when aggregate credits with group credit balances exceed £10,000 – a special situation arranged to enable Regent Holdings to offset group bank balances to that degree.

EXHIBIT 6.4   Consolidated profit and loss statements (£), 1970–4 (year ending 30 September), adjusted

	1970	1971	1972	1973	1974
Sales and work in progress net of discounts	36,000	71,500	100,700	181,000	279,600
Purchases and outwork of discounts	14,000	30,100	30,200	59,800	101,100
Productive wages	7,600	12,700	20,600	31,800	43,500
Gross profit	14,400	28,700	49,900	89,400	135,000
Rent, rates, electricity, gas, insurance	2,100	2,600	4,400	6,600	11,700
Repairs to property and plant hire of equipment	700	1,300	2,200	2,100	4,000
Postage, stationery, telephone, advertising, etc.	800	1,300	3,400	5,800	9,300
Entertaining, travelling, motor	1,000	1,900	4,000	5,500	8,600
Hire-purchase interest and bank charges	400	1,000	1,900	3,400	7,000
Audit and legal fees	300	300	400	600	800
Sundry write-offs	(100)	400	(100)	400	1,800
Depreciation on					
plant and equipment	900	1,300	2,700	3,900	6,700
motor vehicles	100	400	1,000	2,000	1,800
fixtures and fittings	–	–	–	30	100
Unproductive wages and salaries	–	2,100	5,600	8,100	17,500
Imputed equivalent salaries (directors)	5,300	7,500	13,800	16,500	24,900
Total expenses	11,500	20,000	39,300	55,000	94,200
Profit before directors' additional remuneration	2,900	8,800	10,600	34,400	40,800
Directors' additional remuneration	2,200	3,800	2,900	19,800	26,100
Net management charges receivable	–	1,400	1,100	4,300	4,800
Net management charges payable	–	(1,400)	(1,100)	(4,300)	(4,800)
Reserve for bad and doubtful debt	400	1,700	(400)	4,500	(670)
	2,600	5,500	2,500	24,300	25,400
Net profit	300	3,300	8,100	10,100	15,400

7 R. J. Nevill Ltd

PHILIP GREEN

R. J. Nevill Ltd is a small company which includes a printing business, a sub-post office and a retail shop. It was founded in 1785 in Park Street, Willerton, by a local engraver, Robin Nevill, and has remained a small business, so that in 1976 it employed eighteen people and had a turnover of £87,523. In December 1975 the owner, Harry Brown, who had been suffering from multiple sclerosis for some six years, died and his young family was faced with deciding their own future and that of the company.

Despite a number of attractive take-over offers, Sheila Brown (49) and her two children, Philip (21) and Vicky (19) eventually decided not to sell but to retain their family interest. They took this decision on the assumption that Philip would return to the business in 1977 when he had completed his degree in politics and economics at the University of Wales. In the short term, Sheila would assume the role of managing director. Philip explains,

PHILIP: It was Mum's position which was uppermost in our minds. At 49, she was still relatively young, and yet within the space of eighteen months we had left home and her husband had died. We thought that the ideal solution for her future and for the business would be if she became an active managing director. This would provide her with an interest in life and it would solve the problem of management succession at Nevills; from my own point of view it would also enable me to complete my degree. However, although she did take over as a sub-postmistress and although she did force herself to do some of the routine administration, she never really took to general management.

But as finals grew closer, I became less and less enthusiastic about my prospects. I knew that not many people have such an opportunity handed to them but it wasn't exactly an exciting business and it wasn't as though I was being offered the chairmanship of ICI! What if I really didn't like it? Would I be able to leave? What would I then do?

The company history

Harry Brown joined R. J. Nevill at the end of the Second World War, after seven years as corporal in a Royal Air Force bomb disposal unit. He had no knowledge of printing and it was only through a chance meeting with Richard Hill, the owner of Nevill, that the opportunity to join a small business with potential arose. (The sub-post office had been acquired in 1935. Richard Hill had employed one assistant and the company had shown a turnover of £5590 for 1944.)

The chance to take advantage of his situation arose far sooner than Harry had expected. During the Christmas of 1946 Richard Hill suffered a stroke, from which he subsequently died, and having no relatives he left the partnership to Harry, who immediately re-formed it into a limited-liability company.

During the 1950s, under Harry's management, the business expanded steadily. By this time Willerton had grown from a small market town to a town of some 80,000 people in the middle of the industrial Black Country. As well as the sub-post office, the original printing business had grown to include a small retail shop selling such things as fountain pens, greetings cards and general stationery. This shop was now in the centre of Willerton's shopping area and by 1955 was the mainstay of the whole business, contributing 80 per cent of the £32,965 turnover.

In 1951, to be able to devote more time to selling, Harry appointed two women, Nancy and Jenny, both aged 33, as assistants in the post office and shop, and two men, Bill and Ron, to run the printing machines. In 1956 he decided to take on a sales representative, and through local contacts he heard that Ray Brewin, the representative for a large printing business in Birmingham, was looking for a change of employer. When Ray joined Nevills, bringing with him several new and lucrative customers, his salary was based heavily on commission, in order to minimise the additional fixed cost to the business.

By 1959, turnover exceeded £40,000 and it was clear that the premises in Park Street were inadequate to support future expansion. Harry decided to purchase a new property himself and lease it to R. J. Nevill; eventually he acquired suitable land and buildings which were only 400 yards from the 1785 site. The position of the new site was important, since it was no longer in the shopping centre of the town but down a small side street. However, the acquired buildings, when refurnished, had many advantages. Apart from the new shop, there was an office-furniture showroom, a large storage area, a general office, a machine room, a composing room and several other offices. In 1977 Philip estimated that these premises could support a turnover of up to £250,000.

The change in location necessitated a change in product mix. There was no longer a demand for the large variety of high-volume, low-margin stationery items sold in Park Street. Parker pens, Spicer envelopes, Sharpe's cards and so on were replaced with desks, filing cabinets, venetian blinds and office chairs, as well as commercial stationery. The sub-post office was retained, although catering for different customers, since the demand of the local shoppers for stamps, postal orders and so on was replaced by the demand of factories in the vicinity of the new location for parcel post and National Insurance stamps.

The move was highly successful. By 1969 the company employed fifteen people, turnover had increased to £63,482 and trading profits to £7284. But in the same year Harry was diagnosed as having multiple sclerosis. During the initial expansion of the business he had played a significant role in developing customer relationships, but by 1969 he was concentrating on servicing only a few customers. In 1971 he was forced to give up even this activity and Ray took over his duties. With this change, it was agreed that a representative responsible for servicing as well as selling could not be paid on the basis of commission and in 1971 Ray was paid a salary, without commission potential.

In March 1977, as Philip's finals approached the family reviewed the situation.

PHILIP: The greatest strength of R. J. Nevill Ltd is the loyalty of the staff to the memory of my father, to his family, and to the company. When my father died all the employees assumed, as did I, that I would step into his shoes; my continuing at university was a bit of a shock for them and morale fell to a very low ebb.

The issue is further complicated for me by Mum's position. At the very least she must have a reliable income to maintain, if not increase, her present standard of living. I don't know much about running a business but I certainly know more than she does, even though she is doubtful about my capabilities at the moment. Actually, she is encouraged in this doubt by John, our accountant, who, although he is an old friend of my father's, has always disliked me. I think that he is jealous of me. This wouldn't matter if I felt that I could leave him to look after Mum's financial affairs, but I am not even sure about that. The extent of his financial advice to her has been to keep all her money in the building society (as if she would ever need a mortgage!) and he has told her that, as she is no longer going to work at Nevills, she really shouldn't let them continue to pay for the 'phone and the car. Apart from the rent from the lease of the property, and my father's savings, her only income is the dividend from Nevills!

SHEILA: These last few years have been very disturbing for Philip and I know that he is having second thoughts about the business. That is only natural, but once he comes back home to his family and friends I know that he will settle down very quickly.

He is very young to take on the responsibilities of a business but we do have a loyal and competent staff and John, our accountant, has promised to keep an eye on him. Meanwhile, I am giving him all the support that I can and trying not to show how worried I am.

VICKY: I don't think Philip should go back home, but no-one listens to me. I think that we should just sell the business but Philip and Mum keep asking what the staff would do. Why can't they get another job?

PHILIP: Apart from Mum, there are five key personalities to consider:

Nancy, aged 54, is the manageress of the business. Her son also worked for us for a short while in 1969, but left to join the Police Force. She had a very close relationship with my father, an intimate knowledge of the business's customers and generally has been the administrative mainstay since 1973. I know that she and her husband rely on the secure income, and, along with the others, she will draw a company pension when she retires at 60.

Ray, aged 50, is the sales representative. He has been with us since 1956 and has a very good reputation with the customers, providing the high quality of service they require. However, since the change in his salary structure he has needed constant management, and since the death of my father his motivation had gradually waned to a level bordering on indifference.

Jenny, aged 53, is the chief cashier of the sub-post office. Although the post office was retained in the family name before and after 1975, Jenny has been the *de facto* sub-postmistress since about 1965; she is very efficient and trustworthy.

Bill, aged 54, is the foreman of the printing works. Although his knowledge of the printing methods is sound, he is very slow, uninspiring and prone to make many mistakes. The atmosphere in the printing works is depressing. Also, he has suffered from a weak heart since 1973.

111

John, aged 50, is the company accountant; he is the director of a local firm of accountants, with whom he has been employed since leaving the local grammar school. My father used his services in the form of advice, and over the years they became personal friends. Since 1975, he has taken on the roles of business adviser and family confidant. Unfortunately, during the settlement of my father's estate and the debate over the future of the business, I lacked credibility in the eyes of my mother and sister. Although such phrases as 'of course it is up to you' were frequently used, the advice from him was valued far higher than anything I suggested. To do anything about this situation when I was not actually involved in the day-to-day running of the business was very difficult. It would have been impossible for me to replace him: firstly, I would not have received the necessary support from the family, and, secondly, because of his intimate knowledge of the business, I needed him in the short term.

EXHIBIT 7.1   Report of the directors of R. J. Nevill Ltd

1. The Directors present herewith the audited accounts for the year ended 31 Septembe 1976.

2. RESULTS
The profit for the year and the appropriation thereof are set out in the Profit and Loss Account.

3. DIVIDENDS
The Directors do not recommend the payment of a dividend in respect of the year.

4. PRINCIPAL PRODUCTS AND ACTIVITIES OF THE COMPANY
The principal products and activities of the Company are Retail and Wholesale Stationery, Printing and Sub-Post Office.

5. EXPORTS
The fob sales value of goods exported by the company from the United Kingdom during the year was £ Nil.

6. FIXED ASSETS
The movements in fixed assets during the year are set out in the Note [c] to the Accounts.

7. DIRECTORS
The Directors of the Company at 31 September, 1976 were:—

> Mrs S. J. Brown (Chairman)
> Mr P. N. Brown

8. In accordance with the Articles of Association, Mr P. N. Brown retires by rotation a being eligible, offers himself for re-election.

9. DIRECTORS' INTERESTS
The interests of the Directors of the Company at 31 September 1976 in shares of th Company, according to the register required to be kept by Section 29 of the Companies Act 1967, were respectively at the beginning and end of the year ended 31 March 1976 as follows:—

	Ordinary 50p Shares	
	At 31.9.76	At 31.3.75
Mrs S. J. Brown	4,000*	20
P. N. Brown	3,980*	–

*Both these totals include 3,980 Shares in which Mrs S. J. Brown and Mr P. N. Brown interested under the Terms of the Will of the late Mr H. N. Brown.

Trading account (£)

1975			1976	
10,753		Stock in trade at 31 Sep preceding year	14,834	
1,319		*Less* purchase tax refunded	–	
	9,434			14,834
	52,250	Purchases		57,613
	13,695	Productive wages		16,833
	26,978	gross profit carried down		32,598
	102,357			121,878
		Expenses		
11,784		Non-productive remuneration	14,654	
345		Staff superannuation	359	
481		Telephone	481	
488		Postage, carriage and packing	381	
1,355		Motor expenses	1,199	
62		Advertising	60	
1,197		Incidental trade expenses	1,799	
2,099		Rent, rates and insurance	2,519	
585		Heat, light and water	1,055	
96		Bank charges	109	
877		Repairs and maintenance	810	
93		Renewals of type	67	
324		Discounts allowed	914	
404		Reserve for doubtful debts	(10)	
	20,190			24,397
		Balance transferred to profit and loss		
	11,972	account		14,133
	32,162			38,530
	87,523	By Sales		102,834
	14,834	By Stock in Trade at 31 Sep		19,044
	102,357			121,878
	26,978	By Gross profit brought down		32,598
	4,791	By Sub-post office remuneration		5,643
	393	By Discounts received		289
	32,162			38,530

Profit and loss account (£)

	1976		1975
Trading profit for the year		14,133	11,972
Deduct			
directors' emoluments	8,160		7,000
depreciation of fixed assets	967		629
bank-overdraft interest	266		109
auditors' remuneration	500		400
		9,893	8,138
Profit for the year before taxation		4,240	3,834
Taxation on the profits of the year:			
deferred taxation		1,141	1,510
Profit for the year after taxation		3,099	2,324
Repayment of taxation on previous year	1,509		
Less transfer to taxation deferred account	1,509	–	–
Balance brought forward from previous year		14,353	12,029
Balance carried forward to next year		17,452	14,353

Balance sheet (£)

	1976	1975
Capital and reserves		
Share capital[a]	2,000	2,000
Revenue reserve – profit and loss account	17,452	14,354
Total capital and reserves	19,452	16,354
Assets less liabilities		
Current assets		
Stock[b]	19,044	14,834
Debtors	32,358	20,306
Giro account	16	16
Cash in hand	14	43
	51,432	35,199
Current liabilities		
Creditors and accrued charges	17,911	12,940
Amount due to bankers	8,688	2,881
Taxation	–	1,509
Amounts due to directors	7,465	3,423
	34,064	20,753
Net current assets	17,368	14,446
Fixed assets[c]	4,734	1,908
	22,102	16,354
Deferred taxation[d]	2,650	–
Total net assets	19,452	16,354

Notes

[a]*Share capital*

	Authorised	Issued and fully paid
Ordinary shares of 50p each	4,000	4,000

[b]*Stock* has been valued on a basis consistent with that adopted in previous years and is at the lower of cost or new realisable value.

[c]*Fixed assets*

	Plant machinery fixtures and fittings	Motor vehicles	Total fixed assets
Assets held at 31 Sep 1975 @ cost	12,565	3,244	15,809
Additions during the year @ cost	3,297	575	3,872
Sales @ cost		(1,195)	(1,195)
Cost of assets held at Sep 1976	15,862	2,624	18,486
Aggregate depreciation provided at Sep 1975	12,029	1,871	13,900
Depreciation provided for the year	391	576	967
Depreciation on items sold and eliminated		(1,115)	(1,115)
Aggregate depreciation provided at Sep 1976	12,420	1,332	13,752
Net book value 31 Sep 1976	3,442	1,292	4,734

[d]*Deferred taxation*

	1975	1974
Taxation deferred by capital allowances	670	–
Taxation deferred by stock relief	1,980	–
	2,650	–

8 Gilbern Cars Ltd

SUE BIRLEY

CASE A

Gilbern Cars Ltd was created in 1959 by Giles Smith and Bernard Friese to manufacture high performance cars in kit form. Based at Pentwyn Works, Lantwit Fadre, South Wales, the company always maintained a strong Welsh image and the cars became well known for their distinctive styling and motif – a Welsh dragon. Order books were always full and the company's problem seemed to be one of meeting orders rather than of generating demand. Despite this, in 1972, after three years of mounting losses, the company was facing liquidation for the second time.

The kit car

The development of the kit-car market arose out of the fact that, whilst fully completed cars were liable for purchase tax (in 1972, charged at 25 per cent of manufacturers' selling price), individual components were not. A car assembled by the customer himself from a 'kit' was therefore much cheaper than its equivalent from a recognised manufacturer. Also, because usually only a small number of models were produced each week (see Exhibit 8A.1), the cars attracted enthusiasts: many considered that a well built car could be likened to the specialist, coachwork-built automobile of the vintage era. But there was a difference between a home-built prototype or special and a kit car. A special was a car created by the individual by mating components for the first time and construction could often take many months. Manufacturers of kit cars, however, were not aiming to make assembly too difficult for their customers, as this could seriously restrict their potential market and so all cars came with the difficult and professional jobs already completed. The body and chassis were already mated, the interior trimmed, the doors, bonnet and boot in position and instruments, wiring and hydraulic pipelines fitted in place. The parts that usually had to be added were the engine, gearbox, rear axle, front and rear suspensions, radiator, handbrake, steering gear, propellor shaft and a number of small components, such as the coil and windscreen wipers. There was no need for additional welding of brackets or drilling of holes. The cars were designed to go together like Meccano sets, and it was simply a question of placing items in position and securing them with the appropriate nuts and bolts (two people could complete the job in two or three days). This was particularly important, since the laws relating to purchase tax forbade the manufacturers to offer detailed assembly instructions with the component parts. Additionally, professional assistance was barred. The customer could not, legally, pay a garage to assemble the car, although it was possible to hire space in a garage to do the work. Further, the law insisted that the car would be liable for purchase tax if sold within the first year of registration.

The enthusiast knew his car, enjoyed driving it at speed and frequently did his own servicing. This last point was important, since there was only a small number of garages in the UK that dealt with this unusual group of 'sporty' cars (see Exhibit 8A.1) and other garages tended to be unwilling to carry out even the most simple repair job or service work on them. This was in contrast to the service provided for the mass-produced cars, whose dealers could be found in almost any town. However, whilst his repair bills may have been low, the enthusiast's other costs were not. Most kit cars were made of fibreglass, a material which insurance companies did not like, believing that it was easily damaged and difficult and expensive to repair. Some refused to handle such business altogether, whilst others insisted upon high premiums and penalty payments.

Within this market, the Gilbern was viewed favourably. In 1966 J. H. Haynes in his *Guide to Component Cars* commented,

> The most unusual thing about the Gilbern is that it is a genuine four-seater Grand Touring car which compares favourably with many assembled cars that cost at least twice as much. Two factors contribute to this. First, the standard of engineering is very high and there is no need for alterations to make things fit, which seems to be usual when assembling most kit cars. As a result it only takes between 15 and 20 hours to assemble. Secondly, the car is very quiet, extensive use being made of sound-proofing material. In fact, the whole of the interior is very lavishly trimmed.

The Gilbern Motor Company

In March 1968, in the midst of financial difficulties, Gilbern was bought by ACE Industrial Holdings Ltd, Cardiff, a successful manufacturer of amusement machines (one-arm bandits), for £65,000, an amount which included £10,000 for goodwill. The two founders resigned and Michael Leather and Maurice Collings (a director of ACE) became joint managing directors. At the time of acquisition, the company was making approximately one car per fortnight and employed twenty people.

By April 1969, production had increased to two cars per week, and during the same month a new model was launched. This was the Gilbern Invader, priced at £1450 and powered by the 3-litre Ford engine and transmission unit. However, within a few weeks ACE itself was bought by Clubmans Club, which was itself immediately acquired by Mecca Ltd.

December 1969 saw Gilbern with a trading loss of £69,068 (see Exhibit 7A.2), and, not being particularly interested in the kit-car market, Mecca sold it back to Maurice Collings. By 1971 the trading loss had increased to £95,639, in spite of a doubling of production to four cars per week and an increase in price to £1800 per car. In July 1972, disenchanted by the whole venture, Collings sold the company to Leather for £1 and an interest-free mortgage of £55,000.

During August 1972 a major threat to the kit-car market emerged. Whilst most manufacturers sold a few of their cars already assembled, in the eyes of the customer one of the main attractions was the sort of kit car which gave him a fast, attractive and unusual car very cheaply. The advent of value-added tax (10 per cent on retail price) and the special car tax (10 per cent on manufacturer's selling price) would correct this anomaly. With liquidation already just around the corner, this seemed to be the final blow for Gilbern.

Help came from an unusual source, a Gilbern owner. In November 1971 a young management consultant, Roger Salway, needed a replacement for his sports car and decided to try a Gilbern. As a result of a visit to the factory to collect the car, he began to take a professional interest in the company, and late in August 1972 he joined Michael Leather on a part-time basis as joint managing director with a mission to turn the company round. If successful, Roger Salway would take up an option on 40 per cent of the equity in six months' time. His first decision was to sell the newly developed Mark III Invader fully assembled and to launch the car at the Motor Show in October.

The Financial Times of 16 November 1972 carried the following report:

Miss Wales was brought in to lend additional glamour to the [new Gilbern] Mark III at the London Motor Show last month; now the car is on its own. It is wider and lower than its prececessor, though still falling somewhat short of real sleekness. The body is of glass fibre and the engine, the uprated Ford 3-litre V6. The Invader's claim to be a four-seater is just about accurate, though the back seats are so small that even my three-year-old son complained, and rear leg room is practically non-existent.

The interior, available in several colours, is made and finished entirely by hand and offers thick carpeting, other insulation to reduce noise (which it does) and a redesigned walnut facia. It took me ages to find the ignition, which is hidden away behind the steering wheel and awkward to get at. Standard equipment includes head restraints on the front seats, heated rear screen, hazard warning system, overdrive, steering lock and radio with electrically operated aerial.

Once on the open road (town driving is no fun in such a car) the Gilbern handles well and will accelerate to 60 mph in around nine seconds. Motorway cruising at the permitted 70 mph was effortless: the maximum speed claimed is 125 mph. Braking and cornering were admirable and petrol consumption averaged 20 miles a gallon. This is certainly a car for the enthusiast, with a price of £2493 (including VAT) against just over £1700 for the most expensive three litre Capri.

[Note: dealer margins were $17\frac{1}{2}$ per cent of manufacturer's selling price.]

By November prospects were much happier. The Mark III was selling well in the UK and a large order for 150 cars over three years had been received from Holland. For the first time the company would be exporting its products. With order books overflowing, the problem seemed to be one of meeting demand.

The Gilbern Motor Factory

Exhibit 8A.4 outlines the manufacturing process for the assembled cars. Some disruption was caused to the work flow when the company moved over to fully assembled cars, but this was minor, as the only additional process required was in fact the final assembly.

The distinctive nature of the original kit car was achieved in two ways: firstly by the shape of the body and secondly by the manner in which the mass-produced parts were put together to make a high-performance car. Thus, the manufacturing process involved making the body and some parts of the interior trim (seats were often bought in) and assembling the various bought-out parts. In the latter case, it was not unusual for parts to be altered slightly in order to fit the design of the car or to improve its performance. The resulting unfamiliar engine and chassis were often the reason why garages were unwilling to do repair work.

Raw materials and bought-in sub-assembled parts were a high-cost item for Gilbern Cars, the most expensive items being the engine, the gearbox and the rear-axle assembly, which together could cost between £200 and £250. In order to reduce costs as far as possible, the Gilbern was made of fibreglass, which required little investment other than in a body mould and for the raw materials. By contrast, metal, the material used by most large manufacturers, was expensive and required large capital investment in plant to produce a body shell. It was possible to sub-contract such work to produce a metal body, but this would have increased even further both costs and reliance upon suppliers.

As a general rule, the relationship between the company and its employees was very good: the nature of the product attracted an enthusiastic staff, who seemed content to tolerate the poor working conditions and lack of organisation.

The complete management team comprised

chairman and managing director,
manufacturing director,
sales manager,
buyer,
accountant,
development manager,
three secretaries,
six foremen, and
maintenance engineer.

The engineering department was operated by a working foreman and a chargehand, who were responsible for the activities of three skilled adults and three semi-skilled operators under 21 years of age. In this section bought-out front- and rear-axle assemblies were modified and attached to the basic chassis, which was constructed mainly of $1\frac{1}{4}$-inch square hollow steel tube, cut and welded into a space-frame using sub-assembly and final assembly welding jigs. A number of problems were encountered in this department. For example, all operators constantly worked overtime to compensate for the loss of production incurred from their being withdrawn to deliver new cars or unload lorries of raw materials. (The average overtime rate throughout the factory was 25 per cent. The average wage was £2000 per year and overtime was paid at time and a quarter.) Equipment was felt to be inadequate, leading to, for example, inaccurate cutting or distortion of the chassis during welding. There were no detailed work schedules and operators found it necessary to keep their own rough personal records. The layout was such that the chassis was finally assembled in a position remote from the exit doors, which meant that it had to be manhandled into a location where rolling gear could be attached for removal to the next department.

Only one body mould existed and, owing to the nature of the product and the essential predetermined curing times for the resin, it took almost a whole shift to prepare one body (requiring two men) and at least ten hours for curing. To extract the finished moulding from the jig and prepare for the next lay-up, the foreman and an operator started work at 7 a.m., otherwise repeated operations would fall behind, resulting in a lack of mould maintenance and poor quality. However, a second mould was being constructed and it was intended that this would double nominal capacity within the next six months.

119

The foreman, together with the most skilled operator, worked practically full time on the body mould during the day, with the result that it was impossible for the remaining four operators, who were producing other components (for example, bumpers or doors) of indifferent quality, to be properly supervised or trained. For example, their proportioning of resin and catalyst in the mix was somewhat haphazard and took little account of the current temperature. Also, the mixing of the ingredients was poor, leading either to uneven curing or extended curing (two or three hours longer than normal) owing to the use of insufficient catalyst. As in other departments, working conditions fell short of ideal. A leaking roof led to losses of components from water contamination. The resins in use damaged clothing and footwear, which lasted three months at most. Housekeeping was poor and heating inefficient. This last point affected not only the operators but also slowed down the exothermic reaction of the resin mixtures and was the reason for the extended curing times.

In the body shop, seven operators and a foreman were responsible for the rubbing down and preparation of the car body and other parts prior to painting. After the body had been assembled to the chassis, the foreman carried out the fibreglass bonding operations, which made the assembly a composite structure. The bonnet, boot and doors were offered up and fitted to the main structure and then separated for painting. It was therefore in this department that a considerable amount of work was required to rectify blemishes and air bubbles in the main body. Also, the lack of expertise of moulding-shop operators could lead to poor-quality door mouldings, and the operation of making good often greatly exceeded the time taken for the laying-up of the original moulding.

Including the foreman, seven men were employed in the paint shop, four of whom were relatively inexperienced but who were engaged mainly on rubbing down and polishing. Considerable skill was needed to produce a reasonable finish from the existing materials used. If the final coats were too wet, there was the danger that the fibreglass 'gel' coat would be disturbed, allowing the fibrous structure to show through. However, if the viscosity of the paint used for the final coats was too high, the paint was not wet enough to allow levelling to take place, a problem peculiar to fibreglass. Added to this, the quality of the finish produced from the gun currently used resulted in an 'orange peel' effect, which had to be rectified by hand during the final burnishing and polishing.

The finishing shop was responsible for the final assembly of the car prior to installation of the engine. Whilst waiting time had been significantly reduced by bringing together in the stores kits of parts for each car, delays owing to shortages did sometimes result in incomplete assemblies reaching the engine-installation section. This meant that the three finishing operators were sometimes to be found in the final section completing their work and consequently interfering with the work of the engine-installation crew. As a result, the foreman had to spend a large amount of time on assembly work himself. There was also a degree of frustration caused by the poor-quality work of other departments and by production-engineering problems which had not been dealt with owing to other pressures. For example, in the case of wrongly shaped or distorted brackets, it could take two men up to an hour to fit a front bumper. Owing to this the quality-control inspector also could become involved in assembly and rectification work. Further interference with the smooth flow of production was sometimes caused by an instruction from one of the directors to bring forward a particular car which had only just reached the early stages of the finishing operation.

The engine-installation shop was manned by three operators. They reported directly to the works manager and there appeared to be no direct co-ordination with the work in the finishing shop. In fact, there appeared to be a shortage of engineering skill throughout the factory, as the development engineer was often called upon to deal with minor production-engineering problems. As a result, he was grossly overworked and often complained that he was unable to concentrate upon development work for any useful length of time.

EXHIBIT 8A.1   Minor motor manufactures

	No of dealers in UK	Estimated production per week
Lotus	74	50–70
Reliant (Scimitar)	55	50–70
Morgan	20	3–5
Aston Martin	21	10–20
Jensen	53	10–15
Bristol	58	10
AC	8	<10
Gilbern	26	<10
Ginetta	6	<10
Marcos	n.a.	<10
TVR	19	<10
Clan	n.a.	<5
Fairthorpe	1	<5
Trident	1	<5
		200–300

NB. This accounts for about $\frac{1}{2}$ per cent of the total UK car market.

EXHIBIT 8A.2   Profit and loss account (£) (year ending 31 December)

	1969	1970	1971
Sales			
UK	147,317	162,284	381,467
Overseas	–	–	–
	147,317	162,284	381,467
Trading profit/loss	(60,687)	(59,414)	(76,465)
Less			
depreciation	3,656	4,835	6,256
interest	–	1,844	5,800
directors' remuneration and			
dividends paid	4,725	4,724	7,118
Profit/loss carried forward	(69,086)	(70,817)	(95,639)

EXHIBIT 8A.3   Balance sheet (£) (year ending 31 December)

	1969	1970	1971
Capital employed			
Issued ordinary share capital	10,000	10,000	10,000
Reserves	3,796	3,376	2,986
Ordinary shareholders' interest	13,796	13,376	12,986
Loan capital	40,000	40,000	90,000
Profit and loss account, deferred taxation,			
investment grants	18,362	(51,535)	(147,174)
	72,158	(1,841)	(44,188)
Employment of capital			
Current assets	82,525	75,563	110,840
Current liabilities	41,228	101,347	237,725
Net current assets	41,297	(25,784)	(126,885)
Fixed assets and investments	20,861	17,625	72,697[a]
Goodwill	10,000	10,000	10,000
Net assets	72,158	(1,841)	(44,188)

[a]The premises at Llantwit Fadre are owned by the company and are valued by the directors at £35,000 subject to a mortgage. The directors value the moulds, plant and equipment and office furniture at £10,000.

EXHIBIT 8A.4   Manufacturing process

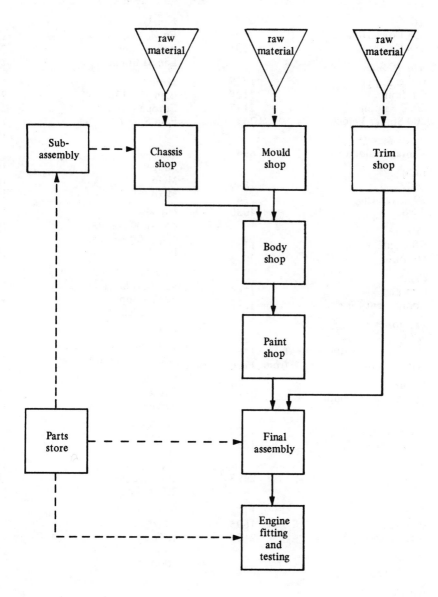

EXHIBIT 8A.5   Comparative price list (£) of sports cars, etc., 1972

AC
428 Convertible	7101
428 Gastback	7101

Alfa Romeo
Guilia Super	1729
GT Junior	2128
2000 Saloon	2177
200 Spider Veloce	2636

Aston Martin
Vantage Saloon	6949

BMW
1602	1899
2000 Touring	2349
3.OS	4030

Citroën
GS Confort	1159
D Estate	2098

Clan[a]
Crusader	1396
Component form	1225

Crayford[a]
William	758
Cortina Convertible	from 1466
Mercedes-Benz Estate	from 1226

Ferrari
246 GT Dino Coupe	5879

Ford
Capri 1300 L	1123
Capri 3000GXL	1831

Gilbern[a]
Invader	2493

Ginetta[a]
G15	1175
G21 1800	1695
G21 3-litre	2125

Jaguar
12V E Type	3367

Jensen
Jensen Healey	1959
Interceptor	6744

Lancia
Fulvia Sedan	1398
Fulvia Sport	2273
Lancia Coupe	2945

Lotus[a]
Elan +2S 130	2720
Europa	2369
Elan Sprint	2346
7S4	1073

MG
Midget	1003
MGB	1390
MGB GT	1546

Morgan[a]
4/4 1600 2-seater	1448
4/4 1600 4-seater	1564
Plus 8	1995

Porsche
914 (left-hand drive)	2527
911T Coupe	4158
Carrera RS	5826

Reliant
Scimitar GTE Overdrive	2398
Scimitar GTE Automatic	2487

Sunbeam
Sport	905
Alpine	1354

Triumph
Spitfire	1053
GT6	1373
TR6 PI	1621
2000 Estate	2071
2.5 PI Estate	2364
Stag	2570

TVR[a]
1600 M	1981
2500 M	2151
3000 M	2278

[a] Available in kit form prior to VAT.

Source: Motor Magazine, 9 Dec 1972.

EXHIBIT 8A.6   Advertisement for Invader Mark III (illustrations omitted)

Safety through Comfort

That's what Gilbern interiors were designed for. Deep bucket seats. Thick pile carpet. Personally selected and colour matched materials. Electrically operated windows. And the air of being exclusively, Gilbern.

INVADER MARK III SPECIFICATION

Engine

Cylinders	6 in 60 deg. Vec.
Main Bearings	4
Cooling System	Water Pump, Electric Fan and Thermostat
Bore	93.7 mm. (3.69 in.)
Stroke	72.4 mm. (2.85 in.)
Displacement	2994 c.c. (182.7 cu. in.)
Valve Gear	Overhead, Push rods and Rockers
Compression Ratio	8.9 to 1 Minimum Octane Rating 97 r.m.
Carburettor	38 DGAS 3A Downdraught
Fuel Pump	AC mechanical
Oil Filter	Full Flow, Renewable Element
Max. Power	140 din at 5000 r.p.m.
Max. Torque	173 lb. ft. at 3500 r.p.m.
Max. b.m.e.p.	146 p.s.i. at 3500 r.p.m.

Transmission

Clutch	Borg and Beck Diaphragm 9.5 in. dia.
Gearbox	4-speed, all syncromesh, with overdrive
Gear Ratios	Overdrive Top 0.82, Top 1.00
	Overdrive Third 1.16, Third 1.41,
	Second 2.21, First 3.16,
	Reverse 3.35
Final Drive	3.09 Hypoid Bevel

Chassis and Body

Construction	Rectangular and Square Tube, Steel
	Chassis, separate GRP Body

Suspension

Front	Independent Double Wishbones, Coil Springs,
	Adjustable Telescopic Dampers, Anti-roll bar
Rear	Live axle, Located by Twin Parallel Trailing
	Radius Arms, Panhard Rod, Co-Axial Coil
	Springs, Adjustable Telescopic Dampers

Steering

Type	Rack and Pinion, with Convoluted Energy
	Absorbing Steering Column
Turns, lock to lock	3.70
Wheel Diameter	14 ins.
Turning Circle	32.6 ft.

Brakes

Make and Type	Girling, Disc Front, Drum Rear
Servo	Girling Power-stop, Vacuum 2.1
Dimensions	Front 9.6 in. dia. Rear 9 in. dia.
	1.75 in. wide shoes
Swept Area	Total 334 sq. in.

Wheels

Type	Sculptured Pressed Steel 5.5 in. Wide Rim
Tyres	G.800 Grand Prix Radial Tubeless Size 185/70 13 ins.

Dimensions

Wheelbase	92.75 ins. (235.6 cm.)
Track: Front	56 in. (142.2 cm.)
Rear	56 in. (142.2 cm.)
Ground Clearance	5.5 in. Unladen (14 cm.)
Overall Length	160.5 in. (407.7 cm.)
Overall Width	67 in. (170.18 cm.)
Overall Height	53 in. (134.6 cm.)
Kerb Weight	2464 lb. (1,120 kg.)

Performance Data

Top Gear m.p.h. per 1000 r.p.m.	22 m.p.h.
Overdrive Top Gear	27 m.p.h.

Equipment

Battery	Lucas 12-volts 53 A/H
Alternator	Lucas 17 ACR 36 AMP
Headlamps	Lucas Quartz Halogen
Reversing Lamps	Twin
Electric Fuses	4
Screen Wiper	2-speed Self Parking
Screen Washers	Electric Type
Interior Heater	Aeroflow System
Heated Rear Screen	
Safety Belts	Anchorages Built-in
Interior Trim	Expanded Vinyl, PVC Headlining
Floor Covering	Pile Carpet
Tool Kit	1
Jack	Scissor Type
Jacking Points	Any Chassis Tube
Electrically Operated Windows	Electric Aerial
Cigar Lighter	Steering Lock
Hazard Warning Lights	Boot Light
Fog and Spot Lamps	Radio with Single Speaker

Maintenance

Fuel Tank	Capacity 12 gallons incl. 2 Reserve
	19.8 Pints including Heater
Cooling System	8 pints SAE 20/50 Oil/Filter change every 6000 miles
Engine Sump	3.25 Pints SAE 80 EP No Change
Gearbox	1.94 Pints SAE 90 EP No Change
Final Drive	4 Front Wishbone Ball Joints every 35,000 miles
Grease	Normal Driving 25 PSI F/R
Tyre Pressures	Fast Driving 27 PSI F/R
Max. Payload	700 lbs

CASE B

By February 1973, production had increased to between seven and eight cars per week and the profit per car to £150 on a selling price of £2500. An offer of a cash infusion of £50,000 had been made by the Industrial and Commercial Finance Corporation (ICFC) in return for 20 per cent of the equity, and had been accepted in early January. But time was running out for Gilbern Cars. During February Salway left the company after a disagreement with Leather, and early in March the offer from the ICFC was reduced to £25,000 for 25 per cent of the equity. In April, with cash flow becoming very tight, the ICFC advanced the company £10,000 prior to the finalising of the legal agreements. It was too late. On 9 July Lloyds Bank appointed a receiver, Mr G. Ehlers, and on 12 July ICFC appointed the same receiver as fifty employees were laid off.

Despite the chronic cash problems, substantial improvements had been made in the manufacturing of the cars. Engine chassis were produced at a rate of seven units per week by one foreman and six welders. A stress analysis of the chassis had been commissioned in an attempt to simplify the process, but, although a preliminary report had been received, no action had been taken.

Two complete moulds existed and had been well maintained. The moulding shop had been refabricated, the heating system redesigned and templates prepared for fibreglass cutting. There was room for additional moulding capacity on the land adjacent to the moulding shop. The maximum throughput of the existing shop and moulds had risen to about eight complete mould sets per week, with an allowance for mould maintenance. The staffing required at this level was one foreman, six laminators and one fibreglass-cutter.

In the trim shop the quality of finishing, floor carpeting and interior trimming was high. Templates existed for most of the fabrics that were cut and some work had been commissioned on redesigning the interior.

A £35,000 DeVilbiss spraying plant had been installed in the paint shop, and had been well maintained. Unfortunately, the claimed throughput and quality of finish had not been achieved with this plant. The staff required was high – one foreman and six assistants – but this was influenced by the amount of warranty and repair work undertaken by the shop. This disrupted the production flow and resulted in increased downtime, as the spray plant was frequently cleaned out for colour changes.

The final-assembly shop had been reorganised but still represented the principal bottleneck to increased production. Problems in this area included unreliable suspension equipment, complex assembly operations and an unsystematic work sequence due to poor parts control. The subsequent operations of engine fitting and testing were inundated with rectifying faults from earlier stages of manufacture.

The method of setting and controlling stock levels, analysis of the relationships between parts call-off, production plans and delivery lead times continued to be organised in a haphazard way, leading to an excess of crisis ordering and high delivery costs. However, most of the work needed in order to use the standard- materials control package on an IBM Data Centre had been undertaken.

The Sunday Times of 22 July 1973 carried the following report:

Negotiations are under way this weekend to save Wales's only car manufacturer, Gilbern, maker of the £2,700, 120 mph Invader Mk III. With the company's debts now over £90,000, Lloyds Bank, the principal creditor, has appointed a receiver.

126

Most of the firm's 60 employees have already been laid off and only a handful are being kept on to finish the last six cars on the assembly at the Lantwit Fadre factory in South Wales. Recent months have seen sales rise to six a week with a two month waiting list. Gilbern dealers met yesterday and assured managing director, Michael Leather, of their full support. [Twelve dealers were present at the meeting.]

The company's main problem appears to have been a persistent lack of capital. Dealers were hopeful yesterday, however, that Leather's efforts to interest a leading Welsh business figure in the company would succeed.

"Snags" hold up signing of deal to save threatened Welsh car firm', the *Birmingham Post* of 21 September 1973 reported,

A Midland-based financier, named yesterday as Mr Anthony M. Peters, is understood to be completing negotiations to buy Gilbern, the Welsh motor company facing closure.

But last night Mr Peters, who is reported to live in the Hampton-in-Arden area, still remained a shadowy figure in the background.

Businessmen and financiers in the Midlands said that they had never heard of him.

And a Gilbern spokesman said: 'He likes to stay in the background and he has asked us to preserve this.' Mr George Ehlers, the Official Receiver, said: 'I can assure you he does exist.'

Mr Peters' name was leaked accidentally yesterday on a company news wire service with a report that he had, in fact, bought the Gilbern assets and announced plans for the future.

Later Gilbern said that its managing director, Mr Michael Leather, had gone to London to sign the contract but 'a couple of snags' had arisen. It was expected that a statement could be made today.

I understood that Mr Peters, who is aged about 33 and has various engineering interests, contacted Mr Jem Marsh, founder of the now defunct Marcos car company, yesterday, and invited him to play a part in Gilbern.

Mr Marsh, who has 15 years' experience in the low volume car business, is to meet Mr Peters in London next week.

In the report which leaked out yesterday it was stated the production of an up-graded Mark III Gilbern Invader would begin immediately under a new company name of Gemketh Ltd, trading as Gilbern Cars.

'Complete reorganisation is being undertaken with special emphasis on systems, safety, quality control and spare parts availability.'

It added, 'plans were being laid in the export field to expand the sales network in Europe.

'There were also plans to diversify into a wide range of glass fibre and engineering products.'

The *Financial Post* of 26 September 1973 elaborated further on Mr Peters' involvement:

How a quiet businessman became owner of Gilbern

A report that Mr Anthony Peters, a 32-year-old Henley-in-Arden businessman read in an English Sunday newspaper, while on holiday in Spain, galvanised him into action.

From his hotel he sent the message: 'Please have all the details on my desk ready for my return.' Today, two months later, he is the new owner of Gilbern, the Welsh car company he had read was going into the hands of the receiver.

Yesterday, Mr Peters, a 6ft 4in, quietly-spoken financier who has built up a group of companies from a £60 loan 14 years ago, talked about his plans for Gilbern.

With the money we paid for Gilbern, and I cannot disclose that, and what is planned in the next five-year programme, we shall be putting between £700,000 and £800,000 into the company,' he said.

'Although I only signed the contract on Monday, a great deal of work has already been done. The first three upgraded Mark III Invaders will be out this week, we are beginning to rebuilt the factory interior to get smooth production, and the archaic administration has been reorganised.

'I think by the end of this year we should have some good reports', he said.

'There are plans to get seven cars a week by November, which has never been done at the factory before. It is a bold statement, but we feel that with our expertise and the enthusiasm at the factory there is no reason why it should not happen.'

Mr Peters talks constantly of 'we' – it is something he has developed over the years. What he really means is 'me', the owner of Antone Group which has interests in finance, property development, fashion, engineering and aircraft charter.

Mr Peters, surprisingly little known in the West Midlands business world – and one senses that he prefers it that way – is reticent to talk about money.

'I suppose you could say I am past the first million. I have not said it yet, or if I am past the second million. I prefer to think that I have built up a very pleasant group with a sound background.'

Mr Peters launched himself into a business career with £60 borrowed to open a hairdressing salon.

'My parents were reasonably well off, but I chose not to use any of their money. By borrowing money I learned the general format of business and how to get along using my own devices.

'I built up the largest independent chain of hairdressing shops in Britain, 38 of them, and at the same time I was buying up other businesses.

'Gilbern was in the situation where it needed a lot of money, it owed something over £100,000 and as we were looking for a company at that time, we bought it because we believe it has tremendous potential.'

Naturally, he will be driving a Gilbern – at least for some of the time. But the Rolls-Royce Silver Shadow parked outside his office window is likely to remain his premier means of travel.

Just six months later, however, on 15 March 1974, the *Pontypridd Observer* printed the following article:

£50,000 to save the Gilbern

Only one thing can save the Gilbern car manufacturing business at Llantwit Fardre from extinction – and that is the intervention of someone prepared to inject about £50,000 into it.

This was disclosed on Monday after a meeting had been held of the directors.

They issued the following letter to creditors and employees of the firm, and to its distributing agents:

'We have to advise you that the position of this company is uncertain and that we consider it to be in the best interests of creditors, shareholders and employees that trading should cease immediately.'

'A petition to wind up the company has been submitted by a shareholder and this will be heard at Pontypridd County Court on Wednesday, May 1st, at 10.30 a.m. Inquiries by letter only should be sent to the registered office.'

At peak production Gilbern employed around 60 people. But because of the three-day working week only one car has been produced weekly of late and last week the 16 workers remaining at the factory were made redundant.

One director of the firm described it as a viable proposition with sufficient orders for the Gilbern Invader Mark III and ample distribution facilities. The only thing lacking was capital to finance production – something of the order of £50,000. He described the £2995 Invader as 'the best car we have ever made'.

Gilbern Cars Ltd, was created in 1959 by Mr Giles Smith and Mr Bernard Friese in an old stable next to a pickle factory. Employing just a handful of employees the firm was producing just two cars a week.

But last year Gilbern plunged £90,000 into the red and Lloyds Bank called in the receiver.

Subsequently, industrialist Mr Anthony Peters intervened to save the firm from going into liquidation and introduced plans to link the manufacture of the plastic bodied cars with light plastic engineering.

It was in February this year that Mr Peters' controlling share in the company was bought by a group of London accountants and businessmen.

9 Morgan Motor Company Ltd

ARTHUR MOORE from material collected by NANCY MARWICK,
ARTHUR MOORE and MARLICE TOMKINSON (London Business
School Masters Programme 1977)

In September 1976, Peter Morgan was optimistic about the future of the Morgan Moto
Company Ltd. The company had been in the hands of his family since his father had
founded it in 1910 with £3000 provided by his grandfather. Now it was producing 400
cars a year and had a full order book until 1979. The company was making profits an
Peter Morgan was enjoying his business – what was there to worry about?

Company history

Peter Morgan's father, known to Morgan devotees by his initials, H. F. S., opened a
garage and started a motor works in 1908. His desire to build and ride motorcycles in
competition grew and led to the construction of the first Morgan, the three-wheeled
cyclecar. Its high power-to-weight ratio gave it a good performance, so H. F. S.,
encouraged by this and funded by his father, purchased machine tools, built an
extension to the garage in Malvern, a small Midlands town, and went into production
1910.

Success in competitions established a reputation for reliability and speed, boosting
sales to a level of 1000 cars per annum by 1913. After World War I the company
continued to grow, with the increasing demand for inexpensive transport. This succes
enabled Morgan to build a new (the present) factory in Malvern and increase producti
to fifty cars per week in 1920.

The three-wheeler continued to win in competitions, especially trials, but increasing
competition from the mass-produced four-wheeled Austin 7 in the mid 1920s forced
Morgan to cut prices. H. F. S. decided to concentrate on consolidating the company's
position as a specialist sports-car manufacturer, developing and emphasising the high
performance of his cars.

The company survived the Depression but found the demand for three-wheeled car
dropping dramatically in the economic upturn of the mid 1930s, and in 1936 H. F. S.
introduced his first four-wheeled car. He was just in time. Sales of three-wheelers had
been 659, 286 and 137 in the years 1934–6 respectively. (The three-wheeler was
eventually discontinued in 1952.)

The new Morgan, the 4/4, was an open two-seater with an 1100 cc engine and use
many Morgan engineering innovations, principally the patented front suspension. Ve
quickly it was successful in competition, and this, with the Morgan name, soon built
sales.

After the war, H. F. S. was fortunate to get many of his skilled workforce back fro
the forces but was hampered by Government restrictions on material supplies, which
were linked to export orders. So he set up agencies abroad to secure supplies.

During the early 1950s the Morgan car was considered 'old-fashioned' in the UK and increasing reliance was placed on overseas markets. By the early 1960s 85 per cent of Morgan's output was being exported to North America, mostly to California. This market collapsed when recession hit the Californian aircraft industry, and the Morgan Motor Co. almost collapsed with it. A vigorous personal effort by Peter Morgan saved the situation in the USA and established new agencies in Canada, Australia and Europe. This kept the company going until 1965, when sales in the UK began to revive.

A new model, the Plus 8, was introduced in 1968, with a very similar body shell to the 4/4 but with a 3500 cc engine. The 1600 cc 4/4 and a four-seater 4/4 made up the product range in 1976. All the models were based on the original 1936 4/4 styling, and, indeed, the last major restyling occurred in 1953, when the current bonnet and raditor grille were introduced.

Ownership of the company passed from the founder (H. F. S.) to a trust for his children when he died in 1959 at the age of seventy-seven. In 1964 the limited company was dissolved to enable a capital redistribution of shares to take place. It was reconstituted in 1970. The shareholders were all Peter Morgan's family.

The product

Exhibit 9.1 presents the specifications of Morgan models as given in a brochure used by the company.

The car was powered by Ford and Rover engines and had a hand-built body, coach-built onto a bought-in chassis. Cars were still made to order and extras such as aluminium bodywork and wire wheels were available.

Exhibit 9.2 lists some of the sports cars and saloons available in 1976, with list price and acceleration times. Listed below are *all* the cars which the magazine *Autocar* showed as having a faster 0–60 m.p.h. acceleration.

Caterham Cars Super 7	£2,979
Porsche 911S	£13,500
Porsche Turbo	£17,500
Aston Martin V8	£14,485
Ferrari 365 GTB4	£16,000

The suspension of the car was stiff, giving an extremely rough ride, which was said by some to be almost jeep-like. 'Dear Roughrider' was the mode of address used by the president of the Morgan Owners' Group in New York in his monthly newsletter. The ride was complemented by the heavy steering, which required only $2\frac{1}{2}$ turns from lock to lock. As *Autocar* (1976) put it, 'Man! – you really steer the Plus 8 using steely wrists and hairy forearms.' The reviewer went on, 'We cannot bring ourselves to disapprove too strongly about the discomforts of the classic style of body.'

Other reviewers commented on the 4/4, 'The only possible reason for buying such a car is the sheer fun of driving it fast on suitable roads' (*Motor*), and 'Morgans . . . produce more amusement than a trainload of Playboy bunnies' (*Automobile Quarterly*).

Producing Morgan cars

In 1976 the factory was essentially the same as in 1919 (see Exhibit 9.3 for the factory layout). An extension in 1972 was the only increase in space since 1925. Customers entering the Malvern Link premises passed into a reception area of Morgan memorabilia with posters and gifts to Peter Morgan showing Morgan's illustrious racing history, which includes a 1962 class win at Le Mans. However, walking through to the parts department and on to the eight crafts shops, it did not take long to find out that 'automation' was a foreign word at Morgan.

Initially Morgan made a large percentage of the car themselves from raw materials, but as mass production prevailed in the industry an increasing percentage of parts were purchased. In 1976 purchases accounted for about 60 per cent of sales (see Exhibit 9.10), the major items being:

	Supplier
Chassis frames	Rubery Owen
Electrics	Lucas
Back axles	G.K.N.
Engines	Ford and Rover
Brakes	Girling
Steering columns and boxes	Cam Gears and A. C. Delco

A small general purpose machine shop was used to manufacture suspension lugs, hubs, hood frames and fuel tanks. It held about thirty machine tools, mostly installed when the factory was re-equipped by the War Office in 1940, and was manned by fourteen operators. Only two new machines had been added in the last thirty years.

The factory was divided into eight craft shops, linked by narrow pedestrian doors; the workers normally worked in groups of eight to ten. The engine, chassis and drive were first assembled in the erecting shop. A Belgian ash frame for the body was then attached and the wooden wheel arches added. The frame was produced by three carpenters in a separate wood mill. One or two men would then spend two days cutting, beating and shaping the metal panels by hand before securing them to the frame in the sheet-metal shop. Cars were pushed from shop to shop via the adjoining yard, as no conveyor system existed and no interior doors were large enough. The cars were finish painted, wired and upholstered before the final test drive.

The stress was on quality from first-class craftsmanship, obviously dependent on a high degree of skill in the employees. Peter Morgan complained of the difficulty he experienced in recruiting apprentices willing to undergo the long 'on-the-job' training. The cost of mistakes during the training was high and the 10 per cent annual labour turnover largely reflected movement of trainees to better-paid, less demanding jobs in the area. Nevertheless, a tremendous loyalty was shown to the company by the workforce. This was typified by several examples of sons (now in their fifties) having followed fathers into Morgan and spent their entire working lives with the company. In spite of being located near the Black Country, only about half of its labour force was unionised and the company had never had a strike.

Marketing

According to Peter Morgan, 'past owners of Morgans are the best salesmen', and the sales effort certainly reflected the statement. Advertising and promotion were very low-key, running at about 1 per cent of turnover, with Morgan placing on its agents, who were paid out of their margins, the chief responsibility for advertising. Morgan's own effort was aimed primarily at displays in the two annual UK motor shows.

The agents were hand-picked by Peter Morgan worldwide (see Exhibit 9.4) and this coverage accounted for the 50 per cent export rate that Morgan were achieving. Exhibit 9.5 presents a breakdown by country of car sales in 1971 and 1975.

Peter Morgan was supported in his selling efforts by Derek Day, the director of sales. Derek had been with the company for twenty-seven years and appeared intensely loyal to 'Mr Peter'. He felt that the key to Morgan's success was its distributors, who knew when they had a hot prospect who was willing to wait three years and be a half mechanic to get the thrill of the 'jeep-like' ride. (Agents usually requested a deposit of £50 on an order for a new Morgan.) Morgan had abandoned the American market when safety regulations and the lack of an engine to meet the emission standards had presented huge barriers. In 1976 the technology for meeting the former had been developed, but the company was waiting for someone to produce a suitable engine. Derek Day considered the US market extremely important and one that should be re-entered as soon as possible. He also felt that 'the problem is not selling cars but making them'.

A price list appears as Exhibit 9.6 and a graph showing second-hand Morgan prices as Exhibit 9.7. Morgans kept their value well and the demand for new cars was sufficient to keep a waiting list of three years. Peter Morgan admitted that a lot of speculators could well be included in the list but was unsure of the effect they could have.

The company received a lot of support from enthusiast clubs established around the world: the Morgan car appeared to stimulate the clannishness of a minority. Each letter from an owner suggesting a modification or improvement or merely complimentary would receive a personal reply from Peter Morgan.

Development and new products

Although Morgan had continued to sell old-established products, the company had pursued a policy of continual development. In 1961 Peter Morgan began work on a new two-seater coupé, the Plus-4-Plus, to have a fibreglass body. He had suggested the idea of the car in his father's last years, but H. F. S. had been against it, partly because he felt it was an affront to the Morgan image and partly because he doubted its technical feasibility. In fact, the car was technically sound when built, but when launched in 1964 it was not a commercial success and production ceased after fewer than 100 models had been made. Derek Day comments, 'The experiment with the Plus-4-Plus was an idea before its time, but it did leave a stigma attached to changing from the classic Morgan and to using new materials.'

In 1966 Maurice Owen was appointed as director of development and engineering. His aim was to develop the new Plus 8 model, using his skills (acquired in his previous job, with Lotus cars) in the use of glass fibre. The car, which cost £40,000 to develop, was launched in 1968. The body and chassis were essentially the same as the Plus 4, but adapted to take the new Rover 3500 cc engine.

Peter Morgan and the Family

Peter Morgan's office reflected the age of the factory and had been described as having 'a dinginess that could almost be considered studied'. Dull brown paintwork and big boards faintly proclaiming the wins of the pre-war years lined the walls. Other memorabilia reflected the trial victories of the three-wheelers at the hands of H. F. S.

Peter Morgan shunned growth-for-growth's-sake. Production had been at the 400 per annum mark for a few years, and, although he talked of 'increasing production by fifty or so', it did not seem to the writers that this was a particularly urgent objective. '. . . if every car on order was finished and available, I would be lucky to get 20–25 per cent "takers". Excuses would be made about not the right time of delivery or lack of funds.'

Nor did it appear that any model change was in the offing: 'We're sticking with a winner . . . but, if interest in the present range wanes, I do in fact have plans available for new markets, and for new and revised models.'

Peter Morgan's philosophy was to produce sports cars at a price a reasonable man could afford to pay. He saw himself as 'more in the business than profit', although profits were essential and the company had to be a thoroughly viable commercial enterprise. 'We are virtually impregnable. We are in a unique position, there is such a demand for our cars.'

When questioned about the age of the plant and the factory, he expressed a willingness to re-equip but saw no point in it if buying out was cheaper.

All the shares were owned by Peter Morgan and his immediate family:

Peter Morgan	48%
Jane Morgan (wife)	2%
Charles Morgan (son)	30%
Lady S. J. Colwyn (daughter)	10%
Mrs G. R. Price (daughter)	10%

Charles Morgan was the 'heir apparent'. He was not in the business at the time, but a photographer for Independent Television News, although, like his father, Charles had competed regularly in events with Morgan cars. He was said to be 'spreading his wings before coming home to the family business.'

When asked about the future, Peter Morgan remarked, 'Morgans will keep on creeping off the production line, made of wood and steel, built by hand and defying anyone who says there is not a place for the small company that refuses to grow.'

EXHIBIT 9.1   Model specifications

4/4 TWO-SEATER AND 4/4 FOUR-SEATER SPECIFICATION

Chassis frame. Deep Z-shape section with five boxed or tubular cross members. Easily detachable front end.

Gearbox. Four speed and reverse. Synchromesh on all forward gears.

Overall ratios. Top 4.1; 3rd 5.7; 2nd 8.3; 1st 12.2; reverse 13.6 to 1.

Transmission and rear axle. Propshaft with needle roller bearing universal joints transmits power to the tubular Salisbury rear axle fitted with Hypoid gears − ratio 4.1 to 1.

Wheels and tyres. Pressed steel rims fixed with four studs and covered by chromium-plated disc. Centre lock wire wheels are an optional extra. Radial tyres − 165 x 15".

Brakes. Girling hydraulic dual brake system on four wheels. 11" dia. discs on front wheels. 9" x $1\frac{3}{4}$" drum brakes on rear. Cable operated hand brake.

Steering gear. Cam gear. Collapsible column. Steering lock ignition switch. Leather-covered spring alloy wheel, giving $2\frac{1}{4}$ turns lock to lock. Turning circle 32' (9.7m).

Suspension. Front wheels − vertically mounted coil springs on sliding axle pin. Double acting tubular shock absorbers. Semi-elliptical rear springs, fitted at both ends with Silentbloc brushes, and controlled by Armstrong hydraulic dampers.

Electrics. Lucas 12 volt equipment: indicators, hazard warning, instrument panel lighting, two-speed wipers and fresh air heater.

Instruments. Steel instrument panel includes speedo with trip mileage, rev. counter: oil fuel, battery gauges and water temp. gauge.

Bodywork. Sheet steel panels on ash wood frame. Black vynide upholstery (alternative colours or leather available at extra cost). Detachable tops can be stowed in luggage compartment or behind rear seats in four seater. Laminated windscreen.

Colours. Deep Brunswick Green, Signal Red, Turquoise Blue, Nut Brown or Royal Ivory. Other colours available at extra cost.

Dimensions (approx.). Wheelbase 8' (244cm.). Track, front 3' 11" (119cm.), rear 4' 1" (124cm.). Length 12' (366cm.). Width 4' 8" (142cm.). Ground clearance 7" (18cm.). Height 4/4 two seater 4' 3" (129cm.). Weight 4/4 two seater 1,624 lbs. (735kg.). 4/4 four seater − 1,680 lbs. (760kg.).

PLUS 8 SPECIFICATION

Chassis frame. Deep Z-shape section with five boxed or tubular cross members. Easily detachable front end.

Gearbox. Five speed and reverse. Rover gearbox. Synchromesh on all forward gears.

Overall ratios. Top 2.76 : 1; 4th 3.31 : 1; 3rd 4.62 : 1; 2nd 6.90 : 1; 1st 10.99 : 1.

Transmission and rear axle. Propshaft with needle roller bearing universal joints transmits power to tubular Salisbury slip axle with Hypoid gears − ratio 3.31 to 1.

Wheels and tyres. Cast aluminium, wide based rims fixed with five studs. Radial tyres 195 x 14". Overseas option 185 x 15".

Brakes. Girling hydraulic, servo-assisted 11" dia. discs on front, 9" x $1\frac{3}{4}$" drum brakes on rear. Fly-off cable operated hand brake.

Steering gear. Cam gear. Collapsible column. Steering lock ignition switch. Leather-covered spring alloy wheel, giving $2\frac{1}{4}$ turns lock to lock. Turning circle 38' (11.5m).

Suspension. Front wheels independently sprung by vertical coil springs and telescopic hydraulic shock absorbers. Semi-elliptic rear springs with lever type hydraulic dampers.

EXHIBIT 9.1   Continued

Electrics. Lucas 12 volt equipment; indicators, hazard warning, instrument panel lighting, two-speed wipers and washer. Twin spotlights and fresh air heater.

Instrument panel. Steel instrument panel includes speedo with trip mileage, rev. counter; oil, fuel, battery gauges and water temp. gauge.

Bodywork. Sheet panels on ash wood frame. Black ambla upholstery (alternative colours or leather available at extra cost). Bucket seats with fore and aft adjustment. Detachable hood can be stowed in the 36″ x 20″ x 12″ (92 x 51 x 30.5cm.) high luggage compartment. Laminated windscreen.

Colours. Deep Brunswick Green, Signal Red, Turquoise Blue, Nut Brown or Royal Ivory. Other colours available at extra cost.

Dimensions. (approx.) – Wheelbase 8′ 2″ (249cm.). Track, front 4′ 4″ (132cm.); rear 4′ 5″ (135cm.). Overall length 12′ 3″ (373cm.). Width 5′ 2″ (158cm.). Ground clearance 7″ (17cm.). Height 4′ 4″ (132cm.). Weight 1,826 lbs. (828kg.).

EXHIBIT 9.2   Sports cars available in 1976

Car	List price (£)	Acceleration Time 0–60 m.p.h. (secs)
MGB	2633	11.0
Morgan 4/4	2779	10.0
Ginetta G21	2948	9.2
Super 7	2979	6.2
TR7	3146	9.6
TVR 1600 M	3481	10.4
Morgan Plus 8	3978	6.7
Panther Lima	4400	6.7
Datsun 260 Z 2 + 2	5247	8.8
Stag – Soft Top	5177	9.7
Reliant Scimitar GTE	5195	9.6

EXHIBIT 9.3   Factory/production layout

| Sales director | Administration offices | | Managing director | A series of eight workshops with approximately ten workers in each. (Each department has its own incentive piece-rate system, tailored to departmental needs) |

Parts department

Final finishing department — cars cleaned, prepared for delivery

One car produced each day (approximately).

Chassis-assembly bay — the chassis is assembled (i.e. bare frame built into a rolling chassis)

Production of each car takes ten days.

Paint bays — cars are undercoated, foiled, undercoated again and given four or five top coats all by hand

Metalworking shop — tin snips cut hoods, etc., from sheet metal

Carpentry shop — Belgian-ash frames handcrafted in this area

Belgian-ash logs delivered here

Machine shop — Morgan produces many of its own components (i.e. hood frames, fuel tanks, etc.). Much of today's equipment originally bought from the Government following World War II

Upholstering/electrical trim shops — upholstering/wiring/instrumented (ready-for-road test)

137

EXHIBIT 9.4   UK agents and overseas distributors

Allon White and Son (Cranfield) Ltd, Cranfield, Beds
John Britten Garages Ltd, Arkley, Barnet, Herts
Burlen Services, Salisbury, Wilts
Cliffsea Car Sales, Leigh-on-Sea, Essex
John Dangerfield Sports Cars, Fishponds, Bristol
F. H. Douglass, Ealing, London, W5
Mike Duncan Ltd, Halesowen, Worcs
Robin Kay, Eastbourne, Sussex
Lifes Motors Ltd, Southport, Lancs
I. and J. MacDonald, Lanchester, Co. Durham
Malvern Sports Car Company, Malvern, Worcs
Otley and Ilkley Motors Ltd, Otley, Yorks
Parker Bros (Stepps) Ltd, Glasgow
Phoenix Motors, Woodbury, Exeter, Devon
Mike Spence (Reading) Ltd, Reading, Berks
Sports Motors (Manchester) Ltd, Manchester
Morris Stapleton Motors, London, SW7
Station Garage, Taplow, Bucks

Australia: K. C. Ward Enterprises, Rhodes, NSW
                    Calder Sports Car Dist. Pty Ltd, Gisborne, Victoria
Austria: Max Bulla, Hauptstr 122, xxxxxx
Belgium: Jacques Elleboudt, Bruxelles 1180
Canada: Sterne Motors, Vancouver, BC
Denmark: Torben Krogh, 7100 Veile
Finland: Kai-Risto Import, Helsinki
France: Jacques Savoye, Paris
Germany: Kenneth W. Flaving, 475 Unna
                    Merz & Pabst, Stuttgart
Holland: BV Nimag, Leidschendam
Italy: Dilia, Genova
        Foreign Cars Italia SRL, Roma
Ireland: William P. Ryan, Dublin
Japan: Toshio Takano, Kanagawa
New Guinea: Lohberger Engineering Pty Ltd, Port Moresby
Spain: Albion SA, Madrid
South Africa: Mrs A. Heinz, Johannesburg
Sweden: A. B. Wendels, Malmö
Switzerland: Rolf Wehrlin, Aesch BL

EXHIBIT 9.5   Morgan exports by country

	1971[a]	*1975*[b]
Europe		
Austria	12	18
Belgium	10	18
Denmark	4	7
France	25	19
Germany	40	82[c]
Holland	6	0
Italy	25	14
Spain	2	3
Sweden	10	3
Switzerland	12	0
	146 (41%)	185 (47%)
Australasia/Asia		
Australia	6	12
New Guinea	4	2
New Zealand	3	2
Japan	10	10
	23 (7%)	26 (7%)
Africa	6 (1%)	5 (1%)
USA	40 (11%)	—
Percentage exports	(60%)	(55%)
Percentage domestic sales	(40%)	(45%)

[a] From J. Bowden, *First and Last of the Real Sports Cars* (1973) p. 177.

[b] From Derek Day.

[c] The doubling of the number of cars sold in Germany was largely accomplished through the appointment of a second German distributor, in northern Germany.

EXHIBIT 9.6   Recommended prices (£) for Morgan cars with effect from 18 October 1976 (home market, right-hand drive)

	Basic	Car tax	VAT	Total
4/4 1600 2-seater	2685	223.75	232.70	3141.45
4/4 1600 4-seater	2880	240.00	249.60	3369.60
Plus 8	3750	312.50	325.00	4387.50
Plus 8—77	4187	348.92	362.87	4898.79

Extras

	Basic	Combined tax
Plus 8		
Special colour paintwork	25.00	4.25
Upholstery carried out in leather (black or colour)	85.00	14.45
Reclining front seats	55.00	9.35
Luggage carrier	27.50	4.68
Spare-wheel cover	5.00	0.85
Headrests	14.00	2.38
4/4		
Wire wheels	77.50	13.18
Special-colour paintwork	25.00	4.25
Upholstery carried out in leather (black or colour) 2-Seater	85.00	14.45
Upholstery carried out in leather (black or colour) 4-Seater	97.50	16.58
Tonneau cover 2-seater	18.50	3.15
Tonneau cover 4-seater	22.00	3.74
Badge bar only	5.00	0.85
Luggage carrier tubular painted (4-seater)	25.00	4.25
Luggage carrier tubular painted (wire-wheeled 2-Seater)	23.00	3.91
Luggage carrier flat steel painted (disc-wheeled 2-Seater)	13.50	2.30
Bucket seats (restall) 2-seater only (including tonneau cover)	70.00	11.90
Reclining and folding seats 2-seater (including tonneau cover)	100.00	17.00
Reclining and folding seats 4-seater	90.00	15.30
Plus 8 type spotlights (pair)	18.00	3.06
Headrests (restall and reclining seats only)	14.00	2.38
3 windscreen wipers	12.50	2.13
Extras applicable to all models		
Seat belts	14.00	2.38
Reversing lights	10.00	1.70
Towing bracket	17.50	2.98
Locking petrol cap	2.00	0.34
Door handles	8.50	1.45
Bonnet strap	8.50	1.45
Undersealing by Carseal	15.00	2.55
Rustproofing by Total Protection Ltd with 5-year guarantee or 100,000 miles	45.00	7.65
Aluminium body and wings	100.00	17.00

The prices of all extras apply only when items are included on a new car in production.

EXHIBIT 9.7   Resale prices of Morgan 4/4

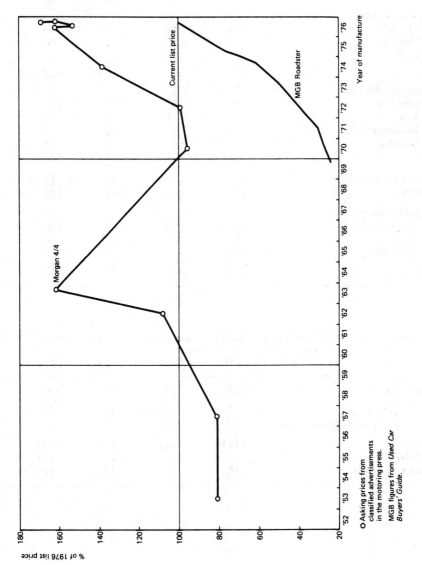

% of 1976 list price

180
160
140
120
100
80
60
40
20

'52 '53 '54 '55 '56 '57 '58 '59 '60 '61 '62 '63 '64 '65 '66 '67 '68 '69 '70 '71 '72 '73 '74 '75 '76

Year of manufacture

Morgan 4/4

Current list price

MGB Roadster

O Asking prices from
classified advertisements
in the motoring press.

MGB figures from *Used Car
Buyers' Guide*.

141

EXHIBIT 9.8 Balance sheet (£ thousand), 1971—5 (year ending 31 May)

	1971	1972	1973	1974	1975
Fixed assets					
Buildings	–	1	60	61	61
Plant	8	6	6	7	8
	8	7	66	68	69
Current assets					
Stock	114	132	175	199	240
Debtors	27	28	37	40	52
Cash	51	39	–	–	12
	192	199	212	239	304
Current liabilities					
Creditors	73	80	117	118	152
Tax	–	4	13	20	12
Dividend	–	–	2	2	2
Overdraft	–	–	4	11	14
	73	84	136	151	180
Net current assets	119	115	76	88	124
Net assets	127	122	142	156	193
Represented by					
Share capital	100	100	100	100	100
Reserves	16	22	40	50	65
Deferred tax	11	–	2	6	28
	127	122	142	156	193

EXHIBIT 9.9 Profit and loss account (£ thousand), 1971—5 (year ending 31 May)

	1971	1972	1973	1974	1975
Turnover	468	527	601	639	801
Profit before tax	27	10	35	23	32
After directors' remuneration	10	10	13	13	13
Tax	(11)	(4)	(15)	(11)	(15)
Dividends	–	–	(2)	(2)	(2)
Retained profit	16	6	18	10	15

EXHIBIT 9.10   Detailed trading accounts, 1974—5

	1974		1975	
	£000	%	£000	%
Turnover	639	100	801	100
Cost of sales				
Raw materials	409		521	
Stock movement	(24)		(40)	
	385	60	481	60
Production wages	138	22	165	21
	523		646	
Gross profit	116	18	155	19
Overheads				
Advertising	8	1	10	1
Other salaries	53		63	
Miscellaneous	32		50	
	93	14	123	15
Profit before tax	23	4	32	4
Number of cars produced		389		391
Average sale price		£1640		£2048
Wages per employee ($n = 80$)		£1730		£2060

10 Barnes and Ward Ltd

SUE BIRLEY

CASE A

Early in September 1970, David Medwin (28) arrived in London from Central Africa to assess on behalf of the shareholders the future of Barnes and Ward Ltd. He discovered an old-fashioned, unprofitable company operating in a declining market. Although his family held a large portion of the shares, David had to take into account the interests of the other shareholders when choosing whether to try to revive the company, to close it down or to put it up for sale.

The company

The Barnes Flooring Company began trading in timber in the 1870s. In 1936 it began to manufacture and instal hardwood flooring. In 1963 it was wholly acquired by an African group in which David's family held over 40 per cent of the issued share capital. At the time, one of the group's main investments was in timber forests in Africa, and Barnes was acquired for two reasons:

(1) as an English outlet for the timber; and
(2) since the other investments were in politically vulnerable countries, a company in the UK would provide a diversification vehicle for the owners of the group.

Almost immediately after the acquisition, in December 1963, Barnes Flooring merged with a local competitor, Ward Timbers, to form the new company of Barnes and Ward Ltd. However, from the time of the acquisition Barnes and Ward were always a worry to the shareholders. Executives from Africa were frequently sent to advise on how to overcome the company's problems. By 1969 the situation had become so serious that they were forced to appoint a well known firm of English management consultants to make specific recommendations on management succession and on overcoming the company's poor marketing performance.

The market

The market in which Barnes and Ward had traditionally competed aimed to provide a high-quality wood floor which did not require further covering, looked attractive and could stand a great deal of wear and tear. Thus, to prevent any dirt penetrating the spores of the wood and at the same time enrich its natural colour, the surface was usually waxed or varnished. With use, this surface would gradually wear away, requiring the floor to be regularly resanded and rewaxed. However, in the 1950s came

144

polyurethane hardglaze seals, such as Ronseal, which gave a much better finish in a variety of colours and lasted longer. This gave new life to the industry.

Wood floors came in three forms – strip, block or mosaic – either presealed or unsealed. The three types were distinguished by the length of wood used for each piece and the resultant variety of designs of floor:

Strip:	random length	by 3 inches
Block:	9 inches	by 3 inches
Mosaic:	4 inches	by 1 inch

The first two were laid individually, but mosaic was arranged in sixteen baskets, each comprising four strips, thus:

The fingers making up each basket were glued onto either a paper or a felt backing to facilitate handling and laying. Although stronger than paper-backed mosaic and easier to lay, feltwood, the more expensive, initially suffered from panel shrinkage. (See Exhibit 10A.3 for the market sizes.)

Whilst block had universal usage, strip had traditionally been used in public buildings such as schools, and mosaic tended to be sold to the speculative housing market. There appeared to be three reasons for this division. First, strip was more expensive than mosaic and the speculative house-builder was price-sensitive; secondly, it was much more pliable and therefore appropriate for any room which might be used for some form of gymnastic activity; and thirdly, and most important of all, concrete slabs replaced joisted sub-floors for ground floors in housing, because of simpler and more economic building methods, thus allowing the use of the shorter, cheaper mosaic.

Most wood floors had a very long lifetime, some lasting for hundreds of years, and consequently the market was perceived by the company to be completely confined to new buildings. Thus, in the majority of cases, the person who made the final decision on the type and make of floor to be laid was the architect. He was, however, greatly influenced, at least in a negative sense, by the flooring contractor, whose technical expertise in laying an even surface which would not lift or bow in the future ensured eventual customer satisfaction. Also, as there was no real product differentiation in the industry, he looked to such factors as price, service and delivery when choosing his supplier. Most manufacturers provided a floor-laying service (sub-contracting) themselves, as well as supplying to other, independent contractors at very competitive terms. This latter factor, plus a shrinkage of demand, had led to overcapacity and a cut-throat price war between manufacturers during the late 1960s. Wood-floor companies tended to be small, with a tradition for quality and service. Their continuing profitability and their production orientation had meant that very few had indulged in any form of diversification and this meant that they were ill equipped to cope with the changing nature of the market.

The total flooring market covered soft-, smooth- and hard-floor finished (soft – carpets; smooth – vinyls and, usually, wood; hard – ceramics, quarry tiles, concrete) and the wood floor could be said to come midway, in both price and customer appeal. For example, at the low end of the hard-floor market was the stone flag, to be found in most old cottages. Although cheap, stone was too heavy for other than the ground floor, cold to the touch and gave an uneven surface. At the high end of the market, the marble tile was very attractive but both cold and expensive and therefore much more likely to be found in an Italian villa than in an English country house. In recent years, however, the market had been changing and the wood-block floor in particular had been faced with competition from a whole new hard-floor spectrum – from boosted concretes to vinyl and vinyl asbestos tiles and sheet. On cost, wear and resilience, blocks performed well, but on appearance and maintenance grounds they were being displaced by more impervious materials, particularly for industrial usage. The new vinyl tiles were easier to wash, had a permanent seal, were quieter, came in a variety of colours and were also cheaper than wood. At the same time, manufacturers of carpet, a previously high-price floor covering, had begun to move down market with materials such as cord or felt, which were cheaper than the traditional wool. Further, both tiles and carpet were made by large companies who sold their products vigorously and aggressively, both to the eventual user and to the architects and specifiers, unlike the small wood-floor manufacturers, who continued to rely upon the loyalty of their traditional customers for sales.

It was within this environment that David began to examine the future of Barnes and Ward Ltd.

Products and sales

Barnes and Ward owned a four-acre site on a canal near the centre of London, convenient for all raw materials to be delivered by barge directly from the docks. On arrival, the wood was stored outside for a minimum of two months for 'drying' before being kiln dried for a further two weeks. The drying process ensured that the moisture was removed, to prevent possible splitting and shrinkage in the future. The wood was then cut, inspected, assembled, sanded (mosaic only) and packed for dispatch (see Exhibit 10A.4). (Mosaic was packed in cardboard boxes which were not waterproof and were difficult to handle with fork-lift trucks.) Much of the work required a high labour content and unfortunately labour turnover was a severe problem. After inspecting the factory and talking to the workers, David came to the conclusion that much of this was owing to the poor working conditions (noisy, old-fashioned machines, repetitive work and poor recreational facilities).

The extensive competition in the market required that orders be satisfied as rapidly as possible, but the bulkiness of the product and the limited space available for storing finished products at Barnes and Ward made this difficult. Tight production scheduling could have eased the problem, but this required close co-operation and communication between production and sales, something which appeared lacking to David.

The company offered the various wooden floors described above in a range of about twelve timbers, a number which was viewed by the assistant to the marketing director as excessive. The products were sold indirectly to the customer through an independent flooring contractor (material sales) or through the company's own contracting service (contract sales). (See Exhibits 10A.5 and 10A.6 for sales analysis.) All contracting sales came from the Greater London area and of this it was estimated that 90 per cent came from the non-domestic environment. Commercial, eductional and health premises seemed to be the principal markets, but no precise data existed on end users. However, statistics on the total Greater London flooring market available in 1970 showed the following:

Type of construction	In specification stage (sq. yds)	In Building stage (sq. yds)
Offices	2,070,000	690,000
Industrial	680,000	650,000
Housing	1,000,000	1,000,000
Educational	1,800,000	2,000,000
Health	2,000,000	2,150,000
Retail	370,000	400,000
	7,920,000	6,890,000

For some time Barnes and Ward had also been selling a plastic-based flooring which was sold in liquid form and was completely self-levelling when poured onto the floor. When hardened it had a marble-like appearance, and it was used extensively in public lavatories as a substitute for tiling. The management viewed it as a 'nice little sideline which needed little capital investment to produce' in a market which, although in its infancy, they considered had great potential. This new seamless floor could be considered as a substitute for most hard-floor finishes. Its major advantages, low maintenance and long life, were first apparent in the hard-finish market, where, by definition, heavy wear and soiling took place. Synthetic seamless floors dealt with this situation better than stone, terrazzo and ceramic surfaces. However, it was estimated that in the next ten years maintenance costs could rise by at least 300 per cent, and therefore the company forecast that seamless floors would soon gain acceptance in the heavy-duty sphere of the smooth-floor market. Taking account of a decline in the total smooth-floor market, it was forecast that by 1985 between 15 and 20 million square yards of seamless flooring would be sold to the smooth-floor market and between 30 and 40 million square yards to the hard-floor market and for use on currently non-floored areas.

Products were priced on a budgeted-cost-plus basis, although when David arrived the budget had not been achieved for the previous five months (see Exhibit 10A.7). This was probably partly because the cost of the timber often varied substantialy over the year, and marketing was rarely in a position to be able to quote a fixed price for a job. Also, although management had no idea of the price elasticity of the market-place, they had the impression that Barnes and Ward was thought to be not very price-competitive. For example, the 1970–71 marketing plan states, 'Barnes and Ward are currently considered by architects and contractors to be a slightly old-fashioned, highly competent, expensive wood block manufacturer, not willing or able to advise on modern floor finishes.'

Timber was bought as a commodity although (unlike cocoa or sugar, for example) no formal market-place existed, and it was therefore not possible to speculate forward through a dealer. Trade contacts and goodwill as well as technical and commercial expertise were therefore essential to the buyer. Barnes and Ward were fortunate in all these respects in their managing director and buyer, Fred Burns, who had worked all his life in the company. Although managing director in name, he had always been buyer in fact – until the advent of the consultants. David says,

> The structure that they imposed made him feel remote from the market and the company and he had reacted by withdrawing further, leaving the company without any real form of leadership. Despite this, there was a very strong bond between him and the employees, many of whom had known him all their working lives and greatly respected him. Also, by the time I arrived on the scene, our timber interests in Africa had been nationalised and we were once more needing the skills of an astute buyer.

The cost of transportation was added, on a per-mile basis, to the price of the materials delivered, and this, plus the fact that the company possessed only three lorries, severely restricted the company's penetration of markets outside London. Normally, a daily delivery service was offered within the London area and a weekly service for customers within a radius of 130 miles. The sales-office manager felt that this was inadequate, even for the London area: 'I understand from one of my customers that they have thirty lorries and load 110 tons of material (equivalent to about 8000 yards of flooring) daily, which is all out on delivery by 11 a.m.' The situation was complicated further by the fact that responsibility for transportation rested with the production function, and marketing felt that orders were often despatched to suit the production schedule rather than customer needs.

Five regional salesmen were responsible for materials sales, three for contract sales and one for seamless floors. Despite the fact that all nine were expected to act as flooring consultants by the customer, none of them had any real technical knowledge and they often had to redirect queries to the factory. Their entire training had involved spending some time (usually a week) in the field with the field-sales manager. In discussion with them David found them to be completely demotivated, so much so that, on their own admission, they were 'not even interested in commission'. The sales-office manager remarked, 'We have had a turnover of nine representatives in $3\frac{1}{2}$ years and this proves in my view that they are not responsible for the increase in the volume of business. Also, it gives a bad image to the company when the customer sees a new representative too often.' David put it thus:

> Very simply, the problem seemed to be that Barnes and Ward just did not know their markets. They didn't know who their customers were, who they should be, what their needs were, what their problems were, or even *where* they were. Lots of the information was known implicitly, but it had not been formalised or written down. There was no real understanding of the term marketing and therefore no marketing

strategy – the product was sold as a commodity and the 'product' was wood floors. Management was wedded to wood.

Organisation and management

After the merger between the Barnes Flooring Company and Ward Timber, very little rationalisation took place. David explains, 'Management did not face up to the difficult decisions which, among other things, required some redundancies at all levels and in particular at the most senior level. Conflicts between the two groups of management inevitably occurred.'

Eventually, in March 1969, the shareholders employed a consulting company obstensibly to study the top-management structure, but in fact to find a way of solving the personal conflicts between the board members. Their preliminary report is shown in Exhibit 10A.1.

David Medwin

David was born in Central Africa, where he spent all his childhood. He obtained a degree in economics from an African university and an MBA from Columbia University in the United States. In 1969, after the death of his father, and after having spent two years with a multinational American bank in London, New York and Johannesburg, he returned to Central Africa to help in the family business. His job was to help sort out the management and organisation problems of the company in Africa, where the investments involved ranching, trading, property, meat distribution, blanket manufacture, wholesaling, timber, hotels and garages. In July 1970 he attended a meeting of the shareholders held to discuss the situation in England. He remarks:

The shareholders were very disenchanted with Barnes and Ward. Not only was the 1970–71 budget unacceptable, but after five months results showed the company to be 20 per cent under budget! They wanted to cut their losses and either liquidate or sell the company. Since my job in Africa was almost finished, I offered to investigate further.

When I arrived at Barnes and Ward I discovered a technically highly-skilled but production-orientated management, most of whom had been with the company all their working lives. There was no real communication or discussion of vital issues and the company was riddled with interdepartmental quarrels and jealousies. The organisation was top-heavy – key executives had become desk-bound and secluded from the market. Moreover, efficiency was lowered by interference from management who had nothing to do and looked for work at head office instead of in the field. Further, the new marketing director, promoted as a result of a recommendation from the consultants, was terribly overburdened. So many functions had literally been thrown into his department that he was not able to concentrate on the priorities – such as selling! In addition, the consultants had tended to take the people most readily available within the organisation and promote them to their level of incompetence. There were however two notable exceptions, in Jeff Kennedy (forty-four), who had been recruited as chief accountant and company-secretary designate, and Tom Cooper (twenty-five), as assistant to the marketing director. When I arrived Tom was about to resign, because he was so frustrated in his attempts to change the company. An extract from a memo which I received from him in August will show what I mean:

Barnes and Ward has not adapted itself to the change in the market place. There were many reasons for this of which you may be more aware than I, since your connection with the company is longer than my own.

After one month with the company I came to the above conclusions and your remark vis-à-vis a dying company in a moribund industry would point to your having reached a similar conclusion rather more quickly.

However, both I and other members of the company have been hampered by the fact that we have been told that 'we must make a success of the field we are in before embarking on new ventures'. My original Marketing Report was a rather more detailed outline of what I have said so far. This was cut and then edited before the report was produced. My point here is that I believe it inviable to promote and continue with hardwood as a staple product. The problem that we have, as I see it, is to develop other revenue-producing commodities/services, and to gradually phase out hardwood. However, no time has been available to properly examine obvious routes to expansion such as package-dealing (i.e. design, planning, systems, supply, fix and to some small extent manufacture).

[David continues]
Barnes and Ward did not have explicit overall objectives. The marketing plan and the consultants' report contained some objectives, but lip-service was paid to them. Even those explicit objectives had not been formally communicated to the rest of the company, which meant that the company had not been mobilised towards achieving them. Unlike the consultants, I felt that Barnes and Ward had a very good team of middle managers who had a wealth of knowledge and experience and who had never really been brought into the decision-making process. These people could make a very valuable contribution to the company and I felt that their views should be sought. If they could participate more in the decision-making process, changes in organisation and policy would be supported and be more effectively communicated to the rest of the staff. Power had been over-concentrated at Barnes and Ward.

Looking at our internal operations, I felt that a number of opportunities existed for simplifying and streamlining operations, but, with the shareholders breathing down my neck, I wasn't sure how much time I had.

EXHIBIT 10A.1   Management consultants' report on Barnes and Ward

ORGANISATION APPRAISAL PRELIMINARY NOTES

Introduction

These preliminary notes summarise the findings and recommendations of the organisation study carried out at Barnes and Ward in February, 1969. These notes precede the formal report, which is in preparation: For this reason, the organisation charts accompanying these notes are copies of draft sketches only.

1   SUMMARY OF COMPANY OBJECTIVES AND DEVELOPMENT POLICY

1.1   Basic Objectives
The basic objectives are to:

- achieve a satisfactory return on the shareholders' investment; this corresponds to a profit before tax of £41,000 being $12\frac{1}{2}$% return on the equity,
- continue to provide a market outlet for Zambian timber; this does not preclude the Company from dealing in other timbers.

1.2   Basic Policy
The basic policy is to:

- expand sales and profits of the existing business
- possibly diversify into other profitable business.

1.3   Resources Available
Finance. £140,000 on deposit account, earning 6% per annum.
Premises and Plant. Fixed assets at the site valued at £215,000. Facilities comprise: main offices, timber wharves, kilns, strip mill and mosaic mill, finished stock stores.
Marketing and Sales. The sales force is just becoming effective after re-organisation, and had five representatives on materials sales, three on contracts sales, and one supporting technical representative on seamless flooring.
Contracts. The installation contracting organisation is well established in the Greater London Council region, and has 24 full-time layers.
Seamless Flooring. This Division has a small production facility and has made only a small penetration of the market.
Commercial Reputation. The Company has a sound reputation in an industry which is not renowned for rapid development.

1.4   Environment
Preliminary study indicates:

- the UK market for hardwood strip and block flooring is virtually static, with demand for each in the region of $\frac{1}{4}$ to $\frac{1}{2}$ million square yards a year;
- the UK market for mosaic floor is between 1 and $1\frac{1}{4}$ million square yards, and is likely to double over the next five years;
- seamless flooring is a growth sector, but there is a trend in demand towards low-cost flooring for industrial and commercial premises.

1.5   Company Development Strategy
Expansion of Existing Business. The basic strategy is to develop the existing manufacturing business nationally, and the installation business in the Greater London Council region.
    In broad terms, to achieve the required profit, the following expansion on current performance is necessary:

151

	£. Values (Sales)
— wood strip and block materials	+10%
— wood mosaic materials	+70%
— seamless flooring	+100%
— installation contracts	+100%

Diversification. It is accepted that B & W does not at present have sufficient Management strength available to assimilate other business operations in new fields. In addition, £140,000 is a small sum upon which to base completely new ventures.

It is therefore considered that diversification in B & W should be limited to additional products which have technology and/or market outlets in common with the existing business.

Diversification in the wider sense (for example, acquisition of other companies in different fields) would be in the nature of a new investment by the Shareholders. It is considered that B & W is not a suitable vehicle for such diversification, which would be better carried out under the responsibility of a Holdings Board representing the Shareholders. The Chairman and Managing Director of B & W might well be members of such a Board.

For these reasons, recommendations for the new B & W organisation are made with only limited diversification in mind.

1.6   Key Activities
Apart from overall planning and direction of the Company, key activities in the organisation are:

Purchasing: timber raw materials.

Financial: control of operating costs in Contracts; evaluation of diversification projects.

Marketing: deployment and control of sales force; market research and sales intelligence; promotion and applications materials; evaluation of diversification projects.

Production: scheduling; optimum utilisation of plant.

Contracts: introducing and negotiating major contracts; control and administration to ensure profitable execution of contracts.

Product Development: identification, evaluation and subsequent development of new or improved materials and methods.

2   THE PRESENT ORGANISATION STRUCTURE

The present organisation structure is shown in Appendix A. It is reasonably sound and workable; existing deficiencies and recommendations for improvement are summarised in the following paragraphs.

2.1   General comments
Levels of activities are not well balanced with staff deployment. This is due to lack of junior clerical supporting staff.

Titles and job specifications are not clearly defined in some instances.

Internal documents and meetings are generally satisfactory.

Management positions are reasonably well covered from the short-term 'stand-in' point of view, with the exception of the Managing Director's position. Management succession is discussed in the section concerning personnel.

2.2   Financial Department
The existing accounting and control systems are sound: staffing is adequate, but it is accepted that there is a case for a junior clerk to take some of the routine load from the senior clerks. The new Accountant/Secretary should be able to cover the combined accounting and Company secretarial functions satisfactorily.

2.3   Contracts Department
A weakness of the present structure is that activities and responsibilities are fragmented between Contracts and Sales Department.

There is a good argument in favour of setting up a completely autonomous, profit-responsible Contracts Division with its own sales force. Such a Division would be in effect a customer of B & W.

A consequence would be that the marketing and selling activities of the Company would be split. This would have important disadvantages:

— the overall strength of the marketing function would be reduced, and exchange of technical and commercial intelligence between materials and contracts sales would be inhibited,
— major architects in the Greater London Council region are important promotional and sales contracts for both materials and contract work.

In the longer term, with diversification in mind, development of strong, integrated marketing function is of prime importance to the Company. It is therefore recommended that a compromise is made:

— Contracts Department to be autonomous and profit-responsible to the Board, under the Managing Director,
— Contracts Office to include estimation, preparation and submission of quotations, ordering of materials etc.,
— a field promotion and selling activities to be provided by Marketing Department,
— financial accounting activities to be provided by Accounts Department.

Contracts field sales staff will answer directly to the Marketing Department, but will be required to co-operate very closely with Contracts Management, who will be responsible for negotiating contracts. Since the heads of departments will be at Board level, the disadvantages usually associated with split responsibilities should be minimal.

2.4   Marketing and Sales
The present structure tends to focus effort upon short-term selling problems, and to inhibit effective planning work. The main causes are:

— lack of junior clerical staff;
— absence of fields sales management;
— lack of staff to provide marketing services.

To introduce effective marketing and planning activities necessary for the Company's development and possible diversification, it is recommended that:

— a Marketing Director is appointed;
— he is provided with a secretary/personal assistant to deal with marketing research, intelligence and publicity services.
— Field Sales Managers are appointed for Materials and Contracts sales;
— a junior clerk/typist is appointed to the Sales Office, to assist with routine work.

2.5   Works Department
The Works is operating satisfactorily. There is a weakness in that lines of authority and responsibility of the Works Director and the Works Manager are interwoven. In effect B & W has two Works Managers, which, in a relatively simple establishment, is not justified. A more suitable structure would be to have a single senior Works executive, with an additional supervisor for the Strip and Block mill.

At present, finished stock stores and finished goods transport are under the control of the Works Department. Since these activities are much more closely associated with the customers, it would be more appropriate for these to be under the control of Marketing. This is not an important matter as the present arrangement operates reasonably well. However, since it is most important that a strong customer-orientation is introduced into the Company, it is recommended that this change should be made in the future, when circumstances are convenient.

2.6   Seamless Materials Division
The Seamless Division has not been very successful. Probably the market for this type of flooring is just opening up in the UK. However, it is considered that in a small company it is not practicable to build up a truly autonomous divisional activity for a specific class of material which has market outlets in common with other products. It is therefore recommended that:

— promotion and selling of seamless materials should be the responsibility of the Marketing Department;
— Contracts Department should be fully capable of advising on, designing and installing seamless and other materials;
— Works Department should be responsible for all production, once the experimental stage has been passed;
— a Product Development Manager should be appointed with responsibilities for — technical development of products, materials and installation techniques; identification and evaluation of new products and of competitors' products; preparation of technical specifications and applicational literature; evaluation of the economics of production and of usage of materials.

   This is a 'staff' position rather than a 'line' position, which would play a major part in diversification planning.

3   PERSONNEL

All senior personnel below the Managing Director were interviewed and assessed. The results are summarised in Appendix B.

4   RECOMMENDED ORGANISATION

Considering the objectives, resources and development policy of the Company, the basic organisation recommendations are shown in Appendix C. This represents the ideal organisation.
   As discussed with the Management, there are variations upon this ideal structure which are acceptable, and which take into account specific skills of individuals and past relationships. These variations concern the structure of the Works Department, and the functional allocation of the Transport and Finished Stock activities. The significant changes are summarised as follows:

4.1   Departmental activities
   Financial Accounting. This Department is unaltered except that the Department head combines Company Secretarial duties with those of Accountant. It is assumed that the new man will be promoted to the Board when he has proved himself. It is accepted that there is sufficient routine clerical work to justify a junior clerk/typist.
   Marketing Department. The new position of Marketing Director is supported by:

— a PA/secretary who is also marketing services officer;
— Fields Sales Managers, one for Materials and one for Contracts. The Contracts FSM should be the 'architects rep.', responsible for dealing with leading architects and institutional staff.

   As the Company's business expands, it is envisaged that there will be requirement for a Sales Manager, and this provides a logical promotional path from field sales.
   The Sales Office Manager is second in seniority and has an additional clerk/typist for routine work.

From the customer-service point of view, it is desirable to place Transport and Finished Stock under Marketing. In the short-term this is not important and these activities may be left under the Works. However, as the Marketing Department gains strength, it is recommended that this change should be made.

Contracts Department. This is now fully integrated, except that initial promotion and selling activities are the responsibility of Marketing. Negotiations, pricing and profits are the responsibility of the Contracts Director. The Department should be allowed to deal with any material, and in the longer term, should not necessarily be restricted to the Greater London Council region.

Works Department. A Works Manager supported by Supervisors is most appropriate for the existing business. It is accepted that the balance of skills, capabilities and personalities of available staff marginally justifies a more complex structure. If this is chosen, Management should be careful to ensure that 'spheres of authority and responsibility' are adjusted to retain optimum working efficiency.

Product Development Department. This replaces the existing Seamless Flooring Division. The scope is widened to cover all products and developments, but executive responsibility is removed and placed with Marketing and Works Departments.

4.2   Company planning, development and diversification

Planning is essentially the responsibility of the Managing Director, supported by the Departmental heads as required. It is assumed that any diversification by B & W, will be concerned with products and/or markets related to existing business. The proposed organisation has adequate marketing, financial accounting and technical effort available to identify, evaluate and plan new projects. Additional specialist and supporting staff necessary to implement new projects would easily be incorporated into the proposed structure.

4.3   Board structure

It is considered that three executive Directors, in addition to the Managing Director, are sufficient for a Company of the size of B & W. It does not follow that Department heads should necessarily be Directors — ability to contribute to the overall planning and direction of the business is the prime criterion. However, it is essential that the major functions of timber purchasing, marketing, finance and technology are represented at Board level. It is therefore recommended that the B & W Board should comprise (under the Chairman and Managing Director) the Marketing Director, the new Contracts Directors, and eventually the new Secretary/Accountant, plus non-executive Directors nominated by the Shareholders. It may be considered desirable to retain the present Works Director on the Board for historical reasons, but the consultants can see no other reason for doing this.

The new structure should enable the Managing Director to delegate routine activities, particularly those associated with Contracts. He will then have more time for monitoring and controlling performance, and for forward planning work.

With expansion and diversification in mind, important activities required of the Chairman are the introduction at high level of new business contracts, and propositions for investment.

If the shareholders are considering additional large-scale investments, involving diversification of interests wider than that envisaged for B & W, it is recommended that this should be handled by a Holdings Board, rather than the executive Board of B & W.

4.4   Management Succession

It is not possible to cover all succession possibilities in a small Company. The best that can be expected is to provide short-term 'stand-in' cover of major activities, and this had been done. From the succession point of view, the important weakness is that there is at present nobody to succeed Mr Burns as Managing Director and timber buyer, although his personal assistant could stand-in for the short-term. It is possible (but not certain) that the Sales Director will prove to be a possible successor in, say, five years' time. The new Secretary/Accountant is expected to be a possible candidate, but is unlikely to have sufficient knowledge of timber. Since timber buying is of prime importance and should be a top-level activity, the most expedient policy is to seek a new Contracts Director who has timber buying skills, and Managing Director potential in the short-term.

Appendix A   Old organisation structure

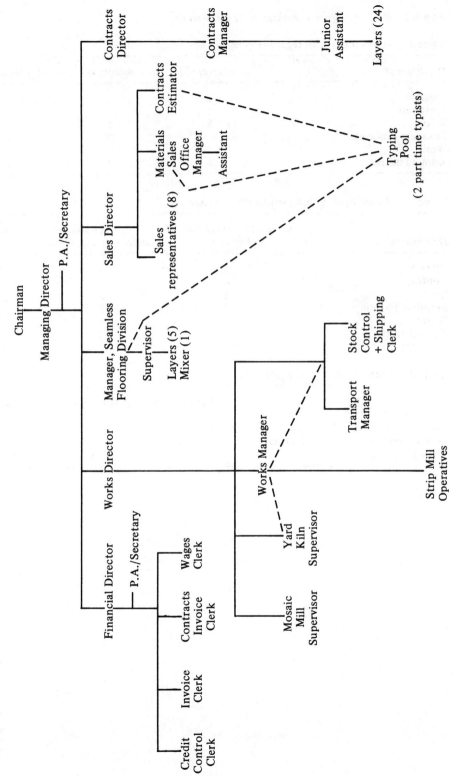

Appendix B   Consultants' management assessment

Table 1   Assessment with regard to present job

Department	Fully capable	Adequate	Inadequate
Finance	1	3	—
Contracts	1	—	1
Sales	5	5	2
Seamless Flooring	—	2	1
Works	2	3	1
Administrative	1	1	—

Table 2   Assessment with regard to future potential

Department	Capable of development to higher level	Correct level, wider responsibilities	Little potentia
Finance	1	3	—
Contracts	—	1	1
Sales	4	6	2
Seamless Flooring	2	1	—
Works	1	3	2
Administrative	—	2	—

Table 3   Present job *v.* future potential

	Fully capable	Adequate	Inadequate
Capable of development to higher level	4	3	1
Correct level, wider responsibilities	6	10	—
Little potential	—	1	4

Appendix C   New organisation structure

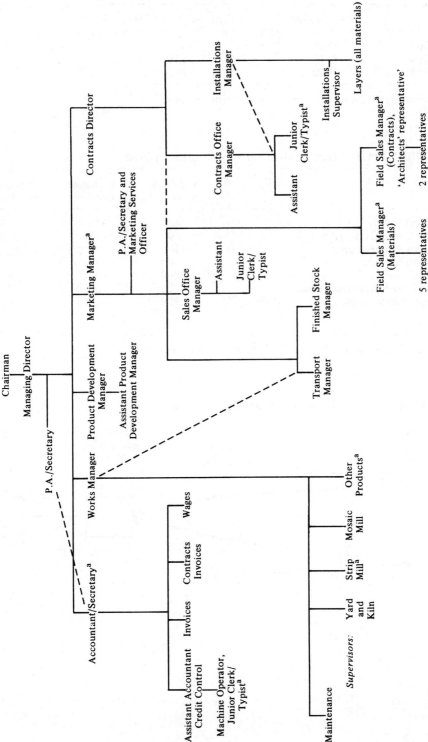

Chairman

Managing Director

P.A./Secretary

Accountant/Secretary[a]

Assistant Accountant
Credit Control

Machine Operator,
Junior Clerk/
Typist[a]

Invoices

Contracts
Invoices

Wages

Works Manager

Supervisors:

Maintenance

Yard
and
Kiln

Strip
Mill[a]

Mosaic
Mill

Other
Products[a]

Product Development
Manager

Assistant Product
Development Manager

Transport
Manager

Finished Stock
Manager

Marketing Manager[a]

P.A./Secretary and
Marketing Services
Officer

Sales Office
Manager

Assistant

Junior
Clerk/
Typist

Field Sales Manager[a]
(Materials)

5 representatives

Contracts Director

Installations
Manager

Contracts Office
Manager

Assistant

Junior
Clerk/Typist[a]

Installations
Supervisor

Layers (all materials)

Field Sales Manager[a]
(Contracts),
'Architects' representative'

2 representatives

[a]*New appointments.*

EXHIBIT 10A.2   The market for hardwood floors (thousand sq. yds)

Year	Total market	Barnes and Ward sales
1967	3425	397
1968	3175	429
1969	2900	435

Note: Data from a report by David Medwin, October 1970.

EXHIBIT 10A.3   Breakdown of hardwood market by product

	Total market (000 sq. yds.)	% change 1967–9	Barnes and Ward share
Imported strip	400	+11.1	6.9
British manufactured mosaic	890	−1.1	26.0
British manufactured block	300	−11.8	32.9
Imported block	100	−16.7	−
British manufactured strip	260	−17.5	17.6
Imported Burma-teak mosaic	700	−30.0	2.5
Other imported mosaic	250	−37.5	6.6
	2900		

Note: Data from a report by David Medwin, October 1970.

EXHIBIT 10A.4   Manufacturing process for mosaic

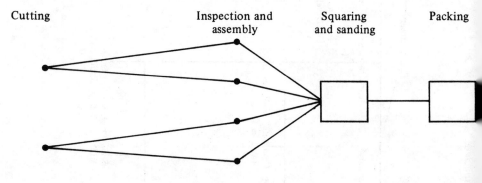

Cutting   Inspection and   Squaring   Packing
                 assembly   and sanding

EXHIBIT 10A.5   Sales by division (£ thousand)

Year (ending March)	Contract	Material	Seamless	Total
1963	425	165	10	600
1964	435	215	35	685
1965	660	290	20	970
1966	550	320	40	910
1967	275	310	30	615
1968	150	360	45	555
1969	220	395	45	660
1970	150	470	65	685

Note: Data from a report by David Medwin, October 1970. Results rounded.

EXHIBIT 10A.6   Percentage gross profit by division

Year (ending March)	Contract	Material	Seamless	Total
1964	18.2	20.1	32.8	20.0
1965	18.1	15.0	26.6	16.6
1966	20.6	22.8	26.9	22.2
1967	18.0	15.8	26.8	16.6
1968	26.7	22.2	34.1	24.3
1969	26.4	22.6	36.4	24.8
1970	24.0	20.0	15.4	20.5

EXHIBIT 10A.7   Material sales activity: wood

(1) Evaluation of situation at end of August 1970

(a) In sq. yds.

	Budget	*Sales*	*Over (under)*	*% over (under)*
Blocks	37,470	30,814	(6,656)	(18)
Strip	22,065	15,889	(6,176)	(28)[a]
Mosaic:				
felt-backed	83,270	78,990	(4,280)	(5)
Mosaic:				
paper-backed	26,555	19,588	(6,967)	(26)
Imported strip	12,485	14,409	1,924	15
Imported mosaic	13,325	17,821	4,496	34
	195,170	177,511	(17,659)	(9)

(b) In £s

	Budget[b]	*Sales*	*Over (under)*	*% over (under)*
Blocks	59,019	48,482	(10,537)	(18)
Strip	44,130	26,062	(18,068)	(41)[a]
Mosaic:				
Felt-backed	81,190	77,985	(3,205)	(4)
Mosaic:				
paper-backed	22,506	16,667	(5,839)	(26)
Imported strip	20,295	22,021	1,726	8.5
Imported mosaic	11,990	15,418	3,428	28.5
	239,130	206,635	(32,495)	(13.5)

162

(2) Projection of current performance of selling price and volume to 31 March 1971, seasonally adjusted

(a) In sq. yds.

	Budget	Sales[c]	Over (under)	% over (under)
Blocks	90,000	66,558	(23,442)	(26)
Strip	53,000	47,320	(5,680)	(11)
Mosaic:				
felt-backed	200,000	170,618	(29,382)	(15)
Mosaic:				
paper-backed	63,775	42,310	(21,465)	(34)
Imported strip	30,000	31,123	1,123	4
Imported mosaic	32,000	38,493	6,493	20
	468,775	396,422	(72,353)	(15)

(b) In £

	Budget	Sales[c]	Over (under)	% over (under)
Blocks	141,750	104,721	(37,029)	(26)
Strip	106,000	96,697	(9,303)	(9)
Mosaic:				
felt-backed	195,000	168,447	(26,553)	(14)
Mosaic:				
paper-backed	54,050	36,000	(18,050)	(33)
Imported strip	48,750	47,565	(1,185)	(2)
Imported mosaic	28,800	33,302	4,502	16
	574,350	486,732	(87,618)	(15)

[a] Larger discrepancy because of price allowance in budget for order not yet delivered.
[b] Trade promotion deducted.
[c] Includes estimated 13,000 yds. strip on contract not yet delivered, at 62s. 2d. sq. yd.

The implications of (2) for the material-sales budget if the other two lines, seamless and sundries, are similarly projected, is a recovery of £150, 109:

	£
Fixed costs	165,627
Loss	15,518

The seasonal adjustment referred to in (2) is based on a historical 10 per cent drop in sales in the second half of the year. The marketing plan and budget were based on a considerable reduction in this seasonal trend, owing to supernormal promotional activity.

EXHIBIT 10A.8   Consolidated profit and loss account (£) (year ending 31 March)

	1963	1964	1965	1966	1967	1968	1969	1970
Sales								
Contracts	423,237	436,959	662,259	549,560	273,663	150,446	222,279	152,961
Material sales	167,094	214,625	291,229	321,603	311,761	360,922	393,886	477,539
Seamless	10,672	29,378	18,647	38,933	32,189	49,827	46,388	60,053
	601,003	680,962	972,135	901,096	617,613	561,195	662,553	690,553
Gross profit	119,531	144,670	168,972	203,222	106,179	138,706	168,834	147,099
Trading expenses	33,746	63,854	83,670	75,479	41,266	50,636	59,466	71,663
Trading profits before deducting:	85,785	80,816	85,302	127,743	64,913	88,070	109,368	75,434
Head-office expenses	35,965	37,716	51,579	40,823	36,337	32,568	34,829	45,786
Directors' expenses (incl. commission to 1969, thereafter nil)	15,408	16,428	16,218	21,552	19,842	23,017	20,871	13,518
Bad debts less recovered	4,581	512	3,592	7,162	(1,596)	276	5,707	4,313
Interest payable (net)								
Loan	–	–	–	17,882	17,882	17,798	17,798	17,798
Other	(122)	431	2,326	3,780	(3,075)	(8,316)	(7,205)	(475)
Profits before taxation	31,499	26,470	16,675	32,617	(4,453)	22,727	35,517	(11,421)
Provision for taxation	20,210	15,584	(524)	14,795	1,079	8,164	17,878	–
Net profits for year	11,289	10,886	17,199	21,879	(3,127)	13,146	17,913	(11,421)
Dividends paid/proposed								
Ordinary shares	7,809	–	–	–	–	6,964	8,357	–
Preference shares	1,099	3,815	10,939	–	–	–	–	–
Unappropriated profits	9,590	16,564	23,604	47,313	44,186	48,596	57,002	51,163

EXHIBIT 10A.9 Consolidated balance sheet (£) (year ending 31 March)

	1963	1964	1965	1966	1967	1968	1969	1970
Fixed assets at cost	191,115	n.a.	410,884	362,837	368,954	361,808	369,627	375,427
Less depreciation	116,500	n.a.	170,948	139,839	150,521	147,293	158,660	169,761
	74,615	177,281	239,936	222,998	218,433	214,515	210,967	205,666
Investments								
Quoted		4,475	4,475	4,475	4,475	4,475	65,049	54,183
Trade	100	100	100	3,350	4,186	586	436	436
	100	4,575	4,575	7,825	8,661	5,061	65,485	54,619
Current assets								
work in progress	45,375	110,046	135,373	92,618	39,804	28,098	20,121	13,540
Less cash received on account	26,863	59,847	73,378	82,983	34,683	24,610	10,557	4,766
	18,512	50,197	61,995	9,365	5,121	3,488	9,564	8,744
Stocks	169,494	227,825	221,159	243,450	163,088	164,023	191,163	206,537
Debtors	133,534	204,722	196,800	228,111	143,600	133,206	169,227	172,313
Cash at bank balances	511	18,494		31,209	161,326	163,859	53,951	30,715
	322,051	501,238	479,954	512,405	473,135	464,576	423,905	418,339
Less Current liabilities								
Creditors	79,861	155,851	90,360	73,303	56,379	42,660	43,584	60,867
Bank loans and overdrafts	11,091		94,163	65,000	55,000	45,000	35,000	25,000
Provision for taxation	19,851	22,902	5,020	23,783	11,372	6,117	19,112	2,738
Provision for dividends	373	3,099				6,964	8,357	
Staff pension and benevolent funds			12,625	10,373	8,930	7,548	6,225	4,913
	111,176	181,852	202,168	172,459	131,681	108,289	112,278	93,518
Net current assets	210,875	319,386	277,786	339,946	341,454	356,287	311,627	324,821
Net assets	285,590	501,242	522,297	570,769	568,548	575,863	588,079	585,106
Total assets	396,766	683,094	724,165	743,228	700,229	684,152	700,357	678,624
Share capital								
Ordinary	2,550	2,692	2,786	2,786	2,786	2,786	2,786	2,786
Preference	30,000	223,528	223,528	223,528	222,473	222,473	222,473	222,473
Loan								
	32,550	226,220	226,314	226,314	225,259	225,259	225,259	225,259
Capital reserves		15,008	25,014	48,188	48,188	49,326	51,003	53,034
Revenue reserves	243,450	243,450	247,365	248,954	250,915	252,682	253,950	256,028
Unappropriated profits	9,590	16,564	23,604	47,313	44,186	48,596	57,867	50,785
	285,590	501,242	522,297	570,769	568,548	575,863	588,079	585,106

CASE B

As a result of his investigations into the declining Barnes and Ward, in September 1970 (see Case A), David Medwin came to the conclusion that it was possible and even desirable to save the business. But time was short and action must be swift if the shareholders were to be mollified. In the market place the strategy was to cut prices, promote aggressively and go for growth. Internally, the organisation was simplified and reduced (see Exhibit 10B.1).

Fortune, in the form of the 1971–72 speculative housing boom, smiled upon Barnes and Ward. Within six months two of their competitors had closed down, and by March 1974 sales had more than doubled and profit before tax had increased from a loss in 1970 to £164,928 (see Exhibit 10B.2). In Tom Cooper's words,

> The price-cutting exercise virtually killed competition, so that by 1974 we controlled almost 75 per cent of the wood-floor market. But we spent so much time trying to meet orders that we had no time to do anything else and it wasn't until 1974, when the bottom dropped out of the speculative housing market, that we began to think about the longer-term future. To help us in this I commissioned a market-research study into the hardwood flooring market.

This case first describes in detail the actions taken in the dash for growth, and secondly summarises the results of the market-research study.

The dash for growth

TOM COPPER: Hitherto the attitude in the company had been that because of the quality of our product Barnes and Ward had a right to expect a higher price. The feeling ran through the company that it was a proud act to obtain a large order at full list price, and that lack of sales were the fault of the salesmen who could not sell. In selling, we concentrated upon the flooring contractors, since they were the only part of our existing market which we could capture readily. With the new, reduced prices, salesmen (to be known as flooring consultants) were encouraged to be more aggressive in their approach to customers. The company had to understand that, as far as the flooring contractor was concerned, the brand name of a product was not of paramount importance. Although Barnes and Ward flooring was recognised as being one of the best-quality wood floorings, the customer was frequently more interested in price, availability, delivery, and the help that the manufacturer could give in obtaining specifications and in advising on installation.

What we had to sell was therefore
- (a) good-quality hardwood flooring in timbers that were required, where these were available to Barnes and Ward;
- (b) a competitive price on which we would negotiate for large orders;
- (c) a regular delivery service within our delivery area, with delivery within one week from order outside this area if required;
- (d) assistance from Barnes and Ward in negotiating with the specifier; and
- (e) advice on installation available from Barnes and Ward consultants.

Promotion

The major promotional change was the writing into the October 1970 price list of low prices for sapele and African teak, mosaics, block and strip; these prices were amplified by mailshots, concurrent with the new price list, stressing the new low prices and emphasising the superiority of African teak over Burma teak. Additionally, a new price list was issued every two months, regardless of price changes, in an effort to keep the name of Barnes and Ward continuously in front of the customer and provide the facility for price changes to be made to take advantage of market conditions.

Service

The need to generate customer loyalty through offering an effective delivery service was approached in the following way.

1. Goods to customers within an approximate range of 125 miles were delivered within one week of order, if so required by the customer, and on a prearranged day within that week. These deliveries were made using Barnes and Ward vehicles.
2. Goods to customers outside the 100–125 mile range were delivered within one week of order, if so required by the customer, using hired transport.
3. Materials and equipment to sites of Barnes and Ward contract operations were delivered at such time as not interfere with the efficiency of those operations.

Customer relations

TOM COOPER: Customer relations were added to the 'product package', since they were a major part of what Barnes and Ward had to sell to the flooring contractor. In any industry where large sums of money are involved, the material supplier is usually blamed by the flooring contractor for any fault which occurs on site. He then attempts to obtain not only the costs of the material which he believes is faulty but also his costs of laying and of wasted time. Barnes and Ward materials were generally of good quality, but however slanderous and abusive the customer he had to be handled with extreme care, and any imputation that the problem occurred through his, rather than our, negligence, even if obviously true, could and did lose customers. We decided that it would usually be expedient to offer partial recompense, or in the case of small problems, complete settlement rather than lose future business.

Organisation structure

DAVID: We got rid of all the organisational frills immediately. For example, in such a small company there was no need for a separate product-development manager, and so he was made redundant giving the company an immediate saving of £3000 per year.

Also, with only two representatives responsible to him, the post of contracts field-sales manager [see Case A] was unnecessary. Even worse, the management consultants had promoted our best salesman to this office job. We returned him to the field and he was delighted. Five of the nine representatives were sacked and the new ones were given both responsibility and power. The marketing director was made totally responsible for the commercial viability of the material-sales operation, matters of internal policy, personnel and pricing being at his discretion. The sales-office manager was given guidelines for negotiating prices for up to 10,000 square yards, orders over this figure being passed to the marketing director.

In the past the salesmen had not been supervised closely enough, because of the field sales-manager's commitment to the seamless-flooring division and to policing head-office functions. Therefore, the marketing director was made directly responsible for checking the sales force. Tom Cooper began to prepare monthly order targets, which were discussed with salesmen, who were retitled 'consultants'! Those who did not obtain their monthly order targets were investigated immediately. Three months' successive failure to meet the target with no satisfactory reason available incurred dismissal. However, a cash prize of £200 was awarded to the man who had, on an aggregated monthly basis, exceeded his target by the greatest percentage margin. Eligibility for this scheme began after three months of service.

The new physical-distribution manager was given full management responsibility for the distribution function, and, instead of reporting to the production director, he now reported directly to the managing director. He was allocated a budget which included sufficient for payment of his staff, particularly drivers, and also salaries for himself and his office staff. He was fully responsible for the distribution of the company's goods in the United Kingdom, the planning and provision of the vehicles necessary to fulfil this function, including the hiring of vehicles and the use of outside transport contractors, and the planning and purchasing of handling equipment and hiring labour. The goods-inward function previously held by him was removed from him, as were all functions not strictly relevant to the distribution activity.

With these actions we had reduced the number of executives in the company, and so Jack Burns, the managing director, became more actively involved in the business, especially in the fields of production, purchasing and contracting, where he excelled. I was appointed chairman. At this point we called a meeting of the whole company, at which I explained our position and gave them all achievable but demanding objectives.

Within two months it had become clear that both the marketing director and the contracts director were inadequate and they were sacked. Tom Cooper, assistant to the marketing director, became the new marketing director. All these organisational changes resulted in an immediate annual saving of £30,000 – quite an encouragement for the shareholders.

Control systems

In order properly to control and monitor the programme the following controls were instituted (* indicates new documentation).

1. Monthly order *versus* target summary. Used by marketing director for checking performance and issued to all consultants* to give an idea of own and overall company position.
2.* Monthly sales/orders totals and aggregates for product lines, showing monthly performance against target, and aggregate against aggregate target, as actual and percentage. Issued by accounts to all managers.
3. Monthly sales/orders totals and aggregates in area and value as currently produced by accounts. Issued to all managers.

4.* Monthly price comparison of 200 sq. yds of Barnes and Ward line/types and equivalent, to be provided by sales-office manager for marketing director on a monthly basis.
5. Monthly stocks and orders listing, as issued by the current circulation list.
6.* Monthly list of deliveries to material-sales customers by line/type. Issued by finished-stock clerk to management committee.
7.* Monthly listing of all trade promotion and price cutting on orders taken.

Diversification

DAVID: Our objective had been to gain a larger share of the hardwood flooring market and we were remarkably successful. By late 1973 we estimated that we had an 80 per cent market share. However, from such a position any further significant increase in turnover had to come from an expanding market and all indications both from the market-place itself and from published figures pointed to a decreasing and weakening market. We had already attempted diversification in two fields, seamless floors and in contract flooring, both of which on the surface at that time had bright futures. But in our haste we had not looked beneath the surface, and in each case the economic structure of the flooring industry proved to be our downfall. There just wasn't sufficient profit to be made at the right price. In the case of seamless, the floor had to be laid down by a skilled person and insufficient skills were available. Also, oil was the main constituent of the product and the 1973 oil crisis was the final blow to the project.

The contract-flooring department began hopefully. Our representatives were given every assistance by the major flooring manufacturers, and in some cases were even trained by them. But we soon discovered that there were too many small flooring contractors operating on very low overheads for any larger company to compete. We just couldn't charge an economic price.

So, we commissioned a market-research study. In the short term, we hoped that it would help us formulate a future marketing policy for flooring and in the long term we wanted information upon which our investment policies could be built.

The market research study

The research was divided into two phases:

1. a quantitative phase, consisting of a series of telephone interviews with flooring contractors; and
2. a qualitative phase, consisting of group discussions and depth interviews.

The study was completed in September 1974 and the following is a digest of the main findings of the study, prepared by Tom Cooper.

QUANTITATIVE SURVEY

The market in 1973

From the information shown in the report, cross-referred with the size of sample, plus total known users, it is possible to indicate Barnes and Ward penetration of the market as follows.

169

(a) BY AREA

Area	Million sq. yds.	Barnes and Ward orders	Barnes and Ward penetration (%)
South East	0.84	0.40	47
South West and Wales	0.27	0.16	59
Midlands	0.20	0.08	40
North	0.55	0.11	20
Other (head office + contracts)		0.01	—
	1.86	0.85	45

Of the above UK total, about 0.38 million square yards are accounted for by two contractors who import or manufacture material for their own use (Tophams, and Beckett and Guthrie). If these are removed, penetration increases in the Southern and Northern areas, and total penetration increased to 64 per cent.

(b) BY PRODUCT

Product	Million sq. yds.	Barnes and Ward orders	Barnes and Ward penetration (%)
Blocks	0.24	0.10	41
Mosaic	1.22	0.65	54
Strip	0.34	0.10	29
	1.78	0.85	48

Again, if corrections are allowed for Tophams, and Beckett and Guthrie, the Barnes and Ward position improved to:

	%
Blocks	66
Mosaic	59
Strip	59
	56

(c) GEOGRAPHICAL AREA BY TOTAL WOOD-FLOORING PERCENTAGE SHARES

	South East	South West	Midlands	North	Wales
Block	9.7	5.2	22.4	20.8	21.8
Mosaic	80.2	75.1	48.7	36.6	44.2
Strip	7.3	15.6	27.0	41.3	29.4
Parquet	2.8	4.1	1.9	1.3	4.6

It is clear from the survey that strip and block flooring are concentrated in the hands of Tophams and to a lesser degree Beckett and Guthrie. This is because of, first, their greater ability to sell to the specifier than the smaller flooring contractor, and, secondly, Barnes and Ward inactivity at this level. Our reasonable penentration in the strip sector, if they are excluded, depends heavily on imported strip, which alone holds 47 per cent of the available market.

(d) BY PRODUCT

This section is the core of the survey and will help to plan the pattern of future activity.

As can seen from the table below, in 1973 there were only four significant types of project where hardwood flooring was used by those interviewed, *viz.* education, housing (speculative and private) and sports.

Project	Percentage usage				
	Barnes and Ward customers			Non-customers	Total
	Large	*Medium*	*Small*		
Speculative housing	11.8	48.2	22.0	1.5	28.3
Hospitals	1.0	0.9	0.7	–	0.9
Education	30.8	16.0	9.7	41.5	20.7
Sports/recreation	18.4	4.8	7.6	7.5	10.2
Dance/disco floors	11.1	3.5	5.2	5.0	6.5
Private housing	17.1	22.6	43.4	34.1	25.6
Offices	3.6	1.0	6.7	5.2	3.3
Industrial	5.1	1.7	2.2	4.2	3.1
Shops	1.1	1.3	2.5	1.0	1.4
	100.0	100.0	100.0	100.0	100.0
Number interviewed	22	44	54	9	129
Total, sq. yds.	222,600	261,056	138,990	24,110	646,756

Note: These data were collected in response to the question, 'For what sort of projects do you in fact lay hardwood flooring?', which was put to the sample of flooring contractors.

The above table is crucial, since all the data in the second, qualitative part of the survey have to do with the attitude of specifiers toward the continuing use of wood in the different sectors.

In terms of geographical distribution, speculative-housing usage is mainly in the South, biased to the South East; private-housing is as above but with a Western bias; education usage appears uniformly distributed; and sports and recreational usages are more likely to occur in the North.

Of major significance however, is the amount of private housing.

(e) BY SPECIFIER

The main specifiers identified in the study were as follows.

		%
Speculative housing		
Builder		57
Developer		15
		72
Private housing		
Owner		39
Builder		32
		71
Education		
Local-authority architect		70
Sports and recreation		
Local-authority architect		43
Owner		34
		77

To summarise, with the exception of private-house owners, 63 per cent of the existing contract market is available through a small number of individuals.

(f) BY PRODUCT AND PROJECT

		%
Speculative housing	Mosaic	91
Private housing	Mosaic	66
	Block ⎫ Strip ⎬	34
Education	Mosaic	41
	Strip	34
	Block	25
Sports and recreation	Strip	80
	Mosaic	20

The market in 1973 v. 1972

Whilst any change in these years will be dwarfed by the change in 1973 to 1974, it is in a sense more significant in that it begins to provide pointers for the reasons in the general long-term decline in the use of wood flooring.

In bold terms the survey states the increase (decrease) in usage 1972 to 1973 is as follows:

	%
Mosaic	(3)
Block	(37)
Strip	(12)

Comparative figures for Barnes and Ward yardage sales for nine months to December 1972 *v.* nine months 1973 are:

	%
Mosaic	(5)
Block	(4)
Strip	(11)

There is good reason to believe, based on total completions for the two years (1973 5 per cent down on 1972), that the mosaic situation was one of no change in terms of yardage per unit. The gain in Barnes and Ward block and strip sales is the result of Beckett and Guthrie's demise as suppliers to the trade, and I am inclined to accept a severe reduction in market size over the period.

Trade opinion and suggestions

This section of the report effectively provides a bridge between the survey and the quantitative/qualitative survey among specifiers.

Two main, and *very important*, points emerge.

1. *Price.* As is echoed in the qualitative survey, the cost of hardwood flooring has now increased to the point where it is no longer a high-class, higher-priced competitor with smooth floor coverings promotable on the grounds that it has a longer life and better appearance, but that it is now bracketed with the cheaper forms of contract carpeting, which have in the last three years become available in hard-wearing qualities at a lower price.

   The implications of this are important. It means that wood flooring will shortly no longer be used to a large extent in institutional and commercial projects as a high-wear floor finish with better appearance than vinyls. This could reduce the size of the market on a 1973 basis by some 30 per cent, cutting almost equally into mosaic, block and strip demand, and necessarily concentrates the potential for wood flooring into the decorative (mainly domestic) and specialist (mainly sports) markets.
2. *Service.* A variety of points are mentioned, the major ones being prices and range instability, closely followed by long and unreliable delivery dates, and, in the North, bad distribution. The impression gained by the researchers was that the bulk of flooring contractors find the situation so unattractive as to preclude their making any active attempt to sell wood floorings. Again the implication is simple. Barnes and Ward so far have depended on the contractors to sell for them. This they are in the main no longer doing.
3. *Promotion.* There was a feeling in the flooring trade that wood flooring requires more promotion that it gets. This was to be expected. It was significant that the suggestions made by the trade for promotion tended to be oriented towards domestic uses of wood flooring rather than contract usage.

QUALITATIVE SURVEY

Speculative housing

It is hard to summarise the views expressed by the specifiers and flooring contractors involved more than they are already summarised in the report itself. However, the keynote would seem to be a genuine liking for wood flooring on the part of the specifier which is being eroded by a need for increased cost control. But the need for increased cost control on the part of the speculative builder has also resulted in the elimination or

downgrading of a large number of finishes, such as doors, joinery, etc. There is no way
to combat this trend, and it is almost certain that hardwood-flooring usage in this sector
will decline to use either in a few very expensive dwellings where the builder needs to
give the impression of a good finish, or by some builders – i.e Bovis – who have a
marketing strategy regarding product designed on the basis of maximum differentiation
from competition and a quality impression. A further problem with timber flooring is
the need to provide electricity for sanding and the unreliability of the material when laid
on a damp screed.

However, the view that the demand for close carpeting has suddenly made wood
flooring redundant is contradicted by a large consumer survey carried out in 1972, to
which I had limited access and which detected that this demand had, in fact, been stable
since the mid-1960s.

Private housing

No specific work was done in this sector since it was beyond the original brief, but there
were a number of comments about the increasing use of wood floors in the fast growing
DIY market.

Education

The interviews here tended to confirm that it was only in general purpose, high-traffic
areas that hardwood flooring was likely to be used, particularly where these areas
doubled as gymnasia.

Sports and recreation

It would appear that wood flooring is still considered here, and also that this market is
an expanding one. However, there is a real danger that timber could be eliminated by
the energetic marketing of a whole range of alternatives, such as Granflex Carpet or the
new range of vinyls from the major manufacturers. The need would appear to be, as
always, for cheaper finishes and more adaptable surfaces.

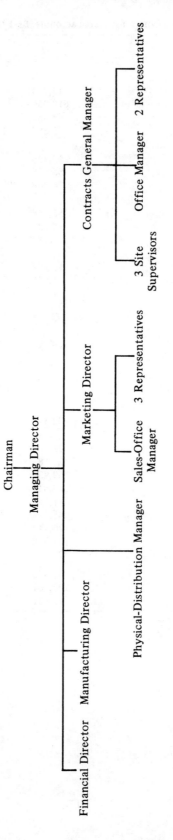

EXHIBIT 10B.1 New organisation structure

EXHIBIT 10B.2   Main items from consolidated accounts (£), 1971−4 (year ending 31 March)

	1971	1972	1973	1974
Sales				
Contracts	142,984	185,970	238,590	246,073
Material sales	618,030	889,579	1,160,544	1,383,188
Seamless flooring	64,355	45,139	48,816	49,426
	825,369	1,120,688	1,447,950	1,678,687
Gross profit	162,426	199,107	313,181	403,306
Trading Expenses	85,458	77,287	88,438	108,011
Trading Profit	76,968	121,820	224,743	295,295
Head-office expenses	52,244	43,809	51,948	65,835
Directors' expenses	15,708	25,081	29,473	33,209
Bad-debt loss recovered	(982)	1,298	1,427	5,819
Interest payable (net)				
Loan	17,798	17,798	17,798	17,798
Other	1,625	2,334	114	(9,534)
Profits before taxation	(12,362)	35,944	112,745	164,928
Provision for taxation	−	13,179	46,058	82,291
Net profits for year	(12,362)	22,765	66,687	75,637
Dividends paid/proposed				
Ordinary shares	−	−	−	−
Preference shares	−	−	−	−
Unappropriated profits	38,546	62,410	129,097	204,734
Fixed assets at book value	196,404	193,796	209,522	219,705
Work in progress (net)	20,181	24,425	42,352	57,055
Stocks	269,930	255,846	236,933	506,303
Debtors and bills receivable	243,637	234,770	328,918	352,521
Cash on hand and at bank	1,455	1,560	2,725	3,720
Quoted investments	48,584	48,584	38,830	38,830
Creditors	70,747	72,668	98,182	191,158
Bank overdraft	137,908	82,456	40,319	126,106
Unrecovered loans	222,473	222,473	222,473	222,473
Capital reserves	52,920	52,930	52,975	52,975
General reserve	243,761	243,761	243,761	243,761
Depreciation reserve	12,831	15,224	17,742	20,260

CASE C

The market-research study commissioned in 1973 and reported in 1974 (see Case B) had indicated four significant areas using hardwood flooring: speculative housing, education, sports and recreation, and private housing. The last was a surprise to the company, and, although there were no data on the breakdown between new and existing houses, there was a hint that wood was being used increasingly in the do-it-yourself market. Barnes and Ward decided to launch their mosaic on the DIY market.

Their major expenditure was in promotion and advertising, for with no High Street presence they had to generate customer demand. The only extra production facility needed was a £2000 shrink-pack machine. Advertisements were placed in all the major DIY and house magazines, such as *House and Garden* and *Ideal Home*. The message was 'Wood is warm' (see Exhibit 10C.1). The objective was to promote the concept of wood floors and at the same time create a brand image. The campaign was highly successful, particularly since the principal competition on the shelf was either cork or vinyl tiles, neither of which had the quality image of wood.

Along with the launch into the DIY market three other changes were made. First, research into the technical aspects of producing presealed floors and thinner floors was instituted. Secondly, merchanting, which had always been a small part of the business, was emphasised: the customer could now buy Barnes and Ward flooring, sealer and adhesive, all from the same shop. Thirdly, the emphasis on contract sales was reduced even further and limited to 'prestige' highly skilled jobs in London. For example, the company was commissioned to lay the stages for the new National Theatre and to maintain the stages at Covent Garden.

TOM: The hardest part of the changes in concentration was not finding the money or the manpower, but in changing from a position similar to a timber merchant to a position almost exactly congruent with that of a flooring manufacturer.

The strategy was so successful that by the summer of 1975 Barnes and Ward flooring was to be found in all the major DIY chain stores. The mosaic mill was running at full capacity all the time.

DAVID: But we hadn't really solved anything. We were still operating in shrinking markets with a senile product range, volatile and increasing raw-material costs and escalating labour costs. The book values of our assets were under 20 per cent of their present-day replacement values. If we were to survive we had to modernise our plant and to do this we needed a minimum gross profit of 30 per cent based on realistic depreciation charges. Potential users believed that wood flooring was difficult and expensive to instal and maintain. They were right. Our existing products could not be promoted for much longer, there were just too few positive attributes to promote!

Resources available

Land and buildings

Of the total site area of about 187,000 square feet (4.3 acres) 89.5 per cent was used. The remaining 10.5 per cent consisted of inaccessible open dumping ground (4500

177

square feet), which could be relatively easily used, and sloping wasteland (1400 square feet), which would be expensive to use productively. Out of the productive 89.5 per cent nearly 35 per cent was used for roads and access.

As at 31 March 1974, the book value of the land, building and equipment totalled £188,767, as compared with a replacement value assessed at £1,139,500 (see Exhibit 10C.3). (The average age of the plant was fifteen years.)

Capacity

The mosaic mill was running at full capacity, but the demand for block and strip was such that the mills were running at only about 40 per cent of capacity. A new mosaic line could double turnover, but this would involve not only the new equipment (see below) but also a substantial increase in working capital to fund stocks.

Approximate costs for new mosaic line:

	£
1 pre-finishing plant	50,000
2 cutting lines (£7000 each)	14,000
4 assemblers (£7000 each)	28,000
1 sander	25,000
1 dust collector	25,000
	142,000

Labour

DAVID: Over the last few years we had witnessed severe inflation. Fortunately, because our wages policy followed the construction industry, which had been more severely depressed than other industries, we had yet to feel the full impact of the wages explosion. Also, with more than 50 per cent of our labour female we had to face the prospect of equal pay.

Between 1971 and 1974, while the total cost of personnel had increased by 76 per cent, the average cost per person had only increased by 11 per cent – the expansion in people had been at the lower, unskilled level, and, with increasing social and political pressure upon companies to increase the wages of the lower paid, this could be a severe problem in the future.

Further, labour turnover was high, and, although the cost had not been quantified, we felt that the resultant costs to the company were high.

Up until then we had rationalised the problem with the argument that 'our labour turnover is no worse than the average for the industry in our area, and, anyway, because of the type of machinery and processes we use, there is little we can do about it'. But do something we must.

Raw materials

The previous three years had seen an explosion in raw timber prices and the cost to Barnes and Ward of their major input had more than doubled. There were two ways in which this cost could be reduced. First, the amount of timber used to produce the finished product, and, second, the cost of carrying the timber, could be reduced. In the first case, Tom had already begun to investigate laminated and veneered products, but he felt that any pay-off would show only in the long term. In the second case, there were no data on the current cost of carrying timber, although there were indications that it was much higher than in the industry. For example, over the previous five years Barnes and Ward had held, on average, 104 days' stock as against the industry average of 81 days.

DAVID: From various internal and external sources we had potentially over £1 million available to finance new developments. However, when one considered the cost of replacing buildings, installing new plant and financing new working capital, what at first sight appeared quite a lot of money was in fact fairly limited. Barnes and Ward had already had its 'stock crisis' and if we were to avoid a 'fixed assets crisis' it was essential that we husband our cash resources and not fritter them away in many small but not significantly profitable expenditures.

At the time we were reasonably liquid but we would eventually probably have to repay the Inland Revenue the deferred taxes arising out of the 1974 stock-relief measures. We would also need to pay annual dividends and in 1985 (10 years away) repay the loan stock of nearly £200,000.

We had about £450,000 of assets within the company which we could liquidate over a fairly short period of time if we found the right investment opportunity and were seriously short of cash. Over and above such internal sources, we had considerable unutilised borrowing capacity, always assuming we had the profits to pay the interest and servicing costs.

There's nothing so good as natural wood flooring . . .

Never has there been a time when wood flooring was out of fashion. Today, it's economic price and natural advantages are being appreciated more than ever.

There is a traditional quality about wood that virtually no other flooring material can claim . . . and with just a minimal amount of attention (no more than you would devote to the care of any good carpet in your home), wood has the ability to give long years of lasting service while still retaining so much of its original, distinctive appearance.

With the B & W range you have the added advantage of being able to select from the finest hardwoods in the world — each chosen for their warmth of colour and richness of pattern as much as for their robust qualities. (Each, we might mention, is a wood grown in abundance in areas of Africa, Brazil, Scandinavia, India and Sri Lanka where deforestation is not possible, nor, indeed, permitted.)

And if it is possible to improve on nature B & W have done so. Many of our floorings have a specially formulated, sealed-in finish that contributes to their glowing appearance, simplifies cleaning and adds even more to their durability.

Another vast improvement our pre-finished laminated flooring makes possible relates to installation. No longer need this be an operation that creates upheaval or disorder in your home, but a job that can be done quickly, cleanly and expertly. At your service, through B & W, are the resources of a nation-wide network of reputable specialists who can lay the natural wood of your choice over any existing concrete or wooden floor. You also have the surety of knowing that we care equally as much as you that our floorings are laid perfectly and to the best possible advantage in your home.

This brochure will introduce you to the B & W range. Each page illustrates colourfully and, we believe, conclusively, that no other flooring looks so naturally at home than natural wood.

With B & W you have the rare opportunity of investing in a product that will never lose its appeal, always add to the value of your home . . . and it's available to you now at a commendably low price.

EXHIBIT 10C.2   Main items from consolidated accounts to 31 March
                 (£000)

		1974		1975
Turnover		1678		2071
Profit before tax		167		80
Profit after tax		78		38
Dividend		–		30
Fixed assets		220		240
Quoted investments		39		39
		259		279
Current assets:				
Stocks and WIP	563		539	
Debtors and prepayments	352		457	
Cash	4		72	
	919		1068	
Less current liabilities:				
Creditors	191		260	
Bank overdraft	126		–	
Corporation tax	100		–	
Dividends	–		30	
	417		290	
Net current assets		502		778
		761		1057
		14		148
		747		909
Financed by:				
Share capital		3		8
Reserves		522		679
Unsecured loans		222		222
		747		909

	Total approx- imate replace- ment value (£)[a]	Total balance- sheet value (£)	Land				
			Original cost (£)	Balance- sheet value (£) 31.3.74	Current value (£) (approx.)	Area used (sq. ft.)	% of site area
Wharf adminis- tration	180,000	43,375	32,855	28,300	124,800	72,560	38.75
Handling and kilning	368,400	46,338	23,700	20,600	90,700	52,752	28.16
Block and strip	242,500	19,655	7,300	6,300	28,000	16,280	8.69
Mosaic	226,400	31,298	5,800	5,000	22,100	12,835	6.85
Seamless	35,500	1,083	800	700	3,100	3,090	1.65
Head office	43,000	43,462	3,950	2,900	12,900	7,471	3.99
Contracts	36,900	3,402	900	800	3,600	2,100	1.12
Transport	6,000	154	Included in wharf administration			430	0.23
Total usage	1,139,500[d]	188,767	75,400	65,400	288,300	167,618	89.48
Site total	–		83,835	73,600	322,200	187,308	100.00
Unused	–		8,900	7,700	33,900	19,700	10.52
Total 'unused' + roads, access, etc.	–		38,100	33,000	145,300	84,488	45.11

[a]Includes land at current value, buildings at replacement value, and equipment at twice original cost.

[b]Refers to budget for 1975–6.

[c]Includes canteen.

[d]Includes roads and access.

General notes

(1) Investment in vehicles not included anywhere.

(2) Capacities based on normal one-shift working; working year of 239 days; normal $37\frac{3}{4}$-hour week.

(3) Replacement values: (i) warehouse, half brick, asbestos lined and roofed – heating and lighting £7 per sq. ft (At cost); (ii) storage £5–6 per sq. ft (At cost); (iii) industrial offices £15 per sq. ft (Goodman and Mann).

Buildings			Equipment					
Original cost (£)	Balance-sheet value (£) 31.3.74	Replacement value (£)	Original cost (£)	Balance-sheet value (£) 31.3.74	Replacement value (£)	Total	Capacity used[b]	Free
17,821	10,801	37,000	9,314c	4,274c	n.a. (19,000)	–	–	–
5,475	2,491	142,700	67,656	23,247	n.a. (135,000)	8,800 m³	7,930 m³	900 m³
8,509	1,000	118,500	48,158	12,355	n.a. (96,000)	120,000 m²	54,873 m²	65,000 m²
12,166	6,948	72,300	66,232	19,350	n.a. (132,000)	459,900 m²	484,557 m²	(24,657 m²)
–	–	28,400	1,794	383	n.a. (4,000)	105,000 m²	26,352 m²	78,000 m²
17,358	31,481	37,100	21,554	9,081	n.a. (43,000)	–	–	–
998	980	13,300	10,022	1,622	n.a. (20,000)	–	–	–
–	–	3,000	1,654	154	n.a. (3,000)	–	–	–
92,327	53,701	452,300	226,384	60,688	n.a. (453,000)	–	–	–
–	–	–	–	–	–	–	–	–
–	–	–	–	–	–	–	–	–
–	–	–	–	–	–	–	–	–

11 Henry Sykes Ltd

SUE BIRLEY and CHRIS HALL

CASE A

'What would you advise me to do, Geoffrey? I feel that Sykes is now too big for my style of management and I would like to retire, having obtained a public quotation. But I do not feel able to do either with all the problems we are facing at the moment.' Harold Paish, chairman and managing director of Henry Sykes Ltd and deputy chairman of Sykes, Lacy-Hulbert, was talking to Geoffrey Scarlett from the Industrial and Commercial Finance Corporation (ICFC), their major financial backer and shareholder, in January 1970.

Henry Sykes Ltd dates back to 1857, when the founder set up in London an engineering concern which claimed to be among the first to specialise in the hire of portable steam engines and other equipment to building and civil engineering contractors. After a few years Henry Sykes began to manufacture various items of contractors' equipment, notably pumps and mortar mills. In 1897 the firm was incorporated as a limited company and by the early 1900s the manufacture for sale and hire of piledrivers, winches and pumps had become the mainstay of the business.

Harold Paish joined the company in 1930. He had left school four years previously, spent one year at the London School of Economics reading economics, and then worked for a firm of stockbrokers. Consequently he had no engineering experience or qualifications when he joined Henry Sykes. Determined to rectify this, he enrolled at the local technical college, and after five years of evening classes he became a qualified engineer. From this time he took a major role in the research and development activities within the firm, and also in its management. By 1937 he was a director of the company and assistant to Mr Mitchener, the managing director. In 1948 he was made managing director, when Mr Mitchener became chairman.

> During this time [Harold remarks] we had achieved steady but unexciting growth and I was convinced we could do better. I felt that we should aim to produce a pump which would stand up to the rigours of the hire business, which would deal more or less with anything which the contractors wanted and yet which would also operate at a low hire charge. In 1954 we clicked, although we did not realise it at the time. We knew we had produced a very good pump that would do a lot of things other pumps would do – but rather better. However, it was very expensive.

The Univac pump was robust and highly versatile, able to handle the pumping of water containing a high proportion of solids, abrasives, screened sewage and sludge. It was an automatic priming pump, would prime and reprime down to a nine-metre vertical suction life in under one minute, and would continue to operate at all depths

184

even when the suction line was exposed to the air. By 1960 the Univac had become a market leader.

This case describes the major events during the next ten years which led to the meeting between Harold Paish and Geoffrey Scarlett in 1970.

The building of the depot organisation

The company's founder, Henry Sykes, had originally set up to hire out portable steam engines. At the time these were a comparatively new innovation, which provided contractors with the first self-contained transportable power unit. As time went by, Sykes also hired out the machines that were driven by these steam engines. By 1910 the company was manufacturing for hire and for sale a considerable range of winches, piledrivers, earth-boring tools, builders' boists, mortar mills and pumps. But hire was not respectable: 'We tried so often to find the right young men to succeed us, but the best ones all turned up their noses at our hire business.' (Paish) This anti-hire attitude remained with the firm until the development of the Univac. Despite the fact that it was twice the price of any other equivalent pump, by September 1960 132 of the 206 pumps on hire were Univacs, and of the old-type reciprocating and centrifugal pumps only seventeen units were on hire; by February 1962, 200 Univacs were on hire; and by 1963 the Univac accounted for 70 per cent of the company's hire revenue.

To cope with this increase in demand for their own product and to meet demand for hire equipment more efficiently than in the past, Harold Paish prepared in 1962 (see Case B) a five-year plan, which envisaged the opening of five strategically placed depots to cover England and Wales, culminating in the provision of a new London depot; in this way all hire could be removed from the works at Charlton and Southwark, leaving them free to develop manufacture unhampered. But the plan broke down because sales grew at an annual rate much greater than the expected 15 per cent (see Exhibit 11A.1 for total production), and in 1966 the hire fleet, by then increased to 1000 units, had to be moved out of the premises at Charlton to leave the necessary facilities for production. After a frantic search in the London area, premises were eventually found on the Slough trading estate, some 20 miles from Central London. Reg Green, who had spent the whole of his working life with Henry Sykes and who at the time was sales manager, became the UK depot general manager. By 1969 there were in all eight depots (see Exhibit 11A.2), run from Slough, each with its own workshop repair facility, and by 1970 the fleet had grown to 2700 units. Most of these were Univacs and the rest submersible and special pumps.

The development of formal accounting systems

Henry Sykes Ltd was one of the first companies to use the services of the ICFC when it was formed in 1945, and from that time the executives of the ICFC had observed the general development of the management of Henry Sykes and in particular that of Harold Paish. An internal memorandum in 1952 remarked that Paish was 'unprepossessing, not a man of the time'. By 1955 he had 'grown in stature and become more confident and decisive'. In 1956, 'although he is a plodder and admits that the firm is stodgy, he has a sound grasp of the business'. This last report goes on to comment that Henry Sykes Ltd had a good reputation with competitors and customers alike, despite the fact that its products were expensive, and a strategy of gradual expansion was favoured. In June 1962 Geoffrey Scarlett was given the responsibility for liaison with Sykes, and after visiting the factory at Charlton he reported that he was 'horrified at the new investment programme [see Case B], which was too lavish . . . £50,000 could have been saved . . . management is completely out of hand . . . educational pressure is needed . . . we suggest appointing an accountant director'. Harold Paish, whilst admitting that labour costs were too high and purchase control poor, refused to appoint an accountant.

In May 1963, after continuous gentle pressure from Geoffrey Scarlett, Paish agreed to appoint a non-executive director who, in Paish's words, should 'know his way round the City and have commercial experience'. Kenneth McGregor, who was on the point of retiring from the Board of Trade and was well known to the chairman of the ICFC, was appointed. Six months later Mr McGregor reported that the two major weaknesses within the company were, first, the lack of accounting control, and, second, the absence of a qualified engineer of senior executive status. Harold Paish 'reluctantly' agreed to a study on the accounting and costing systems.

Alec Potts had been with the ICFC for about three years when he was asked to study the control systems in Henry Sykes. Prior to this he had worked as a management consultant. Potts remarks,

> In spite of all the help and patient assistance I was given, I found it difficult to form a very clear picture of the organisation. I think that this was due to the very piecemeal development of the company over the years since manufacturing had become a more prominent activity. In both the factories, at Charlton and Southwark Street, there was a complete mixture of manufacturing, assembling of custom-built items, hiring and overhauling. When you walked into the place, it was just open space with junk all over the floor – no chance of control at all. In fact, the most disturbing feature was the complete absence of accounting information designed to explain, even in the broadest way, the trading results of the main activities. There were a few loose statistical-type reports and the various costings were there but they were not integrated and overheads were not included. There was, however, always an extensive sales breakdown, particularly for the hire business, which was the barometer for the company.

In his report to the company in September 1964, Alec Potts made the following comments:

> From the trading aspect sales can currently be analysed between the broad categories of:
>
> (i) hire income
> (ii) hire sales
> (iii) spare sales
> (iv) sales of standard new equipment
> (v) sales of special order new equipment.
>
> However, the respective costs of producing these sales are not as easily obtained due mainly to the mixture of production and operating costs in the accounting records. It is necessary to promote a clear split of these costs in order to establish the basis for arriving at the nearest possible comparison with the analysis of sales. It is proposed

that departmentalisation in this context means:—

(i) the setting up of a system for arriving at the true cost of supplying, at factory cost, standard equipment or special equipment, spare parts for stock for subsequent resale or maintenance, and special parts for hire equipment. The factory, therefore, should operate as a supply unit to both sales department – in all its activities – and hire department so far as its hire plant is concerned. All factory direct and overhead costs must be collected through the factory accounts and must be accounted for in production costs.

(ii) the establishment of a hire operating department cost section which should contain all of the expenses concerned with the handling, maintenance and movement control of hire plant and in addition the maintenance of customers equipment.

(iii) a controlled stores system which should serve:

(a) the factory – with stores additional to normal production stocks
(b) hire department – with spares for maintenance of plant or new plant for replenishment of hire equipment stocks
(c) sales department – with spares for resale.

On presenting his report to the company, Alex Potts was invited to join the board as financial director to institute the changes which he had recommended. 'I took the job, despite the fact that I had vowed never to join industry again, because the company and particularly the people in it attracted me a great deal. At the time the constitution of the board was weak. Whilst it was dominated by Paish factions, the Sykes family influence, particularly that of Oswald Sykes, made life difficult.'

Reflecting on this, Harold Paish commented,

I wish I could say that from that time all our troubles were over. They were not. The difficulties were immense; the comparative neglect of years had to be made good and the sheer weight of the growth in the basic accountancy of invoicing and getting in the money, paying the wages and salaries and generally preventing breakdown was hard going. Added to which a merger with a supplier of one of our major components at the beginning of 1966 was distracting [see below]; it absorbed and has continued to absorb a good deal of the energy of our financial director as well as others. We were also at times seriously hampered by shortage of office space.

However, a really first-class product well protected by patents together with a deeply rooted organisation can cover a multitude of sins. By deeply rooted, I mean that there were people who had been so long with the business that by applying some simple ratios they can estimate within reasonable limits the level of current profitability. In 1970 all the senior managers, including myself, continued to forecast sales and control the business by this 'rule of thumb' method. For example, I could forecast to within 2 per cent of what was actually achieved, and, because I controlled the purchasing, I could adjust things accordingly.

The relationship with Scottish Land Developments Ltd

Scottish Land Developments Ltd (SLD) was a small hire firm based in Scotland which in 1961 approached Henry Sykes with a proposal to act as agents for the Univac in

Scotland and the four most northerly counties of England. Paish agreed, with two provisos. First, SLD would not stock any products which were in direct competition with the Univac, and, second, they would not open depots in the south of England. In June 1968, SLD also took over the agency for Ireland.

Relationships between the two companies were cemented even further, in two ways. First, a joint distributorship was set up in Australia in 1967, one-third owned by Henry Sykes and two-thirds by SLD, and, secondly, SLD began to distribute Sykes pumps through its American subsidiary.

But by early 1970 the marriage had begun to crumble. Reg Green comments, 'SLD began to demand a guaranteed 40 per cent of our production. When we explained that we couldn't agree to this, they began using a competitor's pump which had some form of priming and which was in competition with the Univac.'

The merger with Lacy-Hulbert and Co. Ltd

Lacy-Hulbert and Co. Ltd was established in 1901 by C. E. L. Lacy-Hulbert, and in 1965 was being run by Edward Lacy-Hulbert, the son of the founder. Its products included a wide range of reciprocating and rotary vacuum pumps and air compressors, which, under the trade name of 'Boreas', had a wide market as components for use by industry and the defence services. In particular, in co-operation with Henry Sykes the company had developed a range of rotary sliding-vane vacuum pumps designed specifically for the Univac (see Exhibit 11A.3). As a result of this, a high degree of co-operation existed between the two companies, and in 1963 regular quarterly meetings were instituted at which the technical and production staff of each company participated along with senior executives. It was at one of these meetings late in 1965 that Harold Paish became aware that the owner, Edward Lacy-Hulbert (sixty), was looking around for a buyer, and he proposed a merger of the two companies. In the new company, formed in January 1966 and named Sykes, Lacy-Hulbert Ltd, the major shareholders were Edward Lacy-Hulbert, with 21 per cent of the equity; the ICFC, with 18 per cent; and the directors of Henry Sykes, with 5 per cent. Edward Lacy-Hulbert was asked to take the chair of the new holding company and Harold Paish became deputy chairman. (See Exhibits 11A.4–6 for the accounts of Lacy-Hulbert.)

In spite of the merger, there was no effective co-operation between the two subsidiaries, and, although formal board meetings took place, there was no management team at the top. By 1970, the profits of Lacy-Hulbert had declined to a trading loss and the relations between the Paish camp and the chairman were very poor.
HAROLD PAISH says:

> Instead of retiring and taking a back seat, he became very outspoken. He disliked the hire business and always wanted to get rid of it, but he couldn't because all the business in the company was done by the Sykes board.
>
> Also, whereas he ran a Rolls-Royce and a Porsche on the company, our approach was quite different. As old Mr Sykes used to relate, our philosophy has always been 'don't take a taxi when there is a tram around'.

HAROLD ROSE, professor of finance at the London Business School, was appointed to the board as a non-executive director in 1969, at the suggestion of the ICFC.

Harold Paish was not an aggressive man, and therefore there was no one to stand up to Lacy-Hulbert, who had an upper-class manner and always managed to turn aside any serious discussion. Every board meeting which I attended caused me an intense feeling of frustration: nothing ever really happened.

KENNETH McGREGOR: The companies continued to be managed as completely separate units. Lacy-Hulbert didn't appear to like the idea of anyone trying to encroach on the complete financial and managerial autonomy of his own family firm.

ALEC POTTS: The acquisition of Lacy-Hulbert was a natural, since for years they were our sole supplier of vacuum pumps. Lacy-Hulbert was an excellent chairman. He gave people their heads even when he did not agree with them. Paish did not care about being chairman but Lacy-Hulbert did; he was an Englishman of the highest repute – a gentleman's gentleman. He was very active in City circles, had been president of his trade association, the British Compressed Air Society, and gained his OBE for his social work in Croydon. He was a man with ambition.

EDWARD LACY-HULBERT: Henry Sykes was one of our major customers, so much so that Harold and I used to have quarterly lunch meetings to discuss forecast sales. At one of these meetings, discussion turned to the future of the two companies and Harold suggested a merger. It seemed an ideal combination, since it would serve as an outlet for our product, facilitate distribution and at the same time help me to make suitable provision for death duties. Also, Sykes was sub-contracting a lot of work which I felt that we could do.

Although I took over the Chairmanship of the holding company, I remained heavily committed at Lacy-Hulbert and did not interfere in the day-to-day running of Henry Sykes. However, I did feel that there were far too many hire depots and if I had my way I would have closed down a number, which were underemployed. Also relationships between the two firms were not as they should be. We had never been able to get anyone at Sykes interested in Lacy-Hulbert and none of their sub-contract work has come our way.

Succession

In November 1962 Mitchener retired at the age of 87 and Paish became chairman and managing director of Henry Sykes. From the outset it was clear that some provision had to be made for future succession, particularly as Harold Paish did not feel happy in his new position, which exposed him directly to the company's shareholders; and so, says Paish, 'a management committee [see Exhibit 11A.7] was formed and we indeed found that we had a wealth of hitherto underused ability. This team showed itself fully capable of running the business during the first three or four years of the period of rapid expansion.

But by 1968 no-one had emerged from within the company as an embryo managing director to succeed Harold Paish, and so, at the suggestion of the ICFC, John Tyzack, management consultants, were asked to investigate the situation. As a result of their report, Jack Foster was appointed marketing director with a view to his becoming managing director of the group within a couple of years. But within a year it was clear to all concerned that whilst Foster was very able, he was not comfortable in a small but fast-growing company. Harold Paish's first attempt to provide succession from outside the firm had failed.

EXHIBIT 11A.1	Henry Sykes Ltd: total production (units)

Year	Production
1960–4 (inclusive)	2200
1965	1100
1966	1400
1967	1740
1968	1950
1969	2380

EXHIBIT 11A.2 Henry Sykes Ltd: hire depots in 1969

1961	Sandbach, Cheshire
1964	Coleford, Somerset
1964	Portsmouth, Hampshire
1964	Thetford, Norfolk
1965	Slough, Buckinghamshire
1968	Castleford, Yorkshire
1969	Pontypridd, Glamorgan
1969	Birmingham

EXHIBIT 11A.3 Henry Sykes Ltd: purchases from Lacy-Hulbert and Co. Ltd

Year	Purchases of vacuum pump units and spares: percentage of Lacy-Hulbert Ltd turnover
1961	13.4
1965	17.4
1967	34.0
1970	29.9

EXHIBIT 11A.4 Extracts from Lacy-Hulbert and Co. Ltd accounts

Year	Profit before tax (£)	Dividend Rate (%)	Net amount (£)
1960	42,917	5	953
1961	56,272	15	2858
1962	51,850	15	2858
1963	46,680	30	5716
1964	73,087	30	5680

Ordinary capital = £31,109
On 20 December 1965, the Lacy-Hulbert family holdings were

	%
Edward Lacy-Hulbert	42.5
Mrs Lacy-Hulbert	2.9
Other family	13.2
	60.6

EXHIBIT 11A.5   Lacy-Hulbert and Co. Ltd: balance sheet (£) (year ending 31 December)

	1964	1965
Share capital issued and fully paid	31,109	31,109
Capital reserves[a]	3,012	77,108
Revenue reserves and undistributed profits	211,210	237,692
Total share capital and reserves	245,331	345,909
Tax equalisation account	–	5,125
	245,331	351,034
Fixed assets		
Freehold properties	56,554	134,429
Plant and other equipment	46,749	50,716
Motor vehicles	8,400	7,270
	111,703	192,415
Trade investment – at cost	3	3
Current assets		
Stock and work in progress	129,862	143,782
Debtors and prepayments	58,151	65,524
Due from Henry Sykes Ltd	4,987	14,351
Due from Sykes Lacy-Hulbert Ltd	–	62
Quoted investments (market value £100)	5	5
Insurance policy (surrender value £8392)	8,553	9,049
Short-term loans	35,000	35,000
Cash at bank and in hand	4,950	10,877
	241,508	278,650
Current liabilities		
Creditors and accrued charges	77,641	84,637
Corporation tax payable 1 Jan 1967	27,500	29,000
Proposed dividend	2,742	6,397
	107,883	120,034
Net current assets	133,625	158,616
Net assets	245,331	351,034
[a] Surplus arising on sale of assets	3,012	3,012
Surplus arising on revaluation of properties	–	74,096
	3,012	77,108

EXHIBIT 11A.6   Lacy-Hulbert and Co. Ltd: profit and loss account (£) (year ending 31 December)

	1964		1965	
Profit for the year before taxation		73,087		67,43?
After charging				
depreciation	12,007		10,787	
directors' emoluments	15,533		17,543	
auditors' remuneration	186		637	
cost of increase in capital	–		3,014	
interest received	(1,015)		(2,322)	
Taxation				
Corporation tax	–		29,000	
Income tax	26,103		429	
Profits tax	11,000		–	
		37,103		29,42?
Profit after tax		35,984		38,00?
Unappropriated profit brought forward		180,826		211,21?
Profit available for appropriation		216,810		249,21?
Deduct				
transfer to tax equalisation account	–		5,125	
proposed dividend (net)	5,600		6,397	
		5,600		11,52?
Unappropriated profit carried forward		211,200		237,69?

192

EXHIBIT 11A.7   Henry Sykes Ltd: management structure

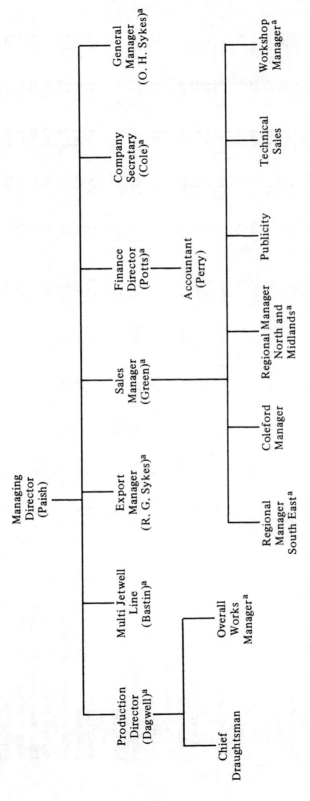

[a]Members of Management Committee.

193

EXHIBIT 11A.8   Henry Sykes Ltd: balance sheets (£ thousand), (year ending 31 December)

	1949	1954	1961	1962	1963	1964	1965	1966	1967	1968	1969
Fixed assets	46.6	99.5	283	320	350	396	765	947	1515	1837	2376
Unquoted investments	–	–	–	–	–	–	–	–	12	12	69
Stocks	94.8	161.0	240	276	341	382	706	917	734	1029	1221
Debtors	69.9	109.3	154	150	331	325	486	594	861	1182	1644
Cash	2.9	6.0	–	1	3	3	10	7	6	5	4
Current assets	167.6	276.3	393	427	574	710	1202	1518	1611	2228	2868
Creditors	37.5	51.0	78	84	158	134	303	360	426	551	752
Current tax	17.2	34.0	12	34	14	33	60	110	121	292	362
Bank loan and overdraft	3.0	24.0	74	112	165	178	203	222	349	854	721
Short-term loan			–	–	–	–	–	–	–	–	–
Dividend	1.5	2.6	–	4	4	6	17	41	48	56	53
Current liabilities	59.2	112.6	164	235	340	351	583	733	944	1752	1890
Net assets	155.0	264.2	512	512	584	755	1384	1732	2185	2313	3423
Share capital	35.0	35.0	42	42	131	219	521	586	684	684	904
Reserves	88.9	177.9	328	346	312	301	461	560	745	897	1395
Ordinary shareholder funds	123.9	212.9	370	388	443	520	982	1146	1429	1581	2299
Preference shares	2.4	33.1	22	22	17	100	100	100	100	100	–
Long-term loans – unsecured	18.0	5.4	2	2	–	–	100	100	100	100	928
Long-term loans – secured	–	–	95	95	105	105	180	330	318	383	–
Deferred tax	10.7	13.0	23	3	17	30	–	26	168	46	64
Deferred government grants	–	–	–	2	2	–	22	30	70	103	131
	155.0	264.4	512	512	584	755	1384	1732	2185	2313	3423

EXHIBIT 11A.9   Henry Sykes Ltd: profit and loss analysis
(£ thousand) (year ending 31 December)

Year	Turnover	Pretax + interest post fees	Interest
1935	43.3	1.6	
1940	94.7	17.0	
1945	102	(6.2)	
1946	115	4.3	
1947	156	10.3	
1948	216	35.2	
1949	247	28.4	
1950	268	18.3	
1951	328	48.1	
1952	387	59.5	0.8
1953	407	69.5	0.7
1954	389	33.9	0.6
1955	426	54.1	1.9
1956	427	15.8	2.3
1957	456	34.3	3.6
1958	549	38.1	1.5
1959	476	16.0	3.5
1960	569	37.6	8.3
1961	662	89.8	12.2
1962	642	36.3	11.9
1963	836	66.9	14.0
1964	1100	132	15.8
1965	n.a.	n.a.	
1966	1906	305	41.1
1967	2492	365	50.3
1968[a]	3313	441	85.2
1969	4244	582	104

[a] 53 weeks.

195

EXHIBIT 11A.10   Sykes, Lacy-Hulbert Ltd: extracts from the accounts (£ thousand), 1969

(1)   Turnover: Henry Sykes Ltd   3892
                             Lacy-Hulbert and Co. Ltd   520
                                                                          4412
                             Less
                             inter-company sales   168
                                                                          4244

(2)   Profits: Henry Sykes Ltd   545
                             Lacy-Hulbert and Co. Ltd   46
                                                                           591
                             Less
                             holding-company expenses and unrealised
                                 inter-company profit   9
                                                                           582

(3)   The total value of goods exported was £542,771, of which direct exports amounted to £424,885.

(4)   The average number of persons, including directors, employed by the company and its subsidiaries in the UK during the year was 1023.

(5)   Directors shareholdings. The directors' interests in the ordinary shares of the company at the end of the year, which had not changed since the beginning of the year, were as follows:

	Number of 5s. shares
E. Lacy-Hulbert	413,768
H. P. S. Paish	105,329
H. L. Dagwell	7,629
R. J. Foster	10,000
L. Jenkinson	10.800
K. McGregor	7,500
O. H. Sykes	72,280

EXHIBIT 11A.11   Building and construction industry trends

| | | Wholesale-price index | |
	Value of output (£ million)	*Construction materials (1954 = 100)*	*Building materials other than fuel (1963 = 100)*
1955	1864	104.7	
1956	2077	104.5	
1957	2144	113.7	
1958	2177	114.2	
1959	2399	113.4	
1960	2581	115.1	
1961	2845	118.1	
1962	3011	120.4	
1963	3110	121.9	100.0
1964	3614		104.4
1965	3851		106.4
1966	4039		109.6
1967	4307		106.7
1968	4569		120.7
1969	5697		126.1

Source: Annual Abstract of Statistics published by the Central Statistical Office.

CASE B

This case traces the financial relationship between Henry Sykes Ltd and the ICFC to the point when in 1973 Sykes, Lacy-Hulbert is faced with an acquisition bid from the Hanson Trust, a large holding company with interests in the building and construction industry.

The financing of Henry Sykes Ltd by the ICFC

During the first half of this century, Henry Sykes was chronically undercapitalised. To quote Harold Paish,

> It was always so short of working capital that, although it declared dividends, the invariable practice was to ask that the dividend cheques be returned and the money placed on deposit at call with the company. Interest was not paid but credited to the deposit account.

Long- and well as short-term financing was also a problem for the company: for example, during the early 1930s it was decided to move one of the three works from Wembley to new premises to be built at Charlton in South London, an exercise which involved a capital expenditure of some £10,000. But, instead of raising long-term capital for this, the company used up the whole of its short-term borrowing power by way of bank overdraft and shareholders' deposits and thus entered the full blast of the slump in 1932 and 1933 with no reserve borrowing power whatsoever. Harold Paish explained that the only way to remain solvent in face of subsequent trading losses was to reduce the inventory, which was preponderantly used machinery available for hire and therefore not at that time a liquid asset. There was no money available to buy materials for production and there were practically no orders for new machines. The shops were kept running by doing jobbing and repair work.

> Our objectives in 1934 were very clear [says Harold Paish]. We had had a bad fright. We must make our business more profitable than it had been previously and at the same time we must restore liquidity. There was no thought or hope of raising fresh capital.

But by 1945 it was clear that a major investment of new equipment was vital if the company was to continue to survive. In order to raise the money, Mitchener approached the bank to increase the overdraft from £5000 to £7000. The request was refused and, continues Paish,

> It was then that we were introduced to the newly started ICFC by one of our major shareholders who knew John Kinross, the then deputy chairman of ICFC. They made their enquiries and in 1946 we had the first instalment of an unsecured loan of £18,000 on a net asset base of £92,000. In point of fact the net increase in working capital was only £12,000, as the balance was used to pay off some old debentures and the remnants of the shareholders' deposits. However, the fact that ICFC had shown such touching faith in our capabilities galvanised the bank into action. They actually complained that we should have borrowed the money from them!

197

With the injection of new money and the increased overdraft facilities, turnover doubled in the three years 1946–8. However, the company was suffering, as we had done no forward cash budgeting. We had raised money to finance machine tools. We had given no thought to the financing of work in progress, stock and debtors, and, when, as was inevitable with rapid growth, money ran short, we 'drew in our horns', i.e. curtailed purchases to the detriment of productivity and profits.

However, ICFC were not unduly dismayed and put in another £30,000 in 1950 by way of preference shares despite their wish for ordinary shares, and again the next three years showed apparently highly satisfactory growth both in turnover and profits. The trouble was that it was too easy in the boom conditions of the time and we did not have any serious problems – or rather we thought we had not and this was extremely dangerous.

However, the ICFC was not quite as unconcerned as Paish had thought. Reference was made repeatedly in the files to the lack of management structure. It appeared that, despite his advancing years, Mitchener was 'still very much in control', and it was not until 1949, after some pressure from the ICFC, that Paish was allowed to participate in discussions with the ICFC.

By the end of 1950 the company was showing a trading profit of £61,000 from a turnover of £199,000, and a capital employed of £180,000, funded as below:

	£ thousand
Ordinary shares	35
Reserves	93
	128
Preference shares	30
ICFC loan	16
Other	3
	177
Bank overdraft	3
Capital employed	180

In 1952 the company approached the bank a second time for an increase in the overdraft limit and was again refused. Undeterred, Paish proposed to approach ICFC for £30,000 to increase the hire stocks and capitalise on the higher margins from that side of the business. Mitchener disagreed, but Paish had the support of the board, and so Mitchener, now 76, handed over the decision, and with it the management of the company, to his patient assistant.

The application for funds and the change in management sparked off an ICFC visit, the first major appraisal since 1947. Unfortunately, the visit was not a success. An internal ICFC memorandum commented that Paish was 'undisciplined in speech and thought', that 'the plant was old with high labour costs and low output', and that it was 'a good business, but results are disappointing'. The memorandum concluded that the application was a borderline case, but that, if it were decided to go ahead, the ICFC should opt for ordinary shares, because

(1) of the possibility of monopoly profits in the business;

198

(2) shares were widely held, thus offering little resistance to purchase; and

(3) low current profits would mean a low share price, when in fact the net asset backing was substantial (it was estimated that a reasonable price would be 25s), against a net asset value of 75s.).

This plan was unacceptable to Henry Sykes Ltd and so ICFC finally offered a further loan of £30,000, but with the tickler of an increased interest rate on the preference shares in order to compensate for the extra risk from the loan. Paish rejected these terms also and after some negotiation managed to increase the overdraft limit from National Westminster. In retaliation, the ICFC declared its intention to charge a fee of £150 per annum if the overdraft exceeded the original overdraft limit of £30,000.

Relations between the two parties consequently became rather cool and remained so for three years, until an exploratory meeting again in 1955, when the ICFC was plesantly surprised. Paish had 'grown in stature . . . more confident and decisive', although 'not a ball of fire'.

By that time the company was testing a new pump, the Univac, and money was required for this development and for the proposed two new properties at Southwark and Charlton. At £100,000 this was the biggest funding yet, and the ICFC's thoughts turned again to equity funding. The ICFC was allowed to take up 7000 ordinary shares and in return Henry Sykes was given a consolidated loan of £40,000 for the first stage of the project. As a token of goodwill, the £150 fee was dropped.

'On reflection,' says Harold Paish, 'we needed the funds because the expenses had soared and again no proper provision had been made for working capital.' This feeling was echoed within the ICFC as those connected with Sykes became increasingly concerned about the lack of financial control in the company. Nevertheless, whenever members of the family indicated a wish to liquidate their shares, the ICFC made an offer to purchase, and by 1958 it owned in total 19 per cent of the equity.

Complaints continued to be made about the low level of profits and the poor state (or non-existence) of management-control systems, and finally the ICFC suggested the appointment of a director who was also an accountant. However, it was not until 1963 that the first non-executive director, Mr McGregor, was nominated by the ICFC and appointed. Meanwhile, the expansion of the depot system, started in the late 1950s and continued into the 1960s was funded by the ICFC through both debt and equity.

To return to Harold Paish:

By 1962, Henry Sykes was already very much committed to ICFC. We said to them we believed there were prospects of doubling the business within the next five years and we produced a very amateurish effort showing what capital would be required and why. The total amounted to what was to us then the enormous sum of £550,000.

Their plan required a five-year loan of £165,000 from the ICFC. Such ambition required a full visit from the ICFC, which insisted on waiting for the 1963 results before making a final decision. These results showed a satisfactory turnover of £840,000 and a trading profit of £89,000. After further negotiation, the ICFC agreed to a loan, but reduced the amount to that required for three years instead of five. Harold Paish comments,

In view of our past record it was a very courageous decision on the part of ICFC in

199

general and Geoffrey Scarlett in particular. It was the major turning point in our history. In fact, we exactly doubled our turnover in three years instead of five; the extra resources employed came to just over £500,000, of which rather over half came from cash flow. After that effort finance for us has not been a headache.

However, after only two years, Henry Sykes returned to the ICFC for money to fund the unexpectedly rapid growth and a loan of £225,000 and an underwritten rights issue were agreed in September 1965. This funded the Slough premises for the hire business and the merger with the compressor-pump manufacturer Lacy-Hulbert and Co. Ltd (see Case A).

The financial plan of 1966 required funds for nine more depots and a major export drive. The medium-term goal was public floatation in the spring of 1968, something which would certainly have suited the ICFC. An internal memo at the time commented, 'Henry Sykes has an insatiable appetite for finance due to continued expectations . . . approaching the limit of ICFC's operations.'

By October 1966 the 1965 accounts were finished. Henry Sykes and Lacy-Hulbert continued to operate in all respects as two separate companies, despite the merger. The results of the former improved and the latter continued to slide downhill, and executives in the ICFC, which now had a substantial investment in the company (see below), began to express concern at Mr Lacy-Hulbert's influence as chairman over the new group. Despite this concern, executives continued to keep a low profile, following their general policy of influencing and persuading at arm's length, rather than becoming directly involved in the management.

By the end of 1966 the ICFC had a total investment in the group of £563,000:

	£ thousand
Henry Sykes Ltd	
7% secured loan stock	105
8% secured loan stock	225
7½% preference shares	100
Sykes, Lacy-Hulbert Ltd	
8% secured loan stock	60
0.4 m 5s. ordinary shares	73 (equal to 18% of the equity)
	563

In May 1967 Harold Paish estimated that he needed to raise £560,000 to prepare the company for flotation. Much of this would come from an increase in bank borrowing and credit facilities, but the ICFC was asked to find £196,000. Because of the issue of flotation, it was suggested that the management structure should be examined, and John Tyzack, a firm of management consultants, was hired to investigate the individuals within, and the structure of, the management team. Tyzack reported that the company should not be floated until a successor to Harold Paish had been found. It was doubted whether Lacy-Hulbert could or even wanted to fulfil such a role.

With the appointment of Foster in 1968 as managing-director designate (see Case A), the goal was to go public in autumn 1969. In mid 1969, flotation was shelved as more organisational problems were identified, and the ICFCs consulting arm was called in: its investigations showed that the companies' problems continued to be the poor management information.

The bid by Hanson Trust

Whereas the 1960s provided a series of internal problems, the 1970s saw challenges and problems coming from the external environment. In March 1970 the Hanson Trust proposed a merger between its subsidiary Scottish Land Developments Ltd (SLD) (see Case A) and Sykes, Lacy-Hulbert (SLH) (the holding company formed in 1966). This was turned down only to be followed by an approach by Woodall-Duckham. A year later, a Ralli subsidiary made loud noises, but it too was rejected.

Meanwhile, in January 1972, Tony Hepper was appointed the new chief executive and chairman-designate, after answering a newspaper advertisement.

The Financial Times of 3 January 1972 reported,

When the liquidator moved into Upper Clyde Shipbuilders in June last year, Mr Tony Hepper, UCS's first and last Chairman, left to spend two months abroad. The point of calling in Hepper is, says Lacy-Hulbert, to provide management continuity (both he and Paish are close to retirement age) and, eventually, to get a public quote . . . Not yet 49, Hepper is young enough to start out on a new career with confidence. He has already acquired plenty of varied experience, being with Courtaulds and Cape Asbestos (a directorship he still holds) before joining Thomas Tilling. After being chairman of six Tilling subsidiaries, he was seconded to the DEA and then, via a Shipbuilding Industry Board working party, to the Upper Clyde job. He is still unwilling to say much more than describing UCS as '$3\frac{1}{2}$ years of sheer hell'. But he clearly feels bitter about other senior men who left UCS when things began to go wrong. 'I was the only person who saw it through. In the middle of '69 I was left alone like the boy on the burning deck.'

But, despite the external face, Tony Hepper's appointment had created problems at Sykes, Lacy-Hulbert. Edward Lacy-Hulbert had been violently against the appointment, but was voted down by the board, and, when Tony Hepper produced his plans for the future, 'there was no seat on the board for me'. Disenchanted, he decided to look round for a buyer for his shares:

EDWARD LACY-HULBERT: It was suggested that I might like to buy back Lacy-Hulbert Ltd, but I felt that it was unwise at my age. ICFC jointly with Baring Bros made me an offer but it was a lousy price and I began to feel that they were trying to chisel me out of my shares. I had always been in favour of a merger between SLH and SLD although I felt that the original offer from Hanson came a little too early after the Henry Sykes, Lacy-Hulbert merger. I wasn't aware of any underground feeling between SLH and SLD, but was of the opinion that we could benefit from the very good people that SLD had on their hire side.

On 26 June 1972, I went to see Tony Hepper at Charlton, with a representative from the Hanson Trust, who put a bid on the table.

TONY HEPPER: The whole thing was clouded by the original merger. The logic behind buying one's supplier is difficult to understand and it would have been better for Henry Sykes if it had not happened. Also with 21 per cent of the equity for a contribution of 10 per cent to the group turnover, Edward Lacy-Hulbert controlled a disproportionate amount of the shares.

When Hanson Trust produced their take-over notice, saying that they were going to communicate it to the rest of the 160 shareholders, it created a maximum reaction, particularly as by this time SLD had broken from us and set up in competition in the south of England.

The Hanson bid for 90p per share was firmly rejected by the SLH board, as was the increased bid, for 100p, made on 31 August. Within a few days, Richards and Wallington, Europe's largest hirer of cranes, countered with a bid at 110p per share. On 19 September Hanson bought Edward Lacy-Hulbert's 21 per cent of Sykes, Lacy-Hulbert for an undisclosed amount. In October *The Financial Times* reported,

Mr E. Lacy-Hulbert has bought 46,845 shares in Sykes, Lacy-Hulbert . . . In a letter to the SLH Chairman, Mr Lacy-Hulbert maintains he bought the shares from former Lacy-Hulbert holders who had asked him to find a cash buyer.

'In view of my long association with many of them, not only as shareholders but as present and former colleagues or employees, I felt that I ought to do something for them personally,' he added.

These shares were subsequently sold to the Hanson Trust.

On 8 February 1973, the Richards and Wallington bid was finally dropped, leaving the arena clear. According to *The Financial Times*, 'R and W claimed [that] . . . further information had been requested but "is still not available". So the Company "consider that they cannot leave the matter any longer".'

Meanwhile the ICFC had been buying further shares in SLH, and by February 1973 its holding had increased from 23 to 41 per cent. The total investment in the company was considerable, for as well as ordinary shares the ICFC was responsible for

	£ thousand
9% unsecured loan stock	110
7⅞% mortgage	313
Short-term loan	200
7½% preference shares	100
	723

The financial press confidently expected a bid for the rest of the shares to be forthcoming from it. Instead, in May 1973, Hanson increased its bid from 110p per share to 150p. The ICFC and the board of SLH had to make a decision.

EXHIBIT 11B.1   The Hanson Trust Ltd

Main product groups: agricultural products, building materials, construction equipment, industrial services, speciality products.

Extracts from consolidated profit and loss account (£ thousand) (year ending 27 September)

	1969	1970	1971	1972
Turnover	48,490	47,139	28,794	36,396
Investment income	21	80	35	92
Interest received	50	50	268	122
Net profit before tax	2,210	2,367	2,871	4,467
Profit after tax	1,093	1,283	1,710	2,724
Dividend	475	639	823	1,429

Analysis of turnover and profit before tax (£ thousand) (year ending 27 September)

	1970		1971		1972	
	Turnover	Profit before tax	Turnover	Profit before tax	Turnover	Profit before tax
Agricultural products[a]	2,515	487	2,823	553	3,546	611
Building materials	3,031	379	5,150	829	8,500	2,026
Construction equipment	10,079	740	10,674	909	10,500	577
Industrial services	6,459	518	6,174	528	6,509	728
Property	151	72	3,973	442	7,341	1,283
Discontinued services	24,904	697				
Parent-company executive		(526)		(390)		(758)
	47,139	2,367	28,794	2,871	36,396	4,467

[a] Including SLD.

203

EXHIBIT 11B.2   Extracts from ICFC accounts (£ thousand) (year
                 ending 31 March)

Investments

	1972	*1973*
Debentures and secured loans	80,076	81,476
Unsecured loans	7,650	11,378
Redeemable preference shares	8,272	7,906
Non-redeemable preference shares	2,825	2,852
Preferred ordinary shares	7,429	8,893
Ordinary shares	27,432	35,050

*Subsidiaries not consolidated (i.e. technical subsidiaries under section
154 of the Companies Act)*

	1972	*1973*
Shares	3,614	5,221
Loans	229	2,296
Unquoted equity investments (net book amount)	19,999	20,275

Financial facilities, 31 March 1973

	Customers	
	Numbers	*Percentage*
<10,000	493	20.7
10,001–20,000	451	19.0
20,001–50,000	596	25.0
50,001–100,000	371	15.6
100,001–200,000	238	10.0
200,001–300,000	85	3.6
300,001–500,000	55	2.3
>500,001	47	2.0
Post-delivery finance for shipbuilding	24	1.0
Ships under charter	19	0.8
	2379	100.0

EXHIBIT 11B.3   Henry Sykes Ltd: extracts from profit and loss
                 account (£ thousand) (year ending 31 December)

	1970	1971	1972
Turnover	4401	4936	5420
Trading profit	284	383	451
Interest charges	200	239	211
	84	144	239
Profits of associated companies	–	61	69
Profit before tax	84	205	308
Tax	34	85	148
Profit after tax	50	120	160

EXHIBIT 11B.4   Henry Sykes Ltd: extracts from balance sheet
                 (£ thousand) (year ending 31 December)

	1970	1971	1972
Fixed assets	2723	2849	2987
Unquoted investments	154	203	320
Stocks	1651	1359	1196
Debtors	1880	1612	1884
Cash	5	28	12
Current assets	3536	2999	3092
Creditors	1008	687	755
Current tax	200	20	68
Bank loan and overdraft	1439	1087	1530
Short-term loan	300	640	200
Dividend	20	30	42
Current liabilities	2967	2464	2595
Net assets	3447	3587	3714
Share capital	904	904	904
Reserves	1418	1478	1586
Ordinary shareholder funds	2322	2382	2490
Preference shares	–	–	–
Long-term loans – unsecured	910	942	930
Long-term loans – secured	–	–	–
Deferred tax	107	173	228
Deferred government grants	108	90	65
	3447	3587	3714

EXHIBIT 11B.5   Henry Sykes Ltd: consolidated profit and loss account (£) (year ending 31 December 1973)

Turnover	7,180,018
Trading profit before interest and tax[a]	878,718
Interest charges[b]	223,419
Profit after interest charges	655,299
Share of profits of associated companies	188,551
Total profit before tax and extraordinary item	843,850
Taxation	412,857
Profit after tax but before extraordinary item	430,993
Extraordinary item[c]	215,254
Profit for the year	646,247
Profit retained	
by subsidiaries	446,884
by associated companies	97,585
	544,469
Dividends paid and proposed	
Preference shares	5,250
Ordinary shares	96,528
	101,778

[a] After charging £366,474 depreciation.
[b] Bank loans and overdrafts repayable in five years: £146,829.
  Loans not wholly repayable in five years: £76,590.
[c] Surplus, net of capital gains tax arising from the disposal of freehold property.

General notes
Total value of goods exported was £1,016,078, of which direct exports amounted to £664,001.
  The average number of persons employed in the UK during the year was 1024 and their aggregate remuneration was £1,975,628.

Assets employed

Fixed assets (net book value)	2,979,426
Unquoted investments[a]	326,629

Current assets

Stock and work in progress	1,350,931
Debtors	2,482,224
Cash at bank and in hand	81,236
	3,914,391

Current liabilities:

Creditors	1,322,797
Current tax	285,973
Bank loans and overdrafts (secured)	1,048,702
Short-term loan	–
Dividends payable	96,528
	2,754,000

Net current assets	1,160,391
Net assets	4,466,446

Representing

Issued share capital of Henry Sykes Ltd[b]	904,403
Reserves[c]	2,155,084
	3,059,487
Long-term loans[d]	915,433
Deferred tax	447,292
Deferred government grants	44,234
	4,466,446

[a] Associated companies: Henry Sykes Pumps Australia Pty Ltd and Hewden–Sykes Pumps Ltd (Scotland)

Unquoted shares at cost	87,100
Share of post-acquisition retained profits and relevant reserves	179,135
Loan accounts	60,394
	326,629

[b] Issued and fully paid:

3,217,611 ordinary shares of 25p	804,403
100,000 $7\frac{1}{2}$% cumulative redeemable preference shares 1979–84 at £1	100,000
	904,403

[c] Share premium account	213,734
Preference-share redemption account	100,000
Loan-redemption account	117,000
Surplus arising on revaluation of properties	248,965
Arising on consolidation	(1,787)
Retained profits	1,298,037
Share of post-acquisition retained profits of associated companies	179,135
	2,155,084

[d] Holding company:

9% unsecured loan stock 1987/89	550,000
Subsidiaries:	
9% consolidated secured loan	295,000
$8\frac{1}{4}$% secured loan	11,475
10% loan	58,958
	915,433

CASE C

On 30 May 1973, Tony Hepper replied to the bid from the Hanson Trust (see Case B) in a letter to the shareholders (see Exhibit 11C.1). On 30 June, the London *Evening Standard* reported,

Hanson drops £5m Sykes bid

Mr James Hanson's Hanson Trust has dropped its near £5,000,000 bid for Sykes, Lacy-Hulbert, the public but unquoted pumps company. Hanson is clearly not pleased with the Industrial and Commercial Finance Corporation; a key figure in the proposed deal.

ICFC has 41 per cent of the Sykes shares and was firmly against the 150p per share bid. Fair enough, but what peeved Hanson was that a higher bid – 180p – it later made privately also got the ICFC thumbs down.

As ICFC's blessing was really vital to the success of the offer Hanson didn't think it worth putting it out to the other shareholders. Hanson itself has around 20% of the Sykes shares and the Sykes board 4%.

The Hanson camp obviously thinks its 'secret' offer was very good and that ICFC should have supported it. Certainly it showed a big profit to ICFC: nearly half of its shares were bought last March at 110p.

GEOFFREY SCARLETT, who by this time had joined the board of Henry Sykes, comments:

We felt at ICFC that a merger between SLD and Henry Sykes would not be to the long-term benefit of Sykes for three major reasons. First, the management of the two companies had already tried to work together and failed. Second, Henry Sykes's strength lay in the fact that it was a small company and Hanson refused to give any guarantees about the future business or the jobs of the employees. Third, we did not like the predatory way in which they did business.

KENNETH McGREGOR: The Sykes Board had always been close to its employees and we found the Hanson flat refusal about jobs the last straw, coupled with the fact that we saw them as financiers rather than serious producers.

HAROLD ROSE: What could Hanson do for the business? SLD, in the end, did not do well at all, whilst Henry Sykes were continuing to increase their share of the market [see Exhibit 11C.2]. Their overseas joint ventures turned out to be failures, both Australia and America failing because of control problems.

ALEC POTTS: I feel that everyone got far more worked up than was really necessary in the circumstances, and the real reason for this was that Edward Lacy-Hulbert was for the merger. Nevertheless, the situation was made worse when SLD came into England. It created antagonism throughout the ranks of the company as well as at board level.

The Hanson episode had not only diverted the Henry Sykes board from their main objective of obtaining a public quotation but had also complicated matters. Any shares which were freely available on the open market would enable Hanson further to increase its holding. Further, by this time the stock market itself was on the decline, thus reducing the price which Henry Sykes could expect to command (see Exhibits 11C.3–4).

The Financial Times of 29 October 1973 reported,

In his interim statement, Mr Tony Hepper . . . tells shareholders that the May forecast of profits, before tax and extraordinary items, of about £750,000 for the current year is likely to be exceeded.

In the 28 weeks ended July 15, 1973, profits have expanded sharply from £91,000 to £429,000, exceeding by £121,000 the total for 1972.

Turnover showed an increase from £2.83m to £3.86m. Providing for a heavier tax of £274,000 (£41,000) the net profit was £155,000 against £50,000, to which was added extraordinary items of £157,000 – surplus on property disposal (£215,000, less £58,000 take-over costs).

. . . Mr Hepper explains that the disproportionate tax charge arises principally because relief is not available in respect of foreign subsidiaries losses. The losses include 'a significant loss in exchange' which is likely to be partially reversed in the second half.

Mr Hepper recalls that when setting out the reasons for recommending rejection of the Hanson Trust offer, he said arrangements were in hand to obtain a listing in the autumn.

Since present conditions in the new issue market are 'far from favourable' the directors, in conjunction with the Industrial and Commercial Finance Corporation, have decided that a listing at present would not be in shareholders' best interests. It remains the intention to seek a listing in due course.

It is proposed to change the company's name (from Sykes, Lacy-Hulbert) to Henry Sykes.

But a possible solution to the Sykes dilemma had been found a year earlier. In December 1972 Michael Nightingale was approached by the Sykes board with a view to trading the shares 'over-the-counter' through his company M. J. H. Nightingale and Co. Ltd, investment bankers. (Nightingale operates the over-the-counter market, which involves acting as agent in matching buyers and sellers rather than as principal. Matching as agent differs from positioning as principal in that it involves neither capital risk nor the spread – or jobbers' turn – between buying and selling prices.)

MICHAEL NIGHTINGALE: I went down to Charlton to see Tony Hepper, who was a very worried man. He had only recently taken over and wanted instant marketability to defend himself against the argument that was being put forward that Sykes was unlisted and Unmarketable. Since the philosophy is that you have a market when you have a market and not when you have a listing, Sykes was an obvious candidate to be our second over-the-counter customer.

ALEC POTTS: The OTC market is a poor alternative to a full Stock Exchange listing; the only advantage would be that someone else instead of me would deal with the family sales of company shares.

In May 1973 Nightingale produced its analysis of Sykes, Lacy-Hulbert (see Exhibit 11C.5 for extracts).

MICHAEL NIGHTINGALE: Despite this Hanson never actually approached us to buy any shares. In fact the first shares which we sold (at 125p) were to a few individuals to start something happening. Then the Hanson bid came in at 150p and it had to be beaten or the majority of shareholders might have sold at this price.

The next block of shares (about 5 per cent of the total equity) we sold for 155p to a number of institutions, including Eagle Star and Robert Fleming. Everyone was amazed that this could be done (i.e. the 50 per cent increase) and in fact it did the trick because Hanson was forced to come back with a higher bid, this time at 180p. At this point I felt that ICFC were not sure what to do. Normally their policy is to hang on to shares, although as investors it isn't always possible to do so indefinitely, if a very high price is offered.

Regarding the Hanson bid, my job was to persuade ICFC not to sell at 180p. I still believed that at 180p Sykes was a reasonable 'hold' and that a sale to Hanson at that price would have enabled Hanson to benefit at the expense of the other shareholders. By keeping the company independent all could benefit from the prospective management turnaround under Hepper. Mind you, if Hanson does not eventually take Sykes over, the company and its growth will be warped until his 20 per cent shareholding is removed.

But by July 1975, the situation had not changed. The *Investor's Chronicle* reported,

If and when the new issues market comes back to life, one of the first companies to go public could be Henry Sykes, which has stated repeatedly that it would like a quotation for its shares and has the qualifications to attract a warm welcome from investors.

. . . The record over the last five years is good, as our table shows, and the elimination of a loss-making subsidiary in America, rising export content and contracts in Arab countries should ensure growth in 1975.

. . . The shares are quoted over-the-counter by investment bankers, M. J. H. Nightingale at 120p where our profit forecast puts them on a prospective 'nil' PE [price–earnings] ratio of 6.7 and a yield of 5%, covered three times. Better marketability, through a public quotation, could sustain a better rating and would please two major shareholders, Hanson Trust and ICFC.

	Sales (£m)	Pre-tax profits (£000)	Earnings per share (p)
1970	4.4	111	1.67
1971	4.9	205	3.49
1972	5.4	308	4.73
1973	7.2	844	13.23
1974	8.7	1028	15.01
1975		1290	
		(projected)	

In June 1976 stockbrokers Greene and Co. produced their eleventh study of the plant-hire industry. In their analysis they comment,

In the present economic climate, we do not believe that it is likely that any plant hirer (with the exception possibly of Henry Sykes which already has an 'over-the-counter' quote) should seek a Stock Exchange quotation. Most plant hirers would find it extremely difficult to gain a Stock Exchange valuation approaching the valuation of their rental assets. We think it far more likely that there will be a trend for medium sized units to be taken over by either larger rivals or by larger companies, outside the plant hire trade, but perhaps with a bias towards the construction industry.

Nevertheless, they conclude by recommending the purchase of

Henry Sykes 25p Ordinary Shares at 60p to yield 3.32% on a dividend of 7.96% covered 4.4 times by earnings.
. . . The company has grown enormously in the last few years. Since 1972, turnover has more than doubled and profits more than quadrupled. The recently announced figures for 1975 showed another fine performance with profits up by an outstanding 51%. We expect Sykes to maintain its progress this year and look for a reflection of this in an improving share price. We regard Sykes as an excellent growth stock where the potential for capital appreciation is above average.

By April 1977 the company was continuing to prosper. *The Financial Times* commented,

The current year has started well at Henry Sykes and provided no external forces intervene is expected to show a satisfactory increase in profits over the £1.78m (£1.56m) for 1976, says chairman Mr Tony Hepper.
. . . He attributes this success to the widening of the company's base and much improved overseas sales. Overseas sales represented 32 per cent of total sales of £15.21m compared with 22 per cent the previous year when total sales amounted to £11.62m. Much of those overseas sales were gained in the Middle East where the company's subsidiary in the UAE, Khansaheb–Sykes, has more recently been awarded a contract in Abu Dhabi worth over £1m.
During the year the one third share in Henry Sykes Pumps Australia Pty was sold for £440,000 cash but the company will continue to act as a distributor for Sykes Pumps. In December 1976, a subsidiary was formed in France which took over an existing business and is already contributing to group profits. Since then a new joint venture company has been registered in Bahrain.
Whitehead Harbormaster [acquired in May 1975] the UK subsidiary manufacturing marine propulsion units had a particularly good year with sales doubled and £1.3m exported.

Since, as is apparent, the climate continued to favour Sykes, Tony Hepper decided to take yet another step towards a full Stock Exchange quotation. He appointed stockbrokers Capel-Cure Myers as the company's brokers, with the intention of applying for permission to trade under the Stock Exchange's Rule 163(2), which states that 'In the case of securities of Private Companies specific bargains may be made with the permission of the Council. Applications for permission must be made on forms provided in the Quotations Department and on all Trading Floors.'
To Tony Hepper's surprise, Hanson Trust arranged a private sale of its Sykes shares,

211

by-passing both the over-the-counter market and Stock Exchange trading under Rule 163(2). *The Times* of 18 August 1977 reported,

> Hanson Trust has sold a 21.95 per cent stake in Henry Sykes . . . for £1.87m. The buyers are Hambros Bank and the National Coal Board Superannuation and Pension Funds. They jointly bought the 1.87m shares at £1 each through stock-brokers Capel-Cure Myers.
>
> Sykes shares are traded over-the-counter by M. J. H. Nightingale and Co. Before the deal was announced they were priced at 84p yielding 2.8 per cent with a price earnings ratio of 8. The £1 price puts a capitalisation on the company of £8.5m.
>
> Hambros says the stake will be divided between the two buyers with Hambros taking fractionally more, probably about 12 per cent of the company. A director representing the new shareholders is to be nominated to the Sykes board.
>
> . . . The largest single holding in the company is a 35.71 per cent held by the Industrial and Commercial Finance Corporation.
>
> There was substantial trading in the shares yesterday and the price moved up 15p to 99p. It has been one of the more active over-the-counter stocks in the past year with continuing talk of an imminent full Stock Exchange quotation as soon as was justified.

The way at last seemed clear for a full listing for the company. But, as Margaret Reid of *The Financial Times* reported on 7 September of the same year, the whole question of listings for small companies seemed to be in the melting pot:

> Brisk competition, which the present stock market boom can only intensify, is beginning to develop in the City for the business of dealing in the shares of smaller companies not listed on the Stock Exchange.
>
> The tussle – and that is what it undoubtedly is, however discreetly conducted – is between the Stock Exchange and the fast-growing investment bankers, M. J. H. Nightingale, which runs a so-called over-the-counter market, outside the Exchange, in the shares of 12 companies.
>
> The rivalry is quickening at a time when reviving investor interest in the wake of the stock market's recovery is likely to prompt many family-owned private companies to re-examine the methods by which they could sell some holdings and obtain a market in their shares.
>
> The Stock Exchange, which quotes the shares of some 2,600 companies, last week demonstrated its anxiety about the scarcity of new applicant companies for its listing – there have been only six so far this year, against 132 in 1973, the high noon for new flotations. To encourage more companies to seek a quotation on the Exchange, it reduced from 35 per cent to 25 per cent the proportion of a company's shares which it normally expects – in the interests of a free market – to be held outside the inner ring of a concern's family and other major shareholders before granting a listing.
>
> The Exchange's Council also took, at the end of July, a decision – whose full implementation is still being considered – to give more publicity to the facility under its Rule 163(2) for share dealing through the stock market in shares of unlisted companies.
>
> Enlivening the whole debate about the route by which companies should

ultimately make their way to fully listed and quoted status on the Stock Exchange is the course adopted by two sizeable companies of the Nightingale stable. One is James Burrough, the unlisted Beefeater gin concern, and the other is Henry Sykes.

. . . Since April, the shares of the company, in which the bank-backed Industrial and Commercial Finance Corporation holds 36 per cent and a range of institutions 44 per cent, have been traded under the Stock Exchange rule 163(2), with two jobbers, Bisgood Bishop and Wedd Duriacher Morduant, making a market in them.

The shares now stand around 100p compared with some 50p in April and 118p when Nightingale started making a market in them five years ago. The full listing aimed for late this year should enable the dividend to be raised, should please the institutional investors by providing a wider market and should help the insurance concerns among them by allowing the holding to be reckoned for solvency ratio purposes.

With its size and 80 per cent of its shares no longer privately held, Sykes appears a classic example of the sort of concern which is suitable for stock market listing.

Nightingale, headed by Mr Michael Nightingale, who started the business after a spell at the Harvard Business School and with a leading New York investment banking house, began trading six years ago. His idea – partly based on practice in the US, where there is extensive market-making by investment houses in the shares of companies large and small which are not listed on the New York Stock Exchange – was to match the desire of owners of private companies to sell some shares with the willingness of institutions to take a stake in such businesses.

From a handful of institutions, including the big Prudential Assurance and Eagle Star Insurance initially, there are now some 40–50 institutional investors with holdings in Nightingale companies.

As it happens, the first company in which Nightingale ran an over-the-counter market was Twinlock, the office equipment concern which last year ran into problems and in which the National Enterprise Board took a stake.

The Stock Exchange riposte to Nightingale's progress has something of an 'anything you can do we can do better' flavour. The thinking appears to be that, if it comes to finding buyers for an available commodity in the form of shares in unlisted companies, the Stock Exchange should have incomparable muscle in finding buyers. As one broker said: 'If there were real opportunities for private clients to buy unquoted securities, most firms of brokers would find they had clients who would support these shares.' (Nightingale might reply to this that it has specialised in developing institutional interest in buying shares in the companies where it arranged deals, though stock-brokers might mobilise such interest also.)

Under Rule 163(2), the Stock Exchange has long allowed its members to deal, with the specific permission of the Council, in the shares of companies not listed on the Exchange and therefore not subject to its exacting listing agreement on the provision of information and other matters.

But the facility is not very widely known – people close to the Exchange as well as outside it, have been known to ask: 'Rule 163(2) – what's that now?' Turnover under the arrangement has been tiny compared with the total worth of quoted securities, but Ordinary shares of a number of concerns which are familiar names – including Rangers Football Club, Aston Villa Football Club, Oldham Estates, Granada Group and others – crop up on lists of 163(2) dealings.

In its evidence to the Wilson Committee on financial institutions in July, the Stock

Exchange noted the shrinkage in applications for new listings and added that it was 'currently considering these problems and assessing whether there should be a change in either the listing requirements for new companies or the dealing procedure for less marketable securities'.

Protection of investors through the availability of adequate information is one issue which would arise with any wide extension of dealings in unlisted companies. The Stock Exchange looks at the latest accounts of a company for Rule 163(2) dealings, but does not pretend to scrutinise the concern as it would a listed company. However, stockbrokers regularly arranging 163(2) transactions would keep a closer surveillance. Nightingale imposes extensive information requirements for those in its stable.

Costs of dealing and the method by which sellers can get the best price are other subjects for debate when the merits of different forms of dealing in non-quoted stock are discussed.

But certainly rivalry looks set to develop in the increasingly interesting area of dealings in stocks of unlisted companies. Mr Nightingale, who says co-existence with the Stock Exchange has always been his policy, remarks: 'We uncovered a market which we have been supplying in a small way for six years which was previously not being covered by anybody. Now the Stock Exchange appears to be getting interested in this market. Our speciality is providing an integrated financial advisory, research and market-making service.'

EXHIBIT 11C.1   Letter from Tony Hepper to shareholders, advising rejection of
                 Hanson Trust bid

SYKES, LACY-HULBERT LIMITED

Directors
A. E. Hepper, C.Eng., M.I.Mech.E. (*Chairman*)
H. P. S. Paish (*Deputy Chairman*)
R. J. Foster, D.F.C., A.F.C., M.A.
R. A. Green
J. W. Llewellyn-Jones, F.C.A.
K. McGregor, C.B., C.M.G., M.A.
Professor H. B. Rose
G. W. Scarlett, F.C.A.
G. E. Thompson, B.Sc. (Eng.), C.Eng., F.I.Mech.E.

Registered office:
403/433 Woolwich Road,
Charlton,
London SE7 7AP

Registered in London
No. 864764

30 May 1973

To the Ordinary shareholders:

Dear Shareholder,
    I am writing to give your Board's reasons for advising you to reject the Offer by
Hanson Trust Limited for your shares.

PROFITS AND DIVIDENDS
    Since the reorganisation of the Company early last year there has been a major
improvement in its profitability. You will see from the enclosed Report and Accounts
that the profit before tax of your Company for 1972 was £308,000 compared with
£205,000 in 1971 and that the Board intends to recommend a final dividend at a rate
equivalent to $7\frac{1}{2}$ per cent inclusive of the associated tax credit, compared with $3\frac{3}{4}$ per cent
for 1971. Trading in the first four months of the current year was extremely satisfactory
and the Board expects that, in the absence of unforeseen circumstances, the profit before
tax for 1973 will be about £750,000; this would justify a dividend of not less than the
equivalent of $17\frac{1}{2}$ per cent inclusive of the associated tax credit.

VALUE OF THE OFFER
    Your Company's profits, therefore, show
        — *an increase of 50 per cent for 1972*
    and are forecast to show
        — *a further increase of 144 per cent for 1973.*

    In spite of this profit performance the Hanson Offer values your shares on a
prospective price—earnings ratio of only 11.0 (based on a UK tax charge of 40 per cent).
    Hanson has stated in recent negotiations with your Company that Hanson's pump-hire
subsidiaries should be valued on a prospective price—earnings ratio of 15. *The same basis
of calculation would attribute a value of 204p to your shares, compared with the 150p
which Hanson is offering.*
    *Your Directors, who have been advised by Hill Samuel & Co. Limited, unanimously
consider that 150p per share does not adequately reflect your Company's prospects for
future growth as an independent group.*

EMPLOYEES
    Your Board also believes that the success of the Hanson Offer would be prejudicial to
the interests of the Company's employees. Hanson has stated that 'the merger of the two
depot networks will not involve significant redundancies'. Your Board considers that if
the two businesses were to be combined there would be significant redundancies.

STOCK EXCHANGE LISTING
    Your Board realises that there is at present only a limited market in your shares. The
Board is therefore making arrangements with ICFC to obtain a listing for the shares on
The Stock Exchange in the autumn. This should enable shareholders to acquire or sell
shares as they wish.

215

EXHIBIT 11C.1   Continued

RECOMMENDATION
Your Board therefore strongly advises you to reject the Offer and to ignore the documents sent to you by Hanson. Your Directors and Industrial and Commercial Finance Corporation Limited and its associates who together hold more than 45 per cent of the share capital do not intend to accept the Offer.

Yours sincerely,
Tony Hepper
Chairman.

Appendix I   Profit forecast of Sykes, Lacy-Hulbert Limited

A. BASIS AND ASSUMPTIONS
The profit forecast of SLH and its subsidiaries ('the Group') for the year ending 31 December 1973 made by the Directors of SLH and referred to in page 1 of this letter has been made on the basis of monthly management accounts for the first sixteen weeks of 1973 and detailed forecasts for the remainder of the year. The appropriate share of profits of associated companies (one of which is two-thirds owned by Hanson Trust Limited) has been included on the basis of the budgets of these companies and the management information available to SLH. The profit of around £350,000 before tax which is likely to be realised on the sale of 53b Southwark Street has not been included. The following are the principal assumptions which have been made in the preparation of the forecast:—

1. The present level of activity in the construction industry will be maintained.
2. Weather conditions will be no more adverse to the Group than in 1972.
3. UK prices and wages will be restricted until the end of 1973 by the limits contained in Stage 2 of the Government's counter-inflation programme.
4. The Group's production will not be materially affected by exceptional delays in deliveries from suppliers or by industrial disputes.
5. Changes in rates of exchange will not materially affect Group profits.
6. Completion of the sale of 53b Southwark Street will take place during July 1973.

B. LETTERS
The following are copies of letters received from Deloitte & Co., SLH's auditors, and Hill Samuel & Co. Limited addressed to the Directors of SLH concerning the profit forecast of SLH and its subsidiaries for the year ending 31 December 1973 referred to on page 1 of this document:—

128 Queen Victoria Street,
London, EC4P 4JX
29 May 1973

The Directors,
Sykes, Lacy-Hulbert Limited,
403/433 Woolwich Road,
Charlton, London, SE7 7AP

Dear Sirs,
We have reviewed the accounting bases and calculations for the profit forecast, for which the Directors are solely responsible, of Sykes, Lacy-Hulbert Limited and its subsidiaries, including the appropriate share of profits of associated companies attributable to Sykes, Lacy-Hulbert Limited, for the year ending 31 December 1973 which is referred to in your letter to shareholders to be dated 30 May 1973.
In our opinion the forecast, so far as the accounting bases and calculations are concerned, has been properly compiled on the footing of the assumptions made by the Directors set out in paragraph A of Appendix I to your Letter and is presented on a basis

216

consistent with the accounting practices normally adopted by Sykes, Lacy-Hulbert Limited and its subsidiaries.

> Yours faithfully,
> Deloitte & Co.,
> *Chartered Accountants.*

> 100 Wood Street,
> London, EC2P 2AJ
> *29 May 1973*

The Directors,
Sykes, Lacy-Hulbert Limited,
403/433 Woolwich Road,
Charlton, London, SE7 7AP

Dear Sirs,
    We have discussed with you and with the Company's Auditors, Deloitte & Co., the profit forecast of Sykes, Lacy-Hulbert Limited and its subsidiaries for the year ending 31 December 1973, referred to in your letter to shareholders to be dated 30 May 1973.
    In our opinion the forecast has been made after due and careful enquiry.

> Yours faithfully,
> Hill Samuel & Co. Limited,
> J. G. W. Agnew,
> *Director.*

Deloitte & Co. and Hill Samuel & Co. Limited have given and have not withdrawn their written consents to the publication of their respective letters in the form and context in which they appear above.

Appendix II   Additional information

1. RESPONSIBILITY FOR STATEMENTS

The members of a duly authorised committee of the Board of SLH have taken all reasonable care to ensure that the facts stated and the opinions expressed in this document are fair and accurate and no material factors or considerations have been omitted and all the Directors jointly and severally accept responsibility accordingly.

2. PRICE—EARNINGS RATIOS

The price—earnings ratios quoted on page 1 of this document have been based on the forecast profit before tax of £750,000; for purposes of comparability a notional U.K. tax charge of 40 per cent under the old system of corporation tax has been used and overseas taxes have been estimated on the basis of the rates currently applicable.

3. DIRECTORS' AND OTHER INTERESTS

(i) The Directors of SLH and their immediate families (wives and children under 18) are beneficially interested in the following Ordinary shares of SLH:—

	Ordinary Shares of 25p each
H. P. S. Paish	103,329
R. J. Foster	10,000
R. A. Green	7,489
J. W. Llewellyn-Jones	2,000
K. McGregor	7,500
G. E. Thompson	1,000

Mr G. W. Scarlett is a Director of ICFC which is beneficially interested in 1,126,485 Ordinary shares of SLH (35.01 per cent) and 100,000 7½ per cent £1 Cumulative Redeemable Preference Shares 1979/84 of SLH (100 per cent).

(ii) The following dealings have taken place in the shares of SLH since 7 May 1972:—

		Date	Ordinary Shares	Price
H. P. S. Paish	sold	March 1973	2,000	110p
J. W. Llewellyn-Jones	purchased	March 1973	2,000	110p

(iii) Save as disclosed in this document neither SLH nor any of its subsidiaries nor any of its Directors, nor any person acting in concert with any such person, is interested in any of the share or loan capital of SLH or Hanson, or has dealt therein since 7 May 1972.

(iv) No Director of SLH has a service contract with SLH or any of its subsidiaries which has more than 12 months to run.

4. DOCUMENTS FOR INSPECTION

Copies of the letters of Deloitte & Co. and Hill Samuel & Co. Limited and their written consents referred to in Appendix I are available for inspection at the offices of Slaughter and May, 35 Basinghall Street, London, EC2V 5DB during usual business hours while the Hanson Offer remains open for acceptance.

5. DEFINITIONS

Throughout this document SLH refers to Sykes, Lacy-Hulbert Limited, ICFC refers to Industrial and Commercial Finance Corporation Limited and Hanson refers to Hanson Trust Limited.

EXHIBIT 11C.2   Financial performance of major plant-hire firms (£ thousand)

	Year end	Turnover	Trading profit	Pre-tax profit
Bristol Plant Ltd	31 Mar			
1971		1,887	711	118
1972		1,686	598	145
1973		2,405	639	214
H. Cox and Sons (Plant Hire) Ltd	31 Mar			
1970		968	388	196
1971		1,082	381	102
1972		1,198	500	212
1973		2,164	829	384
Hewden Stuart Plant Ltd	31 Jan			
1970		3,162	1,160	535
1971		5,077	1,801	680
1972 (incl. acquisition)		9,496	2,516	695
1973		14,410	3,179	1,202
L. Lipton Ltd	31 Dec			
1970		2,202	762	398
1971		2,078	643	332
1972		2,427	578	119
Richards and Wallington Industries Ltd	31 Dec			
1969		7,934	2,864	1,170
1970		8,782	2,722	1,002
1971		10,444	2,948	1,277
1972		13,068	3,370	1,471
G. W. Sparrow and Sons Ltd	31 Dec			
1969		1,693	536	216
1970		2,408	769	340
1971		2,593	981	367
1972		3,488	1,231	428
Henry Sykes Ltd	29 Dec			
1970		4,401	603	111
1971		4,936	765	205
1972		5,420	855	308
Vibroplant Holdings Ltd	31 Mar			
1970		1,963	908	424
1971		2,394	1,122	543
1972		2,422	1,119	602
1973		3,501	2,031	1,160

EXHIBIT 11C.3   Number of newly floated public companies

	1969	1970	1971	1972	1973
Jan	13	10	9	7	15
Feb	10	6	3	5	8
Mar	22	9	5	16	3
Apr	7	6	6	8	11
May	12	2	10	23	12
June	9	2	9	26	13
July	9	15	8	18	8
Aug	3	5	7	15	4
Sep	4	7	3	12	4
Oct	3	5	11	13	
Nov	11	10	11	24	
Dec	13	13	16	7	
	116	90	98	176	(78)

Source: Stock Exchange Fact Book.

EXHIBIT 11C.4   *The Financial Times* Share Index

	1969	1970	1971	1972	1973
Jan	485	400	325	500	490
Feb	420	390	320	510	454
Mar	415	375	360	525	445
Apr	425	340	385	530	464
May	395	325	370	500	457
June	385	340	395	505	459
July	375	340	400	520	431
Aug	380	350	415	505	423
Sept	375	360	405	492	
Oct	375	335	410	481	
Nov	395	330	450	492	
Dec	415	335	480	502	

EXHIBIT 11C.5   M. J. H. Nightingale and Co. Ltd, investment bankers: extracts from
investment manager's summary of Sykes, Lacy-Hulbert Ltd

Issued Ordinary Shares: 3,217,611
(Issued Capital: £804,403 Par value £0.25)
Recent Price: 155 pence

Summary

We believe that Sykes ordinary shares are now an excellent opportunity for long-term
capital appreciation.

A price of 155p does not adequately reflect the growth of a Company whose earnings
are expected to more than double by the end of 1973 and triple by the end of 1974.
These increases will reduce the Sykes price/earnings ratio from 20.8 to only 12.1 times
1973 earnings and less than 10 times 1974 earnings.

Excellent investment opportunity

Sykes shares are an excellent opportunity to invest in:

1. *The UK leader in water control and pumping services* to the civil engineering industry,
   including integrated research, manufacturing, sales and, above all, a large, highly
   efficient and profitable hire fleet.
2. *Dynamic new management* led by Mr A. E. Hepper which has tripled Sykes pre-tax
   profits in the last 18 months, and is projected to triple profits again in the next
   18 months.
3. *An investment 'double-play'*, that is, substantial capital appreciation arising from a
   combination of a major increase in Sykes' earnings and a substantial upgrading in its
   price/earnings multiple.

Classic 'asset' situation

Sykes was a classic 'asset' situation in 1970, with strengths in many areas, although not in
profits. The Company was:

1. *Old-established* as an engineering and plant-hire business founded in 1857.
2. *Highly regarded as experts* in pumps for temporary and emergency water control with
   civil engineering contractors and local authorities throughout the UK. This high
   reputation was based on the engineering creativity of Mr H. P. S. Paish, the Deputy
   Chairman, and the 'Univac' and 'Velovac' pump patents, trade marks and products.
3. *Market leader* as the largest producer and hirer of pumps for the UK construction
   industry (about 60% of the market). Sykes' pumps were technically excellent and
   highly reliable. Its hire service was also outstanding, with local hiring depots
   supported by regional workshops maintaining 'grass-roots' contact so that expert
   advice was available 'on site' within a few hours.

From the financial standpoint, however, Sykes was weak in 1970 with

- *Static earnings per share* for the five years 1965—69, notwithstanding sales growth in
  excess of 25% annually.
- *An earnings collapse* from £251,000 to £42,000 after tax, due to over-expansion,
  inadequate cost control and a down-turn in construction demand.
- *A negligible return* on assets — only 1% after tax on assets of £3.5 million, with assets
  under-stated by about £1 million.

Management 'turn-round'

Mr A. E. Hepper's appointment as Chairman and Chief Executive in mid-1971 began the
management 'turn-round' at Sykes. Mr Hepper, formerly a Director of Thomas Tilling and
Chairman of Upper Clyde Shipbuilders, strengthened the Board with the appointment of
new executive Directors:

— Mr R. J. Foster, Managing Director, formerly Marketing Director.
— Mr R. A. Green, in charge of UK Depot Division, the key profit centre.
— Mr G. E. Thompson, in charge of Production.
— Mr J. W. Llewellyn-Jones, in charge of finance.

Mr G. W. Scarlett, a Director of ICFC (a major Sykes' investor), and Professor H. B. Rose of London Business School, were appointed non-executive Directors.

The new management team, capitalising on Sykes' inherent strengths, immediately embarked on a profit improvement programme including:

1. *Strengthening the UK depots* to further increase the profitability of pump hire and sales.
2. *Cutting production costs* at the Charlton, Tufthorn and Beddington plants.
3. *Reducing assets* employed by pruning inventory and selling off surplus property.
4. *Expanding into new areas* by:

   (a) Selling Sykes' service in new international markets such as the US, Australia and continental Europe.
   (b) Developing new ground-water services in the UK such as contract pumping, well-drilling and de-watering of excavation sites.

Expansion in these new areas was also designed to stabilise Sykes' earning power by reducing its dependence on UK rainfall.

The pay-off from this programme is already evident. It is expected to add further major increases to profits in the three years 1973—75.

Major earnings increase

We estimate that Sykes' earnings should approximately triple by 31st December 1974. Our detailed annual forecasts are:

— 5.3 pence for 1972, a 50% increase over 1971 (or £300,000 pre-tax).
— 12.3 pence for 1973, a 130% increase over 1972 (or £700,000 pre-tax).
— 14.7—18.4 pence for 1974, a 20—50% increase over 1973 (or £800,000 to £1,000,000 pre-tax).

For comparative purposes with 1972 and earlier years, the 1973 and 1974 forecasts are based on a 40% Corporation Tax rate.

Higher price/earnings multiples

Sykes' shares have sold at low multiples of earnings in the past. These low multiples only 5 to 10 times earnings in the years 1965—69, were due to the Company's low profitability, the poor marketability of its shares, and questionable investment status as a family-controlled pump manufacturer with a market capitalisation of only £1.5 million.

We anticipate that Sykes' shares will sell at much higher multiples in future, probably in the 14—18 range, as a result of:

1. *Improving earnings*, and particularly improving earnings quality, with more diversified sources of profit backed up by stronger management.
2. *Wider marketability* of the Company's shares as a result of the over-the-counter market now being made by M. J. H. Nightingale and Co. Limited.
3. *Improved recognition* by the public of Sykes as an investment in a high-quality international plant-hire specialist with a £5 million market capitalisation.

Sykes now appears to be under-valued in relation to specialist plant-hire companies. It is now selling at only 12.1 times prospective 1973 earnings, and less than 10 times prospective 1974 earnings, the earnings for both years being 'recovery' earnings. Equivalent companies are now selling at 12 to 15 times 1972 earnings.

Moreover, and probably more important, the plant-hire sector appears to be under-valued in relation to the market as a whole. Plant hire shares were selling at 15—20 times 1972 earnings a year ago, and current prices are down 9—40% from their 1972 'highs', notwithstanding the striking improvements in earnings now being reported.

Limited downside risk

We believe that the downside risk in Sykes' shares is limited in view of:

1. *Strong asset backing* in both financial and non-financial terms. Sykes' assets of 105p per share underpin the market price of 155p, with the shares selling at 145% of book value. Comparable plant hire companies now sell at between 200—400% of book value. Sykes' market franchise in the UK construction industry is probably an even more important asset.
2. *Possible bids*. Sykes has been subject to repeated merger discussions and two bids by competitors during the past 18 months, all seeking to capitalise on its recovery prospects. Richards & Wallington bid 115p per share in the autumn of 1972 and the Hanson Trust bid 150p per share in May 1973, having acquired a 21% holding from the former Chairman of Lacy-Hulbert Limited in late 1972.

The Sykes Board has rejected all such approaches in the past. It believes that Sykes' shareholders should reap the rewards of the current profit improvement programme, and that Sykes' specialist skills should not be diluted in a larger group. We therefore believe that the Hanson bid will be rejected.

However, Sykes' shares will continue to remain underpinned by the prospect of a bid if its present management fails to produce results.

EXHIBIT 11C.6   Henry Sykes Ltd: profit and loss account (£ thousand) (year ending 31 December)

	1970	1971	1972	1973	1974	1975	1976
Turnover	4,401	4,936	5,420	7,180	8,657	11,622	15,210
Trading profit	284	383	451	879	1,079	1,567	1,805
Interest charges	200	239	211	223	231	267	266
	84	144	239	655	848	1,300	1,539
Profits of associated companies	–	61	69	189	180	257	236
Pre-tax profit	84	205	308	844	1,028	1,557	1,775
Total tax	34	85	148	413	540	819	885
Post-tax profit	50	120	160	431	488	738	890
Extraordinary items	–	–	–	215[a]	–	–	65[b]
Profit for year	50	120	160	646	488	738	825

[a] Sale of Southwark Street.
[b] Disposal of a foreign subsidiary.

EXHIBIT 11C.7   Henry Sykes Ltd: balance sheet (£ thousand), (year ending 31 December)

	1970	1971	1972	1973	1974	1975	1976
Fixed assets	2723	2849	2987	2979	3204	4464	4887
Goodwill	–	–	–	–	–	–	195
Unquoted investments	154	203	320	327	505	556	140
Stocks	1651	1359	1196	1301	2503	3402	3758
Debtors	1880	1612	1884	2482	2509	3343	4502
Cash	5	28	12	81	43	145	69
Amount due on sale of investment	–	–	–	–	–	–	490
Current assets	3536	2999	3092	3914	5056	6890	8819
Creditors	1008	687	755	1323	1644	2516	2816
Current tax	200	20	68	286	353	173	607
Bank loan and overdraft	1439	1087	1530	1049	1488	737	606
Short-term loan	300	640	200	–	35	35	35
Dividend	20	30	42	97	71	78	90
Current liabilities	2967	2464	2595	2754	3591	3539	4154
Net assets	3447	3587	3714	4466	5073	8371	9887
Share capital	904	904	904	904	904	953	2233[a]
Reserves	1418	1478	1586	2155	2537	4092	3299
Ordinary shareholder funds	2322	2382	2490	3059	3441	5045	5532
Long-term loans	910	942	930	915	839	1760	2400
Deferred tax	107	173	228	447	765	1551	1948
Deferred government grants	108	90	65	44	28	15	7
	3447	3587	3714	4466	5073	8371	9887

[a] During the year, new shares were issued as a result of the capitalisation of the share-premium account.